AUTHENTIC WINE

AUTHENTIC WINE

Toward Natural and Sustainable Winemaking

Jamie Goode and Sam Harrop MW

UNIVERSITY OF CALIFORNIA PRESS

Berkeley   Los Angeles   London

University of California Press, one of the most distinguished university presses in the United States, enriches lives around the world by advancing scholarship in the humanities, social sciences, and natural sciences. Its activities are supported by the UC Press Foundation and by philanthropic contributions from individuals and institutions. For more information, visit www.ucpress.edu.

University of California Press
Berkeley and Los Angeles, California

University of California Press, Ltd.
London, England

Library of Congress Cataloging-in-Publication Data

Goode, Jamie.
  Authentic wine : toward natural and sustainable winemaking / Jamie Goode and Sam Harrop.
    p. cm.
  Includes index.
  ISBN 978-0-520-26563-9 (cloth : alk. paper)
  1. Wine and wine making. 2. Organic wines. 3. Organic viticulture. I. Harrop, Sam. II. Title.
  TP548.G6259 2011
  641.2'2—dc22

                                                                    2010052392

Manufactured in the United States of America
19 18 17 16 15 14 13 12 11
10 9 8 7 6 5 4 3 2 1

In keeping with a commitment to support environmentally responsible and sustainable printing practices, UC Press has printed this book on Rolland Enviro100, a 100% post-consumer fiber paper that is FSC certified, deinked, processed chlorine-free, and manufactured with renewable biogas energy. It is acid-free and EcoLogo certified. ∞

Jacket design and illustration by Claudia Smelser.

Note: All the photographs in this book were taken by Jamie Goode.

CONTENTS

PREFACE

Anyone who thinks they know all the answers is a long way
from making interesting wine.

MAC FORBES, WINEGROWER FROM AUSTRALIA'S YARRA VALLEY

We believe that wine is special, and one of the things that make it special is that it is, in essence, a natural product. We argue that this naturalness is important for wine, and any attempt to make wine less natural by allowing winemakers greater freedom to make more additions could severely damage the image of wine and its continued specialness. Indeed, it is not a huge exaggeration to suggest that we are at a crossroads in the history of wine. In the worst-case scenario, wine becomes increasingly industrial and manufactured, a homogenised mass with only a tiny niche of authentic wines remaining, the preserve of only a few lucky souls who can still access them. In the best-case scenario, the wine trade embraces and celebrates the fact that wine is a natural product and takes steps to preserve its diversity and authenticity—steps that will ensure healthy growth and development of the market for wine.

It is for this reason that we began writing this book with the working title of *Natural Wine.* However, we soon realized that "natural" was too narrow a label. Naturalness has its place, but it should be part of a wider body of considerations. As a result, we came up with the term "authentic wine" to describe a wine made in consideration of not just naturalness, but also a broader range of important factors, including environmental impact, marketing, and sustainable viticulture.

We think that this is a timely book, coinciding with an awakening awareness among the general consumer population of "green" issues such as sustainability and carbon footprints. Increasingly, people are looking at what they are eating and drinking in a more critical fashion: Where does it come from? How is it made? What is its environmental impact? How is it packaged? This awareness throws open a door of opportunity to the wine trade to promote the intrinsic naturalness of wine and, where necessary, to put its house in order by addressing the issue of sustainability of wine production.

So what do you expect to find in the pages of a book titled *Authentic Wine*? A campaigning voice, strident polemics, and an agenda aiming to convert winemakers to the natural wine movement? Or an angry denunciation of the direction the wine industry is taking? Or maybe some undiluted romanticism, yearning after a long-past golden age of wine? Well, this book is none of these, although you'll probably find elements of all three themes scattered around the text. Instead, this is a practical book, driven by curiosity and a passion for interesting wine. By coining the term authentic wine, we aim to differentiate between wines that are headed in the direction of homogenization, and wines whose origins have their roots in terroir, which are made from appropriately right fruit, free from faults, and made sustainably. We believe the future of the global wine industry depends on a push towards more authentic wine, and we discuss how winemakers can work, within the constraints of their individual situations, to best achieve this goal. As well as attempting to give a few answers, we'll be asking lots of questions: what is meant by the term *natural*? Is wine different from other alcoholic beverages, and why? Is there such a thing as "fake" wine? What is the appropriate use of technology in winemaking? What additions to wine should be allowed, and who gets to decide? And, practically, how can winemakers adjust their methods to make more honest, expressive, and interesting wines?

Because this book is the joint effort of a scientist-turned-wine-writer and a practicing winemaker, our hope is that it will be solidly grounded in reality while being sympathetic to the mystery and art of wine. Unlike other attempts to cover similar ground, our aim is to address the subject of natural wine with a pragmatic rather than a dogmatic approach, free of the sort of ideology that has the potential to stifle imaginative, openminded thinking.

We take a rather scientific approach in places, but this is not because we think that science alone can make interesting wine. It is just that science is a powerful tool to help unlock understanding. However, it is by no means the only legitimate or useful way of viewing wine.

Our argument is that authenticity and naturalness are concepts vital to the future health of the global wine industry, and we discuss how winemakers can best achieve the goal of making true, honest, natural wines that express best what their vineyards give them. Through the text runs a strong theme: wine is unique and special, and we should do what we can to keep it that way.

ACKNOWLEDGMENTS

We would like to thank all our colleagues, friends, and acquaintances who have contributed to this book: there are far too many to name, but you know who you are. It has been our experience that the wine trade is unlike any other in terms of its spirit of collegiality, and the hospitality and cooperative spirit of most of its members. In addition, some of the chapters and sections of boxed copy in this book began their life as articles for *The World of Fine Wine* and *Meininger's Wine Business International*, and we would like to thank these excellent publications for their permission to incorporate modified sections of these texts into this book.

Jamie Goode
Sam Harrop

1

INTRODUCTION

Some nine thousand years ago, someone made a lucky discovery: that grapes contained within themselves the constituents to make a satisfying, mood-enhancing, food-compatible, and usefully long-lived drink—wine. So universally appreciated was this near-magical liquid that it soon became a cornerstone of the shared lives of many societies. Wild grapes proved amenable to cultivation; vineyards were a sign of settling, evidence that people who had previously been nomadic were here to stay. In addition to its social role, wine also became infused with religious symbolism.

Remarkably, wine has survived various social upheavals, the end of dynasties and empires, and industrial "progress" and remains with us today. Of course, many of the wines we currently consume, dominated by bold, sweet fruit flavours, would be unrecognizable to drinkers of just a century ago. Yet there are still plenty of wines around that taste much as they would have hundreds of years ago. This is because, here and there, wines are still made in ways that would be familiar to a winegrower from past times. Still others are helped a little by cellar technology but manage to retain a sense of place that connects with history. Thus wine carries with it an important tradition. In New World regions where there is a relatively brief tradition of quality wine production, there exist both wines that reflect the personality of the place they come from and those that could have been made almost anywhere.

WHAT IS NATURAL? WHAT IS AUTHENTIC?

One of the keys to wine's enduring appeal is the belief that it is a "natural" product. But how do we define *natural*? We can start by agreeing that in its most basic form, all wine is natural in that it is not a synthetically produced beverage. Instead, grapes contain—within and without—all that is needed to make wine. One could therefore argue that the more manipulations or additions a wine undergoes, the less natural the resulting product, although this is an overly simplistic view.

In truth, there is no such thing as natural or unnatural wine; rather, the "naturalness" of a wine is most usefully measured on a continuum from least to most natural and takes in many aspects of the cultivation, harvesting, and processing of the raw ingredient: the grape.

To illustrate this point, let's consider the analogy of a garden. If a garden is totally "natural," it is untended, and the only plants growing there will be those that establish themselves. The result will not be completely devoid of appeal, but it won't be a garden in the traditional sense. After several generations it will likely become woodland or scrubland. The term *garden* implies some sort of human intervention by selecting which plants to grow, tending them, and keeping a degree of order. Of course, the gardener does not make anything grow herself or himself; she or he acts merely as a facilitator of this growth. But part of the appeal of a garden is that it allows us to enjoy space that is dominated by plants and nature, even if it is nature at its tamest and most controlled.

The analogy with wine isn't perfect, but it's a useful one. Consider the winemaker (or winegrower, if, like some, you have a natural aversion to the term *winemaker*) as the gardener. A gardener could be said to be taking a natural approach if he or she eschews the worst-offending chemicals and doesn't introduce anything nonliving into the garden—the extreme example would be planting artificial flowers. But you could also raise questions about degrees of naturalness, as you can with wine. Does a garden gnome, or a water feature, or a bench make the garden unnatural? There are all sorts of gardens, from formal Regency-style English gardens to botanic gardens and more functional vegetable gardens. In a way all of these are natural, but some are more natural than others.

If we adhere to a strict concept of naturalness, then there is no such thing as natural wine. But if we accept the idea of a continuum of naturalness, and if we recognize that it is useful to establish just how natural some wines are when compared with others, then a range of choices become available in the vineyard and winery that will shift the wine in one direction or the other along the naturalness continuum. We must draw a line somewhere along the continuum from least natural to most natural, because otherwise anything goes—and in winemaking "anything goes" translates into a huge problem, as we'll discuss in later chapters.

However, perceived naturalness is not the only factor that has maintained wine's appeal over the ages. Another important ingredient has been the link to provenance: the

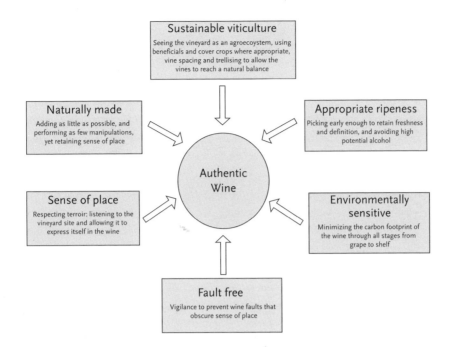

Sustainable viticulture

Seeing the vineyard as an agroecoystem, using beneficials and cover crops where appropriate, vine spacing and trellising to allow the vines to reach a natural balance

Naturally made

Adding as little as possible, and performing as few manipulations, yet retaining sense of place

Appropriate ripeness

Picking early enough to retain freshness and definition, and avoiding high potential alcohol

Authentic Wine

Sense of place

Respecting terroir: listening to the vineyard site and allowing it to express itself in the wine

Environmentally sensitive

Minimizing the carbon footprint of the wine through all stages from grape to shelf

Fault free

Vigilance to prevent wine faults that obscure sense of place

FIGURE 1.1

Elements that make a wine authentic. This is not an exhaustive list: factors such as organics and biodynamics could be added under "sustainable viticulture," and social responsibility and financial sustainability could also be added. In addition, sense of place could encompass "naturally made" and "appropriate ripeness."

FIGURE 1.2

Compost heaps at Rippon Vineyard in New Zealand's Central Otago region. The vineyards are managed using biodynamics.

power of wine to tell the story of its origin. This idea of terroir is intrinsic to wine, but is at great risk of erosion in today's marketplace. Winemakers need to listen to the vineyard and do their best to express it in the final wine. A key part of this is managing vineyards in an effective and sustainable manner. An even more important part of this is picking early enough to retain freshness and definition and avoid high alcohol and the obscure fruit qualities that over-ripeness brings. Linked to terroir is the issue of faults in wine. As controversial as they are misdiagnosed, winemaking faults are often guilty of masking terroir and, in some cases, becoming so entrenched that they become part of it! But it is no longer acceptable just to make fault-free wine that expresses its place; considerations of micro and macro environment are crucial in an age where concerns about global warming have become the domain of many consumers. A wine made with consideration for all of these factors is—in our definition—an authentic wine. We acknowledge that, like naturalness, the concept of authenticity is a shifting paradigm, and that there are limits to its application for individuals and businesses. Larger more hierarchical businesses have greater limitations, but that doesn't mean they shouldn't try to make more authentic wines.

THE FORK IN THE ROAD

The issue of naturalness and authenticity is one of the key current debates in the world of wine, and it is likely to become more heated over the next few years. Why? Because wine is now at a metaphorical fork in the road, and from here it can go one of two ways. The first is to continue down the road taken by New World branded wines: huge volumes, a reliance on technology and marketing, reliability at the cost of individuality, an emphasis on sweet fruit flavours, and a loss of terroir (the possession by wines of a sense of place). The destination? Wine would gradually become indistinguishable from other drinks, and grapes would be seen simply as the raw ingredient in a manufacturing process. It's easy to see how wine is being pushed down this road by changes in retailing practices and demand for branded, homogeneous wine. Marketplace-driven consolidation has hit the wine industry. Players who can't manage large volumes with low margins are in danger of being forced to retreat to the heavily saturated and competitive fine wine niche or to bow out completely. The middle ground, once flush with diversity, has rapidly eroded, and those still in the game are seeing their access to market dry up. This is a real concern because many of the most interesting wines have come from this middle ground: midsized producers with perhaps dozens of hectares, rather than hundreds, who make the sorts of wines that we fell in love with and that persuaded us that wine is interesting in its own right. Nowadays, a small group of large drink companies dominates the world wine market. The accountants and managers rule the roost. Their products hit price points, are made in huge volumes, and don't offend anyone, but they do not excite. They are consistent from vintage to vintage, made to reflect a style rather than a sense of place.

FIGURE 1.3
A raptor post in the middle of Benton Lane's vineyard in Oregon. It attracts raptors that eat gophers, which would otherwise cause damage in the vineyard.

For a vision of where the wine industry might currently be heading, it is worth looking at what has happened to the beer industry in recent years. The big companies and suits (business executives) moved in. The marketeers realized that product quality wasn't the selling point, and instead, they focused on building brands and selling the concepts underlying the brand to consumers rather than talking about the taste of the beer. The result was product homogenisation. Does the wine industry want to tread the same path? There's a real danger that if wine is treated solely as a manufactured product, blended and tweaked to fit the preferences of specially convened panels of "average" consumers, the wine industry will become moribund as a sector. Diversity based on regional, cultural, and winemaking differences will be lost, and any sense of continuity with the past may vanish forever.

The other road involves a retracing of steps and a celebration of what has made wine different and special: a respect for tradition, a sense of place, and an acknowledgment that diversity is valuable and not just an inconvenience. Wine is embedded in the deeper culture. The destination of this road is the rediscovery of "natural," authentic wine. This is wine with a vital connection to the vineyard it came from, wine that is unique to a particular distinguished site. "I believe in the concept of 'naturalness' as it is at the core of the concept of terroir," says renowned Australian winemaker and wine scientist Brian Croser. "Terroir is at the core of the fine wine endeavor and ethic, as it defines

FIGURE 1.4
Terraced vineyards in Portugal's Douro Valley.

the quality factor which is enduring and cannot be competed away by technology. I maintain that the finest, best-balanced, and most unique wines will be made naturally from great expressive terroirs. Not only will the absolute quality across many vintages and tasters aggregate to the best (compared to manufactured wine), but the very ethic itself adds a halo that is in accord with the human spirit trying to reconnect to nature in a largely disconnected life. The spiritual and intellectual needs are in accord with the satisfaction derived from the personality and quality of fine wine."

In addition to changes in the wine industry, the consumer climate is changing. There is a growing awareness of environmental issues in production and packaging of food and drink, as well as the growing awareness of where products come from. Consumers are willing to pay more for organically produced food because they believe that it is better for them, and many claim that food grown with reduced pesticide input in a way that respects the environment actually tastes better. Consumers are also endorsing the concept of food miles and are concerned about the carbon footprint of the food and drink that they buy. It may be that before too long, green issues such as these will have a major impact on the purchasing behaviour of almost all consumers, not just a highly environmentally aware subset, as is currently the case.

Our concept of authentic wine is based on two premises: wine made naturally is more interesting and tastes better, and natural wine production is more sustainable and respectful of the environment. This concept may also offer an effective marketing strategy for wine, which is currently stuck in a price-reduction rut.

In this book we present a wide-ranging, critical look at the way naturalness and authenticity apply to wine. We begin by examining how more natural approaches in the vineyard can have a positive effect on wine quality. We'll discuss the issue of terroir, which is a complex and controversial notion, but one that sits at the heart of fine wine. We argue that there is a moral imperative for winegrowers to work in a sustainable fashion, even if they decide that neither organics nor biodynamics (a specialized form of organic farming popular among winegrowers) is a feasible approach for them. Shifting to the winery, we will discuss the natural wine movement and attempts to make wine with no additives at all, as well as a gradual shift among many growers to try to reduce winemaking inputs to the bare minimum. We'll take a thorough look at exactly what is added to wine, and why. We will also cover attempts to reduce the carbon footprint of wine. We conclude the book by examining whether naturalness can be a helpful marketing angle for the wine industry.

We realize that readers will be coming to this book from different perspectives. Believers in natural wine (whatever it may be) will be looking for a defence of the natural wine position, coupled with a thorough exploration of those wine producers who would position themselves under the natural wine banner. Others will be sceptics who have already decided that the term *natural wine* is nonsense, with no real meaning or usable definition. We hope that whatever your position, you find our exploration of issues of naturalness and authenticity as they relate to wine useful, even if this isn't quite the book you were expecting. The reality is that the topic of naturalness is a highly complex one, bringing together many separate ideas, and it isn't easy to pull out a seamless, tidy narrative. But we firmly believe that it is important to have this discussion.

2

THE DIVERSITY OF WINE
How a Natural Approach Can Help Preserve Wine's Interest

Think, for a moment, of an almost paper-white glass of liquid, just shot with greeny-gold, just tart on your tongue, full of wild flower scents and spring-water freshness. And think of a burnt-umber fluid, as smooth as syrup in the glass, as fat as butter to smell and sea-deep with strange flavours. Both are wine.

Wine is grape-juice. Every drop of liquid filling so many bottles has been drawn out of the ground by the roots of a vine. All these different drinks have at one time been sap in a stick. It is the first of many strange and some— despite modern research—mysterious circumstances which go to make wine not only the most delicious, but the most fascinating, drink in the world.

It would not be so fascinating if there were not so many different kinds. Although there are people who do not care for it, and who think it no more than a nuisance that a wine-list has so many names on it, the whole reason that wine is worth study is its variety.

HUGH JOHNSON, *WINE*, 1966

Hugh Johnson's quote comes from a time when the wine world looked rather different from how it appears today. Then, wine was very much a matter of the classics: chiefly Bordeaux, Burgundy, Champagne, Alsace, Mosel, and Port. The Rhône, so popular with "collectors" today, was considered alongside France's "country wines." Italy and Spain had a token presence on wine lists, and in the New World, perhaps only the Napa Valley of California was seen as significant. Critics had very little influence at this stage. Yet Johnson was able to say that wine "would not be so fascinating if there were not so many different kinds." He was right then; he is right now, when the world market for wine is much larger, and fine wine is made in far more places than it used to be.

Yet the growing popularity of wine has threatened this diversity. Why? As fine wine has gained in popularity in new (and wealthy) markets such as the United States and Asia, incentives for producers to excel have become greater. The rewards, for those who can raise their quality to the very highest level, are huge and make it worth the

FIGURE 2.1

Ancient vines in the vineyard of Wendouree, Clare Valley, Australia.

not-inconsiderable effort and investment of capital. The greater incentives to excel has undoubtedly expanded the category of fine wines, which is a good thing. However, it has also created the problem of how to define the "highest level of quality." In addition, winemakers now have at their disposal a wide array of technological innovations and an ever-expanding catalogue of yeast strains, processing aids, and winemaking additions, which have given them much more creative control over the winemaking process. Have they all used this power wisely?

In the past, fine wine was an aesthetic system, based on benchmarking and learning. Students of wine explored the classic styles and learned to discern what constitutes a great wine as opposed to an ordinary one. It's worth remembering here that wine appreciation operates on two distinct but intersecting levels. First, we have the hedonic level. You sip a wine and then report how much you enjoyed·the experience: how nice did it taste? Second, there is the learned component: people have traditionally learned what constitutes a great example of Bordeaux, white Burgundy, or Champagne. Of course, the two methods of appreciation overlap, and most people use both in tandem. However, a novice is really capable of only the first level of appreciation.

It follows, then, that when experts assess a wine, they do so from inside this tradition of an aesthetic system of fine wine. They don't evaluate a wine just on the basis of what is in the glass, and how much pleasure it brings them. Some knowledge of context is necessary in the process of wine appreciation. To be a good critic, a novice must first seek to gain some knowledge of the wine style he or she is evaluating. When we are tasting blind, there is a limit to what we can say about the wine that is in front of us.

FIGURE 2.2

Vineyards of Châteauneuf-du-Pape in France's Rhône Valley. These vines are grown unsupported in a style called *gobelet* (known in English as "bush vine").

The wine trade has traditionally acted as a custodian of a fine wine tradition, and those entering it have undergone a sort of apprenticeship in wine.

Of course, this aesthetic system of fine wine is terribly Eurocentric and rather elitist, which puts it firmly in the searchlights of those outside the system, who are gunning for a target. The system has also been shaken to its core over the past couple of decades by the emergence of the world's most powerful wine critic, Robert M. Parker, Jr. Probably just a minority of readers of this chapter will be unaware of Parker and his work, so we'll introduce him only briefly.

Robert Parker was a lawyer from Maryland with a passion for wine. In 1978 he began publishing the *Wine Advocate*, a simple magazine, but one that was to revolutionize the fine wine market. Parker's approach was to position himself as a consumers' advocate, and his aim was to give people the sort of impartial guidance that would help them make informed wine-buying decisions. His stroke of genius was to score wines on an easily understandable 100-point scale, where any wine scoring under 80 wasn't much and anything over 90 was pretty special. Parker was rating fine wine, but it could be suggested that he was operating outside the established, British-dominated aesthetic system of fine wine, perhaps unintentionally. Firmly on the side of the consumer, he was positioning himself outside the wine trade with a view to maintaining an independent voice.

FIGURE 2.3
The winery of Mount Difficulty in the Bannockburn subregion of New
Zealand's Central Otago. This area has landscape damage; erosion caused by
sluicing during the gold-mining activities of the nineteenth century is clearly
visible.

Suddenly consumers were empowered. While tasting notes are an important part of
the *Wine Advocate* and his book (*Parker's Wine Buyer's Guide*), it is the scores that make
relative performance transparent. "Parker points" offer a way into wine for those daunted
by its complexity. They introduced an element of competition in the world of fine wine
and enabled overperforming new producers to rub shoulders with the classics: rather
than building a reputation over generations, all that was now needed for entry into the
wine world's elite was a string of scores in the high 90s. They also allowed wine to be
traded by those with no specialist knowledge, because prices track scores, and young
wines with the highest Parker scores have tended to increase in value spectacularly
after release.

Consumers have found Parker points to be a shortcut mechanism for making buying choices, but wine merchants have found them equally useful as a sales tool. Most
wine lists are punctuated by the likes of "RP 92" or even "RP 100" (for something very
special). The ratings, by making fine wine easier to understand and buy, have also been
a significant factor in opening up new markets for fine wine, most specifically in Asia.
"From the perspective of wine buyers and merchants in Asia, Parker's influence can
hardly be overstated," says Nicholas Pegna, managing director of Berry Bros. and Rudd
in Hong Kong. "His views are very, very significant. People do not need to understand
the wines, nor even his notes; they can simply look at the scores. This is vital where
people might not be confident in what they like drinking."

The problem with the Parker phenomenon is that by operating outside the aesthetic system of fine wine, he has changed the way in which quality is defined. The old rule book has been discarded. A Bordeaux wine is assessed not as a Bordeaux wine but as a red wine and suddenly is being compared directly, by means of its score, with a Napa Valley Cabernet or a leading Hermitage from the northern Rhône. Is a Parker score a valid judgment of wine quality? Consumers and merchants think so, and in some fine wine markets a good score is a prerequisite for a high price tag.

This discussion is in no way intended to be read as a criticism of Parker, who is an able, hardworking, and consistent taster, and who deserves his success. But the way his ratings have been understood and used by many, coupled with his huge impact on the fine wine market, hasn't been completely and unreservedly good for wine diversity. Because all wines are now comparable by means of a score, ratings are the effective definition of wine quality. Consequently, some commentators have suggested that there has been movement towards an "international" style of red wine that lacks a real sense of place, because sense of place is not rewarded with points in this new definition of wine quality. A wine that might otherwise be regarded as a good, typical example of a particular appellation may see its score and desirability improve if the grower reduces yields, harvests later, and uses interventionist cellar techniques, such as ageing the wine in barrels made exclusively of new oak, which imparts a distinctive flavour to the wine. So what if it no longer represents a typical reflection of what this patch of ground is capable of? For white wines, there has been less of a trend towards internationalization, perhaps with the exception of Chardonnay. This is because the main focus of critics such as Parker has been on red wines, and for many whites, there has not been a move towards picking later and using lots of new oak.

Some may argue that by making these international-style wines, producers are simply responding to the demands of the market. Well-heeled collectors enjoy these sorts of wines; they are gratifying and, with their dense, sweet, powerful fruit, are quite easy to appreciate. The impression you gain is that many of these collectors don't really care whether a particular wine fits into the aesthetic system of fine wine; they are happy as long as they have a cellar of suitably highly rated wines. In this new synthesis of fine wine, typicity (the way a wine displays characteristics shared among wines from this particular location) and diversity are unwelcome complications. They are irrelevant. Indeed, notions of terroir are seen as undemocratic tools used by members of the wine establishment to maintain their privileged position. But others contend that the new, simplified world of fine wine, with its easily understood measure of quality, is impoverished and less interesting because it fails to celebrate diversity and individuality in their own right.

Is the whole fine wine venture heading for the disaster of dull uniformity? Probably not. While too many wines are being made in the international style, a quick comparison of the wine list of a good merchant today with one from thirty years ago will show that we've never been so lucky. It's fair to say that the real situation is complex, and the critical viewpoint outlined above is somewhat simplistic. There's room for a diversity of wine styles, even within a particular region, and it would be wrong to impose from above a single taste standard on all the producers within an appellation. Besides, who would be the arbiter of this standard? Additionally, the world of wine can't be expected to stand still. Innovation, experimentation, and progress are inevitable whenever wine-growers are intelligently curious. However, one person's idea of progress is another's idea of iconoclastic trashing of valued traditions, and the positive gloss of the modernizers, who argue that there is now more fine wine being made than ever before, fails to mask entirely the disturbing trend towards darker, richer, more alcoholic red wines. An interesting aside in this context is that the whole discussion of the influence of critics and the changing nature of fine wine styles concerns to a large extent red wines. There hasn't been a similar fight over top whites—notably white Burgundy, German Riesling, Alsace whites, Champagne, and Sauternes. These are wine regions for which Parker points are less important in driving sales.

Thus the first great pressure on wine diversity is a new, simplistic definition of wine quality that treats all wines the same and fails to recognize sense of place as a valid criterion of assessment. This definition has led to a shift in wine style as producers who make high-scoring wines reap substantial rewards.

Another great, rather more ordinary pressure on wine diversity stems from changes in the way wine is sold. The key issue for winemakers worldwide is access to the market. Wine producers used to make wine and then try to sell it. Many still do, with varying degrees of success. Increasingly, however, this approach doesn't work. People in many countries now largely buy wine as part of their supermarket shopping. As a result, the wine trade is consolidating into two rather different markets. At one pole we have the fine wine niche, dominated by the classics, which are sold by specialist merchants to a discerning market of wine geeks and wealthy restaurant diners. At the other we have wine for the masses: wine as a commodity, dominated by branded wines and sold through supermarkets and convenience stores. The middle ground is disappearing fast, which is a minitragedy, because this is where much of the diversity lies.

Modern retailing doesn't suit interesting wine well. Generally speaking, wine is best made by families because of the continuity they offer; making good wine is a long-term investment that usually requires tying up large sums of capital, notably in vineyard ownership, for many years. Families also are usually better able to manage small to medium-sized properties of tens of hectares rather than hundreds. Modern retailing needs volume, demands high margins, and slashes prices to the bone. In this environment it is difficult for smaller producers who aren't able to climb to the relative safety of the fine wine niche to find an outlet for their wines, other than direct sales to consumers and restaurants. Modern retailing much prefers branded wines, made to a style, scalable, and with the inconsistency of vintage variation ironed out, to more idiosyncratic, variable, and honest products made in smaller quantities. Only the big brands have the

FIGURE 2.4

A distinctive terroir: a vine at Château Lafite in Pauillac, Bordeaux, just
before harvest. The distinctive soils allow good drainage, with a steady water
supply that tails off around veraison, the point at which red grapes change
colour from green to reddish black.

marketing budget necessary to get the attention of increasingly distracted consumers.
Hence the sameness apparent in many supermarket wine offerings.

Another pressure on diversity is the societal shift in attention from the local to the
global that has occurred over the past few decades, paralleled by the rise in celebrity
culture. With our tight schedules and limited attention spans, we all end up with the
same sports heroes, listen to the same music, and chat about the love lives of the same
"celebs." The rewards are disproportionately spread: the gulf between the earnings of
the tennis players or golfers ranked 1 to 10 and those ranked, say, 50 to 60 is much larger
than any differences in ability. Wine faces a similar situation. Frequently, when affluent
but time-poor consumers develop an interest in wine, they don't want to fuss with lesser
wines; they want the best. A large portion of available wine spending is therefore focused on relatively few wines, with the rewards going to the top producers from the top
regions. Prices of the very best wines are inflated massively above prices of wines from
producers and regions in the next perceived tier: most collectors can cope only with so
many names, and the few top-ranking producers reap a disproportionate share of the
spoils.

Together, these pressures have reduced wine diversity. It is worrisome that at both
ends of the market, wines are beginning to bunch into a limited number of styles. Go
into your local supermarket, and there'll be a selection of Sauvignon Blancs, Chardon-
nays, Cabernet Sauvignons, Merlots, and Shiraz; if you are lucky, you'll also find some
Rieslings and Pinot Noirs, but not much else. In your local specialist wine shop the wine

FIGURE 2.5
The vineyards of Matetic, San Antonio, Chile, are farmed biodynamically.

FIGURE 2.6
A gnarled old vine in the Arribes region of Spain, near the Portuguese
border, on the international Douro.

selection may seem more diverse, but many of the top reds will taste rather similar, with lots of fruit and some noticeable oak: ripe, sweet flavours offset by some spice and tannin. True, in both outlets consumers will be faced with what looks like a bewildering array of wines, but this impression of diversity is increasingly illusory. Ironically, factors that have led to the democratization of wine, notably, clear labeling of wines by grape variety and bright, accessible, fruity flavours from modern winemaking techniques, could threaten the future of wine diversity if consumers never progress to appreciating and purchasing more individual, interesting wines.

Few would argue with the observation that the fine wine scene now is more diverse and vibrant than it was fifty or even twenty years ago. At the commercial end of the market, consumers are faced with a wider array of better-made and tastier wines. So it seems a little churlish to suggest that all is not well in the world of wine. But if we look below the surface, we can detect a creeping homogenisation that is a cause for some concern. Could salvation come from a switch to a more natural approach to winemaking? Certainly, those winemakers who have made a commitment to work more naturally in their vineyards and to take a less interventionist approach in their cellars seem to be the ones who are making more interesting wines—wines with definition, complexity, and a sense of place. In the following chapters we'll begin exploring why this might be the case, and we'll try to dissect complex but important topics such as terroir and how certain approaches to winemaking help confer that magical property of some-whereness on a bottle of wine.

3

TERROIR

The vine is more affected by the difference of soils than any other fruit tree.
From some it derives a flavour which no culture or management can equal,
it is supposed, upon any other. This flavour—real or imaginary—is sometimes
peculiar to the produce of a few vineyards; sometimes it extends through
the greater part of a small district and sometimes through a considerable
part of a large province.

ADAM SMITH, *AN INQUIRY INTO THE NATURE AND
CAUSES OF THE WEALTH OF NATIONS*, 1776

We begin this pivotal chapter with an abrupt, provocative comment: most writing on terroir is simply nonsense, and many winegrowers take terroir far too seriously. But at the same time we believe that it is one of the most important concepts in wine. In fact, we go so far as to call it the unifying theory of fine wine. Our attitude seems a bit paradoxical: on the one hand, we are claiming that terroir isn't important; on the other, we are saying that it is. Here we'll try to explain why we are taking this seemingly absurd stance.

First, though, we must deal with definitions of terroir, a French term without an equivalent in English. On one level, terroir is a truism. Grapes grown in different places result in wines that taste different. Sometimes the effect is subtle; sometimes it is pronounced. It's hard to imagine anyone disagreeing with this rather simple concept. So terroir exists. But this is terroir defined in a very broad way; when wine writers and winemakers alike wield the term, they are frequently referring to somewhat different notions. Also, a concept framed so broadly is pretty much useless in practice. For discussions of terroir to make sense, we first need to constrain the definition to something a bit more specific. Then we need to try to reconcile the several overlapping definitions of the term *terroir* in common use.

The universal premise underlying the concept of terroir—the simple truism we've already described—is that vineyard differences can affect the flavour of wine. Take a single grape variety and plant it in three different spots. Handle the harvested grapes in the same way, and the wines will taste different. The differences are apparently attributable to the soil and subsoil properties of the vineyard site and to its local climate.

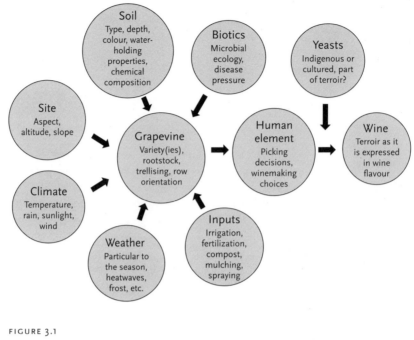

FIGURE 3.1
Influences that shape terroir.

Let's be more precise. Scale is an important factor here. While a Pinot Noir grown in the Yarra Valley will taste different from one grown in Burgundy, even if the wines are made the same way, this isn't usually thought of as a demonstration of terroir. Rather, terroir most commonly refers to a much more local scale. A famous example is that of the late Al Brounstein's Diamond Creek wines. Diamond Creek produces three Cabernet Sauvignon wines from three rather different vineyards on its Napa Valley property. Year by year these wines taste quite different, even though the winemaking is the same. Gravelly Meadow, a 5-acre block on gravelly, free-draining soils (soils which allow rainwater to drain rapidly), is the coolest of the three and produces structured (more grippy or tannic), slightly earthy wines. Red Rock is a 7-acre, north-facing vineyard with a warmer microclimate and soils rich in iron; it produces more accessible (easily enjoyed, fruitier), riper wines. Volcanic Hill is an 8-acre, south-facing, sloping vineyard with volcanic soils and a warm microclimate, producing sturdy, rich, long-lived wines. Somehow, the differences in site leave their imprint on the wine in a way that transcends vintage differences.

At a regional scale, Burgundy illustrates the power of terroir, as well as its limitations. The hillsides of this celebrated region are divided into a patchwork of small vineyards, most owned by a number of growers, while others are *monopoles* (owned by just one grower). There's a strict hierarchy of vineyards here: wine from the lowest rung in the vineyard ladder sells for a mere fraction of the price commanded by wine from the most illustrious Grand Cru vineyards, at the top of the pile. Nestling below the Grand

FIGURE 3.2
Looking towards the village of Vosne-Romanée across some of Burgundy's most prized Grand Cru vineyards.

Crus are the Premier Cru vineyards, with the village-level wines in the rung below. It is striking that each of these vineyards is widely considered to have special characteristics that makes the complication of treating them as separate sites worth the effort. Clearly, the inconvenience that this treatment necessitates in terms of management, winemaking, regulation, and marketing is considered to be worthwhile by vignerons.

That one wine can sell for $150, while another made by the same person from the same grape variety but from a site 200 metres from the first can sell for $25, illustrates the market's recognition of the reality of terroir. But immediately we hit a complication. Two growers can work the same vineyard, yet the wines of one can sell for three times the price of those of another. This is easy to understand if one of these growers lacks the skill to make quality wine, but we could well be talking here about two competent growers who make no obvious mistake in their vinifications. So there is a human element to terroir. The human element is also suggested by the fact that one grower's Chambertin may taste quite different from that of another because of style differences. These style differences may be the result of a conscious decision, or they may be accidental. But the human element of terroir is important. Human input shapes the must and the wine in so many ways that excluding it from the definition of terroir is ludicrous.

Another use of the term is to describe the physical vineyard site itself ("this is a good terroir"; "the terroir consists of schist"). In some ways this is the tightest definition: the terroir is indisputable, in that a geologist could describe it for us in unequivocal terms. A further variation is the French term *goût de terroir*, where characters in the wine are related directly to the soil. In this last definition a mechanism of terroir is alluded to: the vine is picking up flavour from the soil via its roots. We will say more about this

FIGURE 3.3
Mike Weersing of Pyramid Valley
Vineyards in the North Cantebury Hills,
New Zealand, inspects a pit he's just dug
in his vineyard, demonstrating the rare
combination of chalk and claylike loams
that this area possesses.

later. These definitions are rarely made explicit and are mixed and matched by users, often in the same discussion.

TERROIR AND APPELLATIONS

Terroir is central to the French wine industry and also the industries of almost all other European wine countries. It is the principle underlying appellation systems, which form the basis of the regulatory regimes that govern how wine is marketed and sold. While some criticise appellation systems for being restrictive—and they certainly aren't perfect in their implementation—they have had the wonderful effect of preserving wine diversity in the face of increasing competition and economic pressures to react to a changing market. One problem with wine is that change takes a long time to effect. The market decides that it likes Sauvignon Blanc rather than Chardonnay: how do growers respond? They can plant new vineyards or graft over one variety to another, but it will take at least two seasons and possibly three for the new vines to produce. For a top-level wine, we're talking of a much longer time frame. Trying to turn around the wine industry is like turning around a huge coach on a country road. You have to be patient, and there needs to be great willingness. If appellation systems were not in place, the European wine industries would likely have tried to respond to short-term shifts in the mar-

FIGURE 3.4
One of the home vineyards of Pyramid
Valley in Waikiri, North Cantebury, New
Zealand.

ketplace and have gotten themselves into a terrible muddle in the process. Who would
persist with particular combinations of grape variety and site that suddenly fell out of
fashion? They would likely have been lost before they came back into fashion. We accept
that the concept of appellation systems has very real problems, but it has great strengths,
too, although it is probably not suited for the most commercial wine styles.

Does terroir in the broad sense exist in the New World? Emphatically yes. You'll find
flavour differences in wines made from grapes grown in different locations. Any professional who suggests that terroir does not exist in the New World is mistaken. Wine from
a site planted with an incorrect variety may not be great, but it will exhibit terroir if it is
made correctly. The notion that a wine needs minerality to be considered a terroir wine
is flawed; it is a frequent misconception in the wine business. The tangible elements of
terroir vary greatly from one site to the next. The wines that are then made will also vary
greatly. This is not to say that a wine that shows more fruit and less minerality than another has any more or any less terroir in its profile. It has site expression if the winemaker chooses to let it have it. Terroir is often used by elitists in the wine industry looking to protect their plot of dirt to justify higher prices and regular sales for their wine. To
suggest that VdP (Vin de Pays) or IGP (Indication Geographique Protegée) as it is now
known has any less potential for expression of its terroir than an AOC (Appellation
d'Origine Controllée) site is outrageous. In fact, one could argue that because the IGP

FIGURE 3.5
The Douro Valley in northern Portugal, one of the world's most spectacular wine regions. In the foreground is Quinta da Romaneira, on the bank of the Douro River.

winemaker is not bound to follow certain grape growing and winemaking regulations defined in a different time and a different era by unknowns, the potential to produce wines with more intense site expression is greater. Perhaps this is why many winemakers in France and Italy are choosing to label wines IGP or the equivalent even when they are making wines in AOC or DOC (Denominazione di Origine Controllata) areas.

However, the common practice in most New World regions is for each producer to grow a whole slew of different grape varieties and to make a series of varietal wines from a single property. This is beginning to change on two levels. First, there are serious attempts to match grape variety to site when new vineyards are planted or old vineyards are reworked. Most producers recognize that some varieties work in certain locations and not in others, at the level of various spots on their properties and also on a more regional level. It seems that the commercial convenience of being able to offer customers a more or less complete range of popular varieties is giving way to regional specialization, certainly at the higher end of the market. In part, the shift that's occurring in South Africa's wine lands towards Shiraz and other Mediterranean grape varieties and away from the Bordeaux varieties that dominated the industry for so long recognizes a shift in consumer preference; in part, it recognizes that Shiraz, Grenache, and Mourvèdre are rather better suited to these warm-climate vineyards than Cabernet Franc, Cabernet Sauvignon, and Merlot.

There are similar examples elsewhere in the New World. In Australia, the Eden and Clare valleys are known for their Riesling, the Yarra Valley is establishing a reputation for elegant Shiraz, Coonawarra has been known for ages as one of the best places to grow Bordeaux varieties, Margaret River produces perhaps Australia's best Cabernet Sauvignon, the Hunter Valley makes long-lived, unique unoaked Semillons and restrained, ageworthy Shiraz, and the Adelaide Hills region makes top-notch Pinot Noir and Chardonnay. This regionality is presumably an early stage in the development of a terroir-based appellation system. In New Zealand, the Gimblett Gravels in Hawkes Bay is a brilliant example of a good old European-style terroir: it's a special vineyard area some 800 hectares in size with a distinctive geology that imparts distinctive characteristics to the grape varieties grown on it, most particularly Syrah and Bordeaux blends. (We'll explore this vineyard in more detail later in this chapter.) In South Africa, the specific soil types of the Paardeberg in Swartland are producing some very interesting wines, as are the cooler climates and interesting soils of regions such as Elim and Elgin. It's clear that terroir is not restricted to the Old World.

One of the arguments against terroir is that there's often more in common in a range of wines from different appellations made by the same winemaker than there is in wines from the same appellation made by different winemakers. The winemaker's imprint seems to be stronger in some cases than the effect of the shared terroir. Terroir speaks with a quiet voice, if you like, and some sites seem to whisper, while others shout. The site-specific characteristics that lie at the heart of terroir seem to be expressed only where winemakers are able and willing to allow them; too much human intervention can destroy this fragile but important sense of place. Examples are harvesting very late, using extended maceration (the process where crushed grape skins are left in contact with juice before fermentation starts, or after fermentation finishes) to extract every last bit of oomph from the grape skins, or using a lot of new oak.

But terroir can also be lost through too little intervention or simply poor winemaking. Natural wines made with no sulfur dioxide additions often taste very similar, and the winemaking choices have in this case resulted in the loss of a sense of place. A winemaker who lets her or his wines go bretty (referring to the influence of the rogue yeast *Brettanomyces,* covered in the chapter on wine faults) will find that they taste the same as a whole heap of other bretty wines. Secondary and tertiary aromas that might develop from too little intervention in making and a failure to stabilize (the end stage of winemaking where measures are taken to make it chemically stable) a wine before bottling can override any primary site expression. The reactions that cause these faults can also have a great impact on the texture of the wine. Thus terroir is a partnership between the site and the winegrower. This is expressed well in the following quote from Brian Croser:

> The passionate maker of fine wine who is truly committed to the terroir of a few distinguished sites (too many will not allow the devotion of time and intensity of observation

required) will suppress the immediate gratification derived from moulding the wine to conform to fashionable perceptions of quality. For the winemaker devoted to a terroir, the act of winemaking will be the simplest possible, non-interventionist, allowing the terroir to express itself and employing viticultural techniques to coax the best out of the distinguished site. Change to practice will be measured, one parameter at a time, over many vintages so that the effect of change can be correctly interpreted.

Not for the committed custodian of a great terroir the extended grape "hang time" that results in the smell and taste of the death of the terroir; the *surmaturité* that makes varieties and sites taste of dead grape and the grape-must require a radical reconstitution with water and acid before fermentation.

Equally the custodian of a great terroir will be content with the moderate concentration and the savoury mouth feel that is natural to the site and will not employ extended cold maceration and super-extractive technique to make it conform to unnatural unction. The use of oak by the responsible curator of a distinguished site will be as a balancing and complementary condiment, allowing the strength of the site to shine through.

Brian Croser, paper presented at Vinexpo, 2005

Let's explore this partnership between site and grower in the expression of terroir in the finished wine. On the one hand, it can be argued that it is necessary to exclude the human element in definitions of terroir, or else the whole topic becomes excessively complex, with too many variables. On the other hand, we worry that a simple definition of terroir that is restricted to just the characteristics of the site and the way in which the vine adapts to its environment in the process of grape production doesn't fully recognize the reality of the situation. Characteristics that are shared among wines from a particular region because of a combination of cultural and winemaking practices held in common among most growers may mistakenly be believed to come from the soil. Reduction (a wine fault due to the presence of volatile sulfur compounds), a winemaking artefact, is an example here: we have a sneaking suspicion that most of what we think of as "minerality" in wine, one of the bedrocks of terroir discussion, has to do with a combination of acidity and volatile sulfur compounds in wine, such as polyfunctional thiols. Where do "mineral" flavours come from, if not from the soil? One explanation could be that they are due to the presence of reduced sulfur compounds, described commonly by tasters as "reduction" flavours. Wine contains a wide range of these, which at certain levels in specific contexts may be mistaken for terroir character. Dominique Delteil consults for a number of wineries around the world, and his experience is that sulfur characters are often presented by winemakers as "terroir expression." He contends that when sulfur compounds are managed better in the winery, suddenly "that famous terroir appears to be a luscious fruit source!" The perception of these sulfur compounds depends a great deal on the context. Delteil recalls a visit to a grower in Friuli who had a dominant "flinty" character in his wine, caused by a sulfur compound, despite appropriate steps in the winery to manage it. This sulfur compound problem

FIGURE 3.6
A cutaway showing the distinctive terroir of the Awatere Valley in New Zealand's Marlborough region. The gravel and large river pebbles allow good drainage and are covered by thin loamy topsoil.

was finally managed by increasing the fruit expression in the wine, at which point the flinty character became an attribute and not a fault. On other occasions it is likely that sulfur compounds aren't the explanation, and that wines with high levels of acidity are simply being described as "mineralic" by tasters looking for a useful descriptor.

In addition to minerality, another term often associated with terroir is *earthiness*. Where does this quality come from? It's hard to be sure, but in some cases earthy, spicy characters can be contributed to wines by *Brettanomyces*, which is present in a surprisingly large proportion of red wines. At high levels some of the aroma compounds generated by *Brettanomyces* activity contribute more animally, stinky characteristics; at lower levels the aromatic impact of *Brettanomyces* could be mistaken for terroir effects. Reductive sulfur compound aromas and some of the aromas from *Brettanomyces* (e.g., volatile phenols) can be quite difficult to differentiate. We believe that sulfur compounds and *Brettanomyces* activity can equally contribute to a perceived definition of minerality and/or earthiness, both of which are qualities commonly used to provide evidence of terroir in the finished wine.

Terroir isn't just a French concept. According to Santiago Achaval, president of the premium Argentinean winery Achaval-Ferrer, there's also a word in Spanish, *terruño*, that's equivalent to *terroir*. Achaval is an eloquent proponent of this concept. "Our word has the same nuances as the word *terroir*, plus an additional one: it's the land a man belongs to, not the land that belongs to a man. It describes a man's bond with the land where he was born," he says. "We think the concept of terroir is of the highest importance.

TERROIR VERSUS GRAPE VARIETIES

JAMIE GOODE and SAM HARROP

In brief, the difference in approach between the New World and Old World wine industries is that the Old World focuses on terroir, while the New World focuses on grape varieties. In the Old World wines are labeled and marketed depending on where they come from, whereas in the New they are labeled by grape variety. There are pros and cons of each approach.

Varietal labeling is simpler and easier for consumers to understand, but it is less diverse and interesting. Different grape varieties have different flavour characteristics, and by learning just a dozen or so names, consumers can find their way around New World wines quite happily.

The terroir approach is potentially more interesting because it recognizes the influence that vineyard site can have on flavour. It is intellectually more appealing and provides a strong link between wine and local culture, but its subtleties and complexities can confuse consumers.

There are other difficulties with the terroir approach. Implicit in an appellation system is the idea that certain production guidelines, such as maximum yields, standard cultivation practices, mandated grape varieties, and recognized soil types, will result in wines of a consistent style and standard. It's almost as if the skill of the grower and the competence of the winemaking are being taken for granted. And who wrote these guidelines and processes anyway? Even if they were correct at the time, terroir has changed (for example, average temperatures, water relations), and thus winemaking should change to accommodate environmental changes. Because appellations are effectively used as brands, growers who lack competence or who cut corners can cheat the system by gaining the cachet of the appellation even though their wines don't deserve it, although it can be argued that the AOC system is to blame here for not ensuring a quality guarantee.

However, the difference in approach between the Old World and New World wine industries is beginning to break down. It seems that the simpler varietal approach better suits commodity wines, while the appellation approach is better for fine wine. In the Old World rules are beginning to change such that the more commercial wines can be labeled more simply by variety, which enables the creation of stronger brands without expecting cheap wines to have to sell themselves by hanging onto the coattails of more prestigious appellations. And in the New World growers are beginning to work out which varieties grow best in which sites, and various locations are developing a reputation that is strong enough for the wines to be marketed effectively by appellation.

Terroir is for us the only source of originality and personality of a wine. It is also a source of never-ending wonder: how small distances and slight differences in soil composition, exposure, and even surrounding plant life result in very noticeable differences in the wines."

He refutes the idea that terroir is confined to classic Old World regions. "Argentina does have terroirs in the same way as France and Italy do. The difference with those other countries is that the discovery of our terroirs is just now beginning. Both France and Italy have been perfecting their knowledge of their soils and microclimates since the early Middle Ages. Argentina started a century ago, with a hiatus during the turbulent economic times during the 1970s and the 1980s. So there's a lot of exploration to be done until we can really say that we know our terroirs, and that we can design their hierarchy: not every vineyard is capable of expressing a powerful personality through its wine. And as in the rest of the world, there are differences in quality of the wine that are driven only by location."

A brilliant New World illustration of terroir is found in Hawkes Bay, New Zealand, and more specifically in an 800-hectare patch of vineyard land known as the Gimblett Gravels. Almost bizarrely, this important terroir went unplanted until the 1980s, and as recently as 1991 just 20 hectares of vines were planted there. Now, however, it is perhaps the most important patch of ground in New Zealand for making red wines from Syrah and Bordeaux varieties.

The gravel was laid down by the Ngaruroro River, which changed its course after a flood in 1867. Located northwest of Hastings, the whole area is almost completely planted with vines. Some thirty years ago, however, this now extremely valuable land was little regarded: it was not very good for grazing sheep, and nothing much would grow here. The first person to think about growing vines here was Chris Pask, who bought and planted a small block in 1981. Shortly afterwards, he was joined by other pioneers: David Irving, Gavin Yortt, John Kenderdine, and Alan Limmer. But their vineyards were small scale, and it wasn't until the early 1990s that larger plantings were made by the likes of Babich and Villa Maria.

However, the Gimblett Gravels faced a serious problem. In 1988, 150 hectares of this prime vineyard land were bought by a concrete company that wanted to extract the gravel and use it to make roads. A coalition of growers started a campaign against this planning application, and they finally persuaded the council that the best use of this land was for establishing world-class vineyards.

What makes this patch of land so special? First, the gravel is free draining and has low fertility, which results in low-vigour vineyards where the vines concentrate their efforts on ripening fruit rather than on producing lush vegetation. Second, temperatures here are a vital couple of degrees higher than in other parts of Hawkes Bay because the gravelly soils act as a sort of thermal blanket, warming up and then radiating heat. The soils are so free draining that it isn't possible to establish vineyards here without irrigation, although established vineyards can be managed with just a little judicious watering.

Thus we have an interesting example of a world-class terroir where some human input in the form of irrigation is essential. Interestingly, Professor Hans Schultz of Geisenheim, Germany, conducted trials on two plots of Riesling vines on the Schlossberg vineyard in Rüdesheim, which has shallow soils with limited water-holding capacity. One plot was unirrigated, while the other received some irrigation. Professionals who tasted the wines made from each plot on two occasions preferred the wine made with the help of irrigation, although this was the warm 2003 vintage, so the unirrigated vines would have experienced quite a bit of water stress: in this case water stress was not good for quality. This raises an interesting point: some human intervention, in this case irrigation, might lead to wines that more faithfully express their terroirs.

But if we look at this topic from a slightly different perspective, what makes the Gimblett Gravels so special is the quality of the wine produced here. The focus is on Bordeaux varieties, principally Merlot, but also Cabernet Sauvignon and a bit of Malbec and Cabernet Franc. The results are fantastic. Some really exciting Syrah, however, is also being produced, even though there isn't very much of it. Gimblett is mainly red wine territory, but some Chardonnay and Sauvignon Blanc are also grown.

But the concept of terroir is not universally respected or welcomed in the New World. It would be false to suggest that all New World vignerons are on a journey where the destination is a European-style fine wine scene built around terroir. One New World vigneron who objects to the notion of terroir is Sean Thackrey, a California winemaker famous for his single-vineyard Orion wine. "My objection is simply that it's so ruthlessly misused, and with such horrifying hypocrisy," says Thackrey. "It's very true that fruit grown in different places tastes different. In fact, it's a banality, so why exactly all this excess insistence?" Thackrey himself allows terroir to influence his work—"I don't know how it would be possible to observe the delicacies of change in a particular vineyard more attentively than I do in making the Orion"—but he feels that the French overemphasize terroir largely because of economic motives. He describes terroir as "an intensely desirable and bankable proposition because their property can then be sold, transferred and inherited with the full value of the wine produced from its grapes attributable to the property itself." Thus the work of the winemaker and viticulturalist is played down, and the role of the vineyard site is talked up. "The immense psychological imperative to have wine be born from the earth without human intervention other than caretaking—which may in itself be why there is no French word for 'winemaker'—would make a long and complex book in itself," Thackrey suggests. "Personally, I believe that the quality of French wine is due to a French genius for viticulture and winemaking, just as I believe that the quality of French cuisine is due to a French genius for gastronomy."

Portugal's Dirk Niepoort, well known for his groundbreaking Douro table wines, adds a slightly different complexion to the debate: "As a rule, I believe blended wines to be better than single-vineyard wines." This doesn't mean that he's a nonbeliever, though. "I believe that terroir is essential," he says. "I think that a good blender has to be some-

FIGURE 3.7
The famous *galets* of Châteauneuf-du-Pape in France's Rhône region. These
are large river pebbles, but what really matters for terroir is what lies beneath
them.

one who understands, knows, and respects the different terroirs they are working with."
Niepoort maintains that the search for great terroirs is very important to him. "But it is
not only finding the terroirs that is important: it is also important to understand them
and then adapt your winemaking to them."

MECHANISMS OF TERROIR: A TASTE OF THE SOIL?

The idea that one can taste the earth in a wine is appealing, a welcome
link to nature and place in a delocalized world; it has also become a
rallying cry in an increasingly sharp debate over the direction of modern
winemaking. The trouble is, it's not true . . . Terroir flavors are generally
characterized as earthiness and minerality. On the other hand, wines
with flavors of berries or tropical fruits and little or no minerality are
therefore assumed not to have as clear a connection to the earth, which
means they could have come from anywhere, and are thought to bear
the mark of human intervention.

HAROLD MCGEE AND DANIEL PATTERSON, *NEW YORK TIMES MAGAZINE*,
6 MAY 2007

How, then, do soils shape wines? Is it through chemical constituents in the soil being
taken up by the vine roots and affecting wine flavour directly? Some winegrowers seem
to think so, and this idea is implicit in the term *goût de terroir*. They suggest that mineral

flavours in wine, for example, are a direct consequence of minerals in the soil. We disagree, as do others, such as McGee and Patterson.

MINERALITY

The topic of minerality overlaps with the concept of terroir. It is hard not to make the link between great wines and soils. In prospecting for new vineyard areas to plant, it is possible to identify homoclimes—sites whose climate closely matches that of the world's greatest vineyards or wine regions. But how many great wines have resulted from such analysis? In the absence of great soils, climate alone is not enough. Where a producer makes wines from neighbouring sites with different soils and comes up with wines that are quite different, it is tempting to link the soil composition to the flavours in the wine and to conclude that because the main variable is the soil, the soil is responsible for the flavour. So far, so good. The danger arises when the link is extended to an assertion that flavours in the wine have come directly from components in the soil. This is a particularly problematic logical leap for mineral flavours in wine, for reasons we'll discuss later.

"I think that minerality, or something like minerality, is very important in wine," agrees California winegrower Randall Grahm, "and I am exceptionally embarrassed not to have anything like real scientific data to back up that claim." Grahm is one of the most astute and thoughtful commentators on the world of wine. He is so intrigued by the issue of minerality and terroir that a few years ago he carried out a crazy-sounding experiment involving rocks and wine. He took some interesting rocks, washed them, and placed them in a barrel of wine until some flavours had been absorbed.

The rocks chosen—granite, Noyo cobblestone, black slate, and Pami pebbles—resulted in major changes in the texture and mouth feel of the wine, as well as dramatic differences in aromatic compounds and persistence of flavour. Grahm states, "In every case, low doses of minerals added far more complexity and greater persistence on the palate. It is my personal belief that wines richer in minerals just present way differently." He adds that "they seem to have a certain sort of nucleus or density around their center; they are gathered, focused, cohered the way a laser coheres light. It is a different kind of density relative to tannic density, somehow deeper in the wine than the tannins." Of course, the extraction of mineral components at pH 3.6 or so will be quite different from what occurs in soil at around pH 7, even without taking the mechanisms of root uptake into account.

Mineral uptake by the vine is a confusing idea. If we have a slaty Mosel terroir, and the wine tastes of slate, is the slate in the wine coming from the soil? What about Douro wines from schist? The schist soils influence the flavour, but do the wines taste of schist? If Chablis is grown on soils of Kimmeridgean clay and chalk (characteristic soil types found in this region), can this be tasted in the wine? Some people think so. But how is this achieved? Higher-quality soils (say, Grand Cru versus Petit Chablis) tend to result in wines that are more mineralic.

How do we make sense of mineral flavours in wine? It's hard to answer this question precisely, but a small dose of plant physiology can help keep our thinking on the right track. It seems clear that almost all the flavour compounds in wine are made by the vine, or are made from precursors present in the must by yeast metabolism, or come from an extrinsic source such as oak barrels. The plant roots take up a restricted set of compounds, largely water and water-soluble mineral ions. But this observation can be a source of confusion because of the word *mineral*. These mineral ions aren't really the same as mineral flavours. They are pretty much flavourless. There's no real evidence for direct translocation of flavour compounds from soils to wines, even though this is a very seductive idea. We have spoken with a number of plant physiologists about this topic, and the overwhelming conclusion seems to be that there is no flavour transmission from soils to grapes, although soil chemistry could be influencing grape composition indirectly by altering gene expression and thus the synthesis of various compounds in the grapes. Many viticulturalists, however, are convinced that the main impact of soils on wine flavour is mediated via their structure and drainage properties. The most successful terroirs seem to be those that allow a slow, steady supply of water to the vine that tails off after veraison (the stage in ripening when the grapes change colour, expand, and begin to accumulate sugars). Work on regulated deficit irrigation and partial root drying (specialized irrigation techniques working on targeted restriction of water at precise times) indicates that water stress influences plant hormone signaling (abscisic acid is the key hormone involved), which then affects grape development in significant ways.

There is one example, however, of direct flavour transmission from a locale to the wine, and this is eucalyptus. Wines made from grapes grown in vineyards in warm climates with adjoining stands of eucalypti frequently have a hint of mint/eucalyptus to them, which results from aromatic oils from the tree leaves finding their way onto leaves and grapes, getting into the grapes, and surviving the fermentation process. Smoke taint from wildfires is another illustration that the vineyard environment can directly impart flavour to wine, but not via the plant roots.

Let's address a more practical question. What exactly is minerality in wine? What sort of flavours are we talking about? They are not "earthy" tastes—flavours reminiscent of soil—but rather stone or rock flavours. Crisp Chablis with high acidity is frequently mineralic. Muscadet can often be mineralic. Old World wines tend to show more minerality than those from the New World, while riper wines are often less mineralic, so these are observations that need some explanation. There's frequently a gravelly edge in Bordeaux that has a mineral component but also overlaps with a faint hint of greenness. Sauvignon Blanc is frequently described as being minerally. Great examples of both red and white Burgundy frequently have a mineral dimension to them. It seems hard to pick many consistent themes here, and this is just an abbreviated list.

"In the absence of hard data that would show that what we call 'minerality' correlates to certain levels of specific minerals or ratios between minerals or perhaps even to specific redox couples," says Randall Grahm, "Probably the disulfide/thiol couple is the one that is most interesting, as that is the one that is in our sensory wheelhouse." Here Grahm is touching on an interesting idea: that reduction can show itself in a form that leads to the use of the descriptor *mineralic* by tasters. Overall, though, he thinks that minerality in wine has many sources, and that it correlates with the following list of phenomena:

1. Mineral-rich soil, that is, high levels of exchangeable cations
2. Healthy soil microflora
3. Low yields, that is, favorable ratio of rooting mass to fruit volume
4. Old vines
5. Nonirrigated soil, especially soil that is not drip irrigated
6. Maybe smaller trunks and head-trained (*gobelet*) vines (aka bush vines)
7. Later-harvested vines (all things being equal) but not overripe
8. Ability to tolerate oxidative challenge after being open for several days
9. Ability to age and improve in the bottle
10. Mineralizing processes in soil—the presence of particular animals (sheep?), manure, compost

"It is certainly possible to confute 'minerality' with other phenomena," says Grahm. "The presence of *Brettanomyces* (that's more iodine and sweat), 'greenness' (that's likely green seeds or perhaps inclusion of stems), tannin (that's more of a sense of astringency), and various volatile sulfur compounds such as thiols and disulfides." In relation to the last point, he adds a question: "Do minerals in wine tend to make a wine more backward or 'reduced,' or is a tendency toward the formation of thiols just another word for minerality?"

Another thoughtful winegrower with an interesting perspective on minerality is Dirk Niepoort. "Minerality is very, very important for me in wine," he emphasizes. "I believe that minerality comes from (mainly) two factors," he adds. "The logical one is terroir. I'm a firm believer that terroir is very important in great wines, and different terroirs give different wines." But he thinks that the second factor is just as important, and here he develops some of the themes that Grahm has raised. "What many times originated (I say 'originated' because it is disappearing because of crazy modern focus on perfection which originates with the modern winemakers who have to control and correct everything) minerality (and specific character) in certain famous wines and areas was in fact due to certain imperfections in the must due to the terroirs." Niepoort's point is that what many modern winemakers would call wine faults that develop during *élevage* (the process of maturing wines in the cellar) but diminish by the time the wine is bottled impart to the wine characteristics that are complex and in many cases are described as minerality. "For example, because of a lack of a certain nutrient in a must from a certain terroir, off flavours would develop during the fermentation which

FIGURE 3.8
Schist: the distinctive slatelike soils of the Douro Valley in Portugal. These
allow good drainage, and their poor fertility keeps the vines from being
overvigorous.

in the end would give the typical character of that area," he explains. "Certain treatment
habits in the vineyards (such as sulfur treatments done late) create some residue in the
must that influences the fermentation and produce some reduction, which by the time
the wines are bottled is gone but which gives a lot of character." Niepoort concludes
with a lament: "The paranoia of correcting everything means that the wines taste more
and more of the grape variety/varieties and less and less of the terroir, and of course the
wines are tasting all alike. The winemakers are gods!"

Much more can be said about minerality and its importance, but most important, it
would be good to have more solid data on exactly what it is. For New World winemakers
in particular, who have typically struggled to attain mineral complexity in some of their
wines, these data might help in the quest to make ageworthy fine wines on a more
regular basis. "I think that a real comprehensive survey to look at minerality in wine
worldwide is definitely in order," says Grahm. "If I had a jillion-dollar research budget,
this is one of the first things I would study."

While in some circles literalist explanations of terroir are quite common, they are
treated with a degree of incredulity by many New World viticulturalists. Dawid Saay-
man, a South African viticultural expert known for his work on terroir, states, "I don't
believe that the minerals taken up by the vine can register as minerality in the wines.
Minerality appears to me to be more the result of absence of fruitiness." But it's pretty
much a given that wines made from grapes differing only in the soil in which they were
grown taste different. So just what is the scientific explanation for these terroir effects?
The question is important because providing a sound scientific footing for terroir is

a worthy cause. Not only will it lend credibility to the concept in the eyes of sceptics, but it will also help those who are already converted understand and therefore better use terroir effects.

Even if science leaves us with what currently looks like a rather emasculated version of terroir, we don't think that the importance of this cherished concept is necessarily diminished. Winegrowers who use terroir as their guiding philosophical framework and focus on the importance of the soil are responsible for a disproportionately large share of the world's most interesting wines. However it happens that wines from a certain place end up tasting of that place, it is these local differences in flavour that help make wine interesting. If we were to drop the concept of terroir and all that goes with it, we'd lose a good deal of the interest and diversity of wine. Perhaps it would help if we could come up with a term to describe this complicated concept that is less loaded and has less baggage. *Typicity* might do, but we suspect that we are stuck with *terroir* for now.

We end this chapter with another quote from McGee and Patterson's *New York Times Magazine* article "Talk Dirt to Me" (6 May 2007):

> If rocks were the key to the flavor of "somewhereness," then it would be simple to counterfeit terroir with a few mineral saltshakers. But the essence of wine is more elusive than that, and far richer. Scientists and historians continue to illuminate what [famous enologist Émile] Peynaud described as the "dual communion" represented by wine: "on the one hand with nature and the soil, through the mystery of plant growth and the miracle of fermentation, and on the other with man, who wanted wine and who was able to make it by means of knowledge, hard work, patience, care and love."

4

GRAFTED VINES

With their slate soils and steep slopes, the Erdener Prälat, Urziger Würzgarten, and Wehlener Sonnenuhr vineyards of Germany's Mosel region are some of the most spectacular and scarily steep vineyards anywhere. The vines themselves are unusual: they are individually trained with their own stakes, and the majority are planted on their own roots. In the modern world of wine, this is quite uncommon.

In discussions of naturalness, one of the most remarkable and common vineyard manipulations in wine regions everywhere is often forgotten: the fusing of two different species of grapevine. Because *Vitis vinifera* is susceptible to a tiny root-munching aphid called phylloxera, it needs to be grafted onto resistant rootstock. This striking manipulation is the legacy of the global spread of phylloxera from its home in the United States at the end of the nineteenth century. This tiny insect, with its complicated life cycle, caused a vine plague of epic proportions that in the space of a few decades brought the world's wine industry to its knees. Salvation came from an unlikely source—the same as the origin of the problem—native American grapevines. The resistance of American vine rootstocks to phylloxera is therefore the fragile pillar on which the worldwide wine industry now rests; fortunately, it has proved amazingly resilient.

But is grafting "natural"? Are wines from ungrafted vines different? And were the great wines, made from pre-phylloxera vines, any better?

FIGURE 4.1
The famous vineyard of Erdener Prälat in Germany's Mosel region, with centenarian ungrafted Riesling vines.

HOW PHYLLOXERA WAS BEATEN

The second half of the nineteenth century was not a good time to be a winegrower in France. By 1850 the livelihood of a large proportion of the population was tied to the vine and its produce. But within a few decades the French wine industry was shaken to its roots by two natural plagues. One of these, the fungal disease oidium, was remedied fairly quickly by chemical means, but the other, phylloxera, caused devastation on an enormous scale and threatened to eradicate viticulture as we know it from the globe.

The grape varieties responsible for almost all the wines that we drink belong to a single species, *Vitis vinifera* L. One of around a hundred grapevine species found in the wild, it was originally domesticated perhaps as long as nine thousand years ago, in the Neolithic period. Because the hundreds of varieties in common use all belong to the same species, the resulting lack of genetic diversity renders them vulnerable to attack by pest and disease.

The United States has a wide variety of native wild vines. Surprisingly, there is no historical record that these were ever cultivated or that wine was ever made from them, despite their abundance. Eventually, European immigrants to the United States, anxious to produce wines like those of their homelands, turned to the native vines out of necessity when their attempts to grow *Vitis vinifera* varieties had failed. The *vinifera* vines simply lacked innate protection against the mildew and phylloxera that were endemic in the United States, and alongside which the American vine species had coevolved. But while the American varieties grew well and proved robust in the face of disease, their big flaw was that they produced fairly unpalatable wine, with a strong "foxy" taste.

In the Victorian craze for importing novel, exotic plant varieties, aided by the steamship, American vines began to be imported into France early in the nineteenth century, and by 1830 a couple of dozen varieties were growing in French nurseries. These imported vines were disseminated throughout Europe's wine regions by nurserymen and vignerons keen to experiment. They turned out to be carrying a deadly insect (phylloxera) and fungus (oidium) cargo.

The consequences were disastrous. European vineyards were hit first by the fungal disease oidium (powdery mildew). *Oidium tuckeri* (now known as *Uncinula necator*) was first discovered growing on a greenhouse vine in Kent in 1845. This previously unknown fungus almost certainly arrived from the United States on a botanical sample and soon spread throughout Europe. Within a few years wine production in France had collapsed to less than a third of its previous levels. The response of vignerons was one of panic, but this time, science provided an answer fairly rapidly. French scientists discovered that dusting the vines with elemental sulfur provided protection against the fungus, and by 1858 oidium was in retreat, albeit through the use of a chemical solution. In the 1880s, while France was in the throes of dealing with phylloxera, a second fungal disease from America, downy mildew (caused by *Plasmopara viticola*), hit the vines. In this case, another chemical solution was found by serendipity: Bordeaux mixture, a combination of lime, copper sulfate, and water. Interestingly, to this day it is necessary to use some form of chemical protection against oidium and downy mildew when growing *Vitis vinifera* vines. Even biodynamic and organic growers have to use copper and sulfur in their vineyards, although the use of these chemicals is justified by calling them "natural."

The culprit was the root-feeding aphid *Phylloxera vastatrix* (known today by scientists as *Daktulosphaira vitifoliae*). It was introduced by a wine merchant in The Gard. By 1868 the entire southern Rhône was infected, and phylloxera had become endemic throughout Languedoc. Within the space of a decade it had moved through France and gone global, reaching Portugal's Douro by 1872, Spain and Germany two years later, Australia in 1875, and Italy by 1879. The last French wine region to be affected was Champagne, in 1890.

The response to phylloxera was, again, panic. At first, the outward signs—the leaves of affected vines turning yellow and falling prematurely, followed by death—gave no clue about the specific nature of the disease. When affected vines were extracted from the ground, their roots were found to be rotten and crumbling, but no obvious pest was present. The French government commission that was established to investigate the outbreak appointed Professor Jules-Émile Planchon, a botanist, to identify the culprit. He dug up roots of a healthy vine and observed clumps of minute wingless insects happily gorging themselves. Clever parasites don't kill their hosts, and in the United States phylloxera and grapevines had coevolved such that they existed alongside each other. However, this cosy relationship hadn't developed with *Vitis vinifera,* and the arrangement was hopelessly imbalanced: the parasitism by phylloxera was too harsh and resulted in eventual death to the vine.

There are three potential mechanisms for vine damage by phylloxera: removal of photosynthates, physical disruption of the roots, and secondary fungal infections of damaged roots. It is unlikely that the severe, usually fatal vine damage is caused by the first mechanism. It is much more likely that the damage occurs through secondary infections by fungal pathogens.

Initial attempts to halt the spread of phylloxera by uprooting and burning affected vines failed. Some of the proposed treatments sounded surprisingly modern, such as biological control (finding a natural enemy of phylloxera) and planting more attractive hosts for the aphid amid the vines. However, they didn't work. Vignerons growing vines on the plains discovered that where seasonal flooding was possible, it was reasonably effective in killing this subterranean pest. Vineyards in sandy soils were also observed to be immune. Chemists searched rather randomly for a magic bullet. At the time, it was known that carbon disulfide was an effective insecticide, despite the fact that it was highly volatile and explosive when mixed with air. An elaborate array of devices for injecting this rather risky chemical into the root zones were invented, and before long it was seen as the best option for heading off the pest. The problems with carbon disulfide were threefold. It was a relatively expensive treatment that was beyond the economic reach of many vignerons; it needed repeating, year after year; and it wasn't very effective, mitigating the worst symptoms of the malaise without being curative.

Another controversial solution was proposed. American vine species, which had introduced the invader in the first place, had natural protection against phylloxera. Where they had been planted, they thrived, while all around them was a scene of devastation. It was true that the wine they produced tasted fairly bad, but better odd wine than no wine at all, argued the faction that became known as the *américainistes*. Tastings of wines made from the American vines were set up, but the depressing conclusion was that these foxy wines really weren't good enough.

Then someone had a brilliant idea. In 1869 Gaston Bazille, a winegrower, suggested grafting *vinifera* varieties onto American rootstock. With the benefit of hindsight, this seems a brilliant solution, but at the time there were many unknowns. Chief among these were the following: First, how long would the graft last? Second, would the rootstock impart some of that American vine "foxiness" to the wine, altering the qualities of the grapes of the *vinifera* varieties by this unnatural union of scion and stock? Third, how resistant would the various rootstocks be?

One of the first documented applications of this grafting occurred in 1874, when Henri Bouschet displayed an Aramon (*Vitis vinifera*) vine grafted onto American rootstock at the Congrès Viticole in Montpellier. In a short time it became clear that, somewhat counterintuitively, the wine made from *vinifera* vines grafted onto American rootstocks retained the full character of the *vinifera* variety while benefiting from the phylloxera resistance of the American roots. In a rather neat circle, the plague had come from America, but so had the salvation.

However, the battle between the two factions of the chemists (who advocated carbon disulfide) and the *américainistes* (who supported the use of resistant American vines or their rootstocks) continued. The turning point was the International Phylloxera Congress in Bordeaux in 1881, where discussions reached the conclusion that *vinifera* varieties grafted onto American rootstock did indeed maintain their characteristics.

The idea spread. The technique of grafting was easy enough to learn that it could be attempted by just about anyone. The supply of American vines was a more difficult problem because many wine regions began to prohibit their importation in order to prevent the remaining phylloxera-free vineyards from succumbing to the pest. Moreover, not everyone was won over by this radical idea of grafting. Many resisted replanting, with the attendant three-year loss of production, and clung tenaciously to their chemical treatments. In the end, good sense prevailed, and the grafters won the day. The lengthy work of replanting France's vineyards began. It was not a straightforward process, and some of the grander estates, reluctant to pull out their vines, kept them going with insecticide treatments as long as they could. The choice of appropriate grafting material was also complicated by the fact that it took a while to find American vine species that were well adapted to the chalky soils that predominated in some of France's key regions.

One thing that replanting did facilitate was a change in the viticultural landscape, with some sites being abandoned and others being replanted with new varieties. In addition, the choice of rootstock, with its effect on graft parameters such as vigour, became an additional variable, a new item in the viticultural toolbox.

HOW GRAFTING WORKS

Grafting is an ancient practice that takes advantage of the fact that plants don't have an immune system, and thus different varieties or even species can unite and grow as one. It is recorded as far back as 323 BC by Theophrastos for apple trees, and by Cato in his second-century BC *De agri cultura* for grapes. It is easy to see why, when grafting all *vinifera* varieties onto American rootstocks was proposed, growers would have objected: why should they fuse their precious vines with foreign vines that made only bad wine? There is also the widespread emotional—and dare we say spiritual—significance accorded to the soil in which the vine is rooted. Traditional notions of terroir have frequently encompassed a belief that the vine roots are extracting some special component from the soil in which they are growing that confers a sense of place on the wine. In effect, the concept is widely (if unconsciously) held that there is a conversation between the earth and the vine, mediated by the roots, that then determines the character of the wine. According to the viewpoint of biodynamics, this interaction involves unquantified (and probably unquantifiable) life forces: the fact that vines are all grafted must seem to the biodynamic practitioner some sort of admission of defeat, for if the vine were truly in harmony with the life forces of the vineyard, it would be able to repel the damaging attentions of hungry phylloxera, and harm would be averted. But biodynamic growers seem to accept grafting as a necessity.

Physically, grafting involves the union of two plants, the scion and the stock, where the critical area is a thin layer of cells known as the vascular cambium. This cylindrical layer of cells runs close to the outer circumference of the stem or trunk of the plant, producing phloem on the exterior side and xylem on the interior. Phloem is the vascular tissue that conducts sugars and nutrients; xylem is the tissue that conducts water and dissolved minerals, as well as providing structural support. Grafting takes advantage of the wound-healing response in plants. When an incision is made in a plant stem, the response is the growth of dedifferentiated cells (cells that have reverted to an unspecialized state). Thus when branches or trunks that have already initiated secondary growth are damaged, they respond by producing callus, a tissue of undifferentiated cells produced by proliferation near the wound site. This same callus production happens when the scion and the stock are joined. This callus provides the tissue through which vascular continuity is restored. Signals from the vascular tissue of both scion and stock presumably influence the undifferentiated callus cells to become cambial cells, and from these, the new vascular tissue that is seamless between scion and stock develops.

Grafting a *vinifera* vine onto an American vine stock is a relatively simple process. Incisions are made in both the rootstock and scion such that they marry closely, giving some physical resilience to the join. The critical feature is to have the two cambial layers in apposition to each other: typically, the cleft made in the rootstock is designed to allow the maximum area of cambial contact. Most grafting is done with cuttings (bench grafting), but it is also possible to graft in the field. And as well as joining American rootstock to a *vinifera* scion, grafting is commonly used to transplant one *vinifera* variety to another in the vineyard. In any graft situation, both scion and stock retain their separate genetic identities; the graft merely facilitates vascular transport.

ARE WINES FROM UNGRAFTED VINES BETTER?

So we reach the central question. Have vines that have been altered by the grafting union lost something intrinsic to their identity? Were wines made from ungrafted vines, before phylloxera appeared, somehow better? "When I first met wine people, it was the great debate," recalls Hugh Johnson. "There was still lots of evidence of how good wines had been before phylloxera, but I don't remember a single conclusive demonstration that they had become less good since, or that if they had it was blameable on the louse." As the number of surviving pre-phylloxera bottles has diminished, the pre- and post-phylloxera debate has become less voluble, but there are still people in the trade with enough experience of these pre-phylloxera bottles to have formed an opinion. Famous auctioneer and wine expert Michael Broadbent is one. Are the pre-phylloxera wines

FIGURE 4.2

South Australia is currently free of phylloxera; the vineyard owners want it to stay that way.

better? "Who knows?" he replies. "The quality was undoubtedly high from 1844 until 1878: one has read about them and one has tasted them." Fellow auctioneer Serena Sutcliffe is another who has experienced plenty of these old bottles. Are they special? "Yes, they are different: they are more intense; they have total, concentrated heart," says Sutcliffe. "They also have the most incredible scent and long, lingering finish. But you have to mix this in with the fact that yields were so much lower then: so how much is due to that, how much to the original vines? I suspect it is a combination."

Hugh Johnson also elaborates this theme. He agrees that pre-phylloxera wines may have been different, but not necessarily because of grafting onto American rootstocks. "Of course it was not one event," maintains Johnson. "The oidium before it and the mildew at the same time made owners more proactive in their vineyards than they had ever been. They manured like mad to make their vines healthy and strong. They sulfured the vines, used carbon sulfate on the soil, invented Bordeaux mixture. Yields went up dramatically. They started chaptalizing (adding sugar to the must before fermentation), tried to control fermentation temperatures, started bottling much earlier, in fact changed so many things in a short period that it's amazing that some of the 'pre-phylloxera' wines made during this time were as good as they were."

Sutcliffe adds that she doubts that the top wines from top vintages that are made now will last eighty to one hundred years. "But, how many people today require their wines to do that? Virtually no one. We are in the age of instant gratification, so it is perhaps irrelevant." Sutcliffe also adds a possible explanation of the longevity of the old

FIGURE 4.3

Quinta do Noval's celebrated Nacional vineyard is an ungrafted plot within the main vineyard. No one knows how it survives when there is phylloxera all around it.

FIGURE 4.4

Vines trained singly on stakes in the Urziger Würzgarten vineyard of Germany's Mosel.

FIGURE 4.5
Old, ungrafted, untrellised Mourvèdre vines in Australia's Barossa Valley.

wines. "A fascinating fact is that the vast majority of these pre-phylloxera gems are very low in alcohol, often 10 percent or even under, as with some old Ausone from the nineteenth century: absolute proof that alcohol in itself does not assure longevity—perhaps the contrary, so beware all those 14 percent numbers out there! It seems to eat up the wine over time."

As well as experience with pre-phylloxera wines, two further lines of argument might give some insight into whether ungrafted wines are somehow better. First, around the world there are some significant areas where *vinifera* vines are still grown on their own roots. Among the most notable is South Australia, which phylloxera hasn't reached yet, and which is kept clean by a strictly enforced quarantine. The Barossa Valley in particular has a number of old-vine vineyards, planted on their own roots. These Barossa old-vine vineyards make some extremely fine wines, albeit in a rather different style from that of the Old World classic regions, which renders a comparison rather difficult. The Mosel is another region where growing vines on their own roots is feasible. The intensely slaty soils seem to make life impossible for phylloxera. Most Chilean vines are also ungrafted, but Chile has so far struggled to make world-class wines, so these data points are also of limited use. Many of the older vineyards in New Zealand and Oregon are still on their own roots, even though phylloxera has reached these regions. Perhaps more useful is evidence from particular isolated ungrafted vineyards still being cultivated in the middle of wine regions that are otherwise grafted.

One example of an ungrafted vineyard where wines are made that can be compared with those from grafted vines on the same estate is Quinta do Noval's Nacional, a

2.5-hectare vineyard in the Cima Corgo of the Douro Valley, Portugal. This vineyard has never been affected by phylloxera. Each year the grapes are picked, vinified, and matured separately. On average, just 250 cases are produced annually. "Although we don't declare it every year, the Quinta do Noval Nacional is always extraordinary," says Christian Seely, who took over running Quinta do Noval on behalf of insurance company AXA in 1996 (*declaration* is a term used by Port producers for the release of a Vintage Port, the highest category, which usually occurs only three times a decade). "The remarkable thing about the wine is that although we vinify it in exactly the same way as the other wines from Quinta do Noval, it is always very different from any of the other lots of wine from the estate. It marches to quite a different drum than the rest of the vineyard: sometimes it can produce a Vintage Port that is among the greatest wines of the world when the rest of the vineyard is having an LBV (late-bottled vintage, a lower tier of quality than Vintage Port) quality year (as in 1996); in others it is not even of Vintage quality when the rest of the vineyard is making great Vintage Port (as in 1995), but it is always different from the rest of Noval. Even in years such as 1997 for example, when I believe the Quinta do Noval Vintage and the Nacional to be equivalent in quality, the wines have an entirely different character." Even here, though, we can't say that it is the fact that the Nacional vines are ungrafted that makes them produce different wines. There may well be something different about the soil of the Nacional vineyard that neuters the threat of phylloxera. This difference could reasonably be expected to influence the nature of the wine; as Seely puts it, "Nacional is a supreme example of the importance of terroir."

In the Loire, Domaine Henry-Marrionet is the proud owner of an ungrafted vineyard and has been so convinced by the quality of the resulting wines that it has planted more vineyards on their own roots. "Effectively we have the luck to possess the oldest vineyard of France, which was planted in 1850 to the Romorantin variety," explains Jean-Sébastien Marionnet. "She is thus *pré-phylloxérique* and ungrafted and has a surface area of 35 ares [an are is 1/100 of a hectare or 100 m², the same as a 10×10 m plot]. Furthermore, in 1992 we planted 1ha of Gamay and in 2000 2ha of Malbec and 1ha of Sauvignon. In 2002 we also got back 25 ares of Chenin planted in 1979." What is the benefit of this rather risky practice? "Wines coming from ungrafted vines give much more complex aromas, a more pronounced red colour, and greater density, volume, and fatness in the mouth," maintains Marionnet. "The wines from ungrafted vines have more of everything, and greater length. The rootstock acts as a filter."

The second line of argument is theoretical and uses science to answer the question of how grafting *vinifera* varieties onto American rootstocks is likely to affect wine grape quality. These theoretical considerations are more informative.

How does the rootstock affect wine grape quality? It is clear that rootstocks can influence the growth pattern of the scion quite considerably. Apples are instructive here. In the early 1900s scientists at the East Malling Research Institute in Kent (United

Kingdom) did much work on rootstocks for apple trees. There are around twenty well-known rootstocks for apples, and these determine how the apple tree (the scion) will grow. With one rootstock a certain variety of apple will produce a tall tree; with another, the same variety will produce a dwarf plant just 5 feet high. The rootstock not only supplies water and mineral nutrients to the plant but also communicates with the scion by means of hormonal signals. That the roots of grape vines signal to the aerial part of the plant is well known, particularly from work done recently on partial deficit irrigation and precision root drying. The roots are able to signal information about soil water status to the aerial parts of the plant by means of the stress hormone abscisic acid, which is produced in response to deficit. This causes the leaves to close their stomata to avoid losing water before they suffer any water stress. It is likely that the rootstock signals all manner of information by means of plant hormones, and that there is communication the other way also, from shoots to roots. Because the scion and rootstock have subtly different genetic makeups, the choice of rootstock is likely to have physiological consequences for the *vinifera* scion and will, to a degree, shape its growth pattern. This interplay is effectively a new viticultural tool, provided that viticulturalists understand enough about it to manipulate it effectively. This will in turn affect grape, and thus wine, quality. But there is no reason that this should be a negative impact; in many instances it could be positive. Science has no evidence to support the claim that grafted vines produce grapes that are necessarily inferior to those produced by the same variety grown on its own roots.

We think that the fact that so many expert commentators over the ages have argued that there was something special about pre-phylloxera wines strongly suggests that they were very good wines indeed, and perhaps even better than the wines that followed, made from grafted vines. There are numerous confounding factors here, not least that old-vine vineyards were being uprooted at more or less the same time and were being planted with new vines. While no one knows for sure why it is the case, young and adolescent vines simply don't perform as well as their older siblings. It could be this dip in quality following widespread replanting that caused commentators to note a qualitative deficit after phylloxera, which may then have been wrongly attributed to grafting. But other factors involved in replanting could also be responsible for this deficit. From theoretical considerations, it seems that pointing a finger at grafting onto American vines is misguided, and that changes in winemaking, viticultural "advances," and stylistic changes have produced wines that may impress more when young but lack the longevity and purity of the very old wines made before the phylloxera plague hit. Phylloxera was a crisis that led to widespread changes in global viticulture, some good and some perhaps less so. Might there be a future revolution in the vineyard that will begin with the best intentions but result in us lamenting a lost world of wine? We refer here to genetically modified grapevines, currently a long way off, but certainly on the radar.

One other point worth making is that the famous terroir-focused wine regions such as Burgundy and Bordeaux were defined at a time when vines were planted on their own roots. It could be argued that rootstock is a key element in defining terroir. Here we have introduced into the equation another element: the roots of a different species of vine. It is often said that the careful matching of variety to site that is seen in regions such as Bordeaux, Burgundy, and Piedmont took many hundreds of years, and lots of experimentation. Have we had enough time to understand the relationships involved since phylloxera necessitated the introduction of rootstocks?

5

BIODYNAMICS AND ORGANICS

In certain regions of the world, a quiet but influential viticultural revolution has been taking place. Over the past couple of decades, increasing numbers of winegrowers have been adopting a special form of viticulture called biodynamics. This supercharged version of organic viticulture, with its range of sometimes bizarre preparations, adherence to a celestial calendar, and an underlying philosophy that speaks of mysterious life forces, is currently growing in popularity in the vineyards of Europe and is gradually gaining converts in Australia, New Zealand, Chile, the United States, and South Africa.

The Saahs family of Nikolaihof in Austria's Wachau was the first to apply this agricultural system to winegrowing in the 1970s, but in recent years it has taken strong hold in many European wine regions, perhaps most notably Alsace, Burgundy, and the Loire. It's hard to know exactly how many winegrowers are practicing biodynamics, in part because many are in the process of conversion and are currently not certified, and in part because some practice it without explicitly telling anyone, but a rough estimate might be that there are some 750 biodynamic producers worldwide.

Nicolas Joly, unofficial ambassador (or should we say high priest?) of biodynamic viticulture, describes his conversion to *biodynamie* as having its nascence in environmental concerns. When he returned from a spell as a banker in the United States to his family's estate in the Loire in 1977, he decided that he wanted to make wines that expressed the "spot" of Coulée de Serrant. Early in his tenure, he was visited by an official from the Chamber of Agriculture. "They told me that my mother had been running the estate well, but in an old-fashioned way, and it was now time for some modernity. I was

FIGURE 5.1
Digging up cow horns from the vineyard at Millton in Gisborne, New
Zealand.

told that if I started using weed killers, I'd save 14,000 francs."Joly took this advice but
soon regretted it. "Within two years I realized that the colour of the soil was changing;
insects like ladybirds were no longer there; all the partridge had gone." Then fate intervened. Joly read a book on biodynamics. "I wasn't attracted to the green movement, but
this book fascinated me, and I had the crazy idea of trying to practice this concept." If
you speak to growers, you'll often hear them repeat in other settings the sort of journey
that Joly has taken.

Of course, biodynamics isn't the only option open to those who wish to farm their
vineyards more naturally, but it makes sense to begin with it because it has been the
most visible example of the greening of the wine business. We'll then look at other sustainable farming practices that are being applied in vineyards worldwide. It could be argued that many of the sustainable farming practices now applied in vineyards are being
used only because of the green awakening of the wine trade, which might not have occurred but for the pressure biodynamic growers have put on viticulturalists to lessen
their environmental impact. It would be impossible to prove this, of course, but we suspect that the influence of biodynamic winegrowing has gone further than just the vineyards of those who choose to farm this way.

How does biodynamics work? It's essentially organic farming with an extra layer of
practice and philosophy added, although some growers might object to this simplifica-
tion. It has been described by others as "organics plus metaphysics," or "Harry Potter
does viticulture." So first we'll look at organics, and then we'll see what extra is required
of biodynamic producers. This might be seen as a slightly back-to-front approach because biodynamics, which dates back to the 1920s, actually predates the current organic

movement, which began only in the late 1940s. But it's structurally the simplest way of addressing the issues because of the extra elements involved in biodynamics on top of shared common practices.

ORGANIC VITICULTURE

At the heart of organics lies the soil. One thing you'll find in common among organic growers is their emphasis on generating and maintaining healthy soil life. According to advocates of organic growing, soils that are rich in organic materials are able to retain the inorganic mineral ions that plants need for healthy growth; they are also able to provide complex nutrients to the vine at a slow rate that seems to be better for optimal vine growth than rapid delivery that occurs with the use of inorganic fertilizers. In some ways, organics is farming the way it used to be done before the intensive farming of the past fifty years and its reliance on agrochemicals became the norm.

Organics as we know it is actually quite new, even though it reflects older patterns of farming from the preindustrial era. The oldest certifying body is the United Kingdom's Soil Association, which was founded in 1946 by a group of individuals who were concerned about the impact of new forms of intensive agriculture. Specific concerns were the loss of soil through erosion and depletion, the decreased nutritional quality of intensively produced food, the exploitation of animals in intensive units, and the impact of large intensive farming systems on the countryside and wildlife. For many years this remained a small organization, operating out of a farm in Suffolk, but demand for organic products began to grow in the 1970s. A certification system was developed in 1973; today, the Soil Association certifies 80 percent of organic food in the United Kingdom. Interest in organics grew steadily during the 1980s and 1990s. It is estimated that today 4 percent of agricultural land in the United Kingdom is managed organically, and the market for organic products is worth £2.1 billion. The Soil Association is a not-for-profit organization, and fees for inspection and certification are not onerous. Overall, the United Kingdom has nine different bodies that are authorised by the Department for Environment, Food and Rural Affairs (DEFRA) to certify organic farming; throughout the world there are now more than three hundred such bodies, but they all share common philosophies and practices.

CHANGING VIEWS OF THE SOIL

One of the great contributions of organic farming is the way it has changed the way we view the soil. The old-fashioned, "bad-science" view is that soil is merely a physical substrate into which plants root to find support, water, and inorganic mineral ions. This physicochemical view of the soil fails to see it as a living medium, but the organic movement encourages us to consider the life in the soil as critical to good farming. Soil microbes, insects, and arthropods help create the soil's structure, and organic material in the soil is responsible for humus. Humus is degraded organic matter that assists the soil to retain water and aggregate properly, as well as to capture and hold mineral ions and make them available to plants. Living soils have good resistance to compaction and are properly aerated; they are also protected to a degree against erosion. Soil microbes are critical in nutrient cycling, making complex nutrients available to plant roots.

Because of the way the soil was viewed in the past, farmers saw no problem with the use of agrochemicals. As long as these chemicals didn't harm the crop plant, the people applying them were wearing proper protective equipment, and the residues left on the crop were below the legal limits, everything was okay. But this view failed to take into account the effect of the various agrochemicals on the life of the soil itself. If you kill or otherwise change significantly the microbial life or fauna of the soil, you change its properties in important ways. Clean cultivation of vineyards by using herbicides also changes the microbial populations because the plants growing between the rows have been eliminated. This loss of soil biodiversity may not be immediately visible, and the vineyards may look very tidy, but there will be an impact on soil health and fertility.

Farmers aren't all stupid, though, and they haven't deliberately set out to wreck their soils by adopting these brutal agrochemical approaches. Scientists aren't all stupid, either, and while the makers of agrochemicals are clearly motivated by profit, it would be wrong to cast all agribusiness as an evil empire plotting to conspire against the earth. Plant scientists have worked hard towards the goal of helping growers produce more and better-quality crops. However, the scientific model of crop production has in the past been based on a simplified understanding of how nature works, including the outdated view of the soil as an inert substrate. Looking at how we got to where we are now provides a useful perspective.

In 1798, in his *Essay on the Principle of Population*, clergyman Thomas Malthus calculated that the population of the earth tends to increase geometrically, while the provision of food increases only arithmetically. The result? Before very long the population pressure is such that large numbers of people will starve. "The power of population is indefinitely greater than the power in the earth to produce subsistence for man," he warned. This spectre of mass starvation has been referred to as the "Malthusian precipice." We have avoided it so far largely because of the increased efficiency of agriculture.

The dramatic improvement in crop yields that occurred in the 1950s and 1960s is commonly dubbed the "green revolution." It was accomplished by the use of new, high-yielding crop varieties such as the IR8 strain of rice developed at the International Rice Research Institute in Manila and Norman Borlaug's dwarf wheat varieties, as well as the widespread use of fertilizers and pesticides. These advances in agriculture undoubtedly saved many millions, perhaps even billions, of lives. Of course, these advances have come at a price and are associated with some level of environmental degradation and loss of biodiversity. But these losses should be weighed against the number of lives that were saved. It is against this backdrop that a call for a less efficient form of agriculture such as organics would seem to be ill advised: while there would be environmental benefits,

FIGURE 5.2
A huge, steaming compost heap at Beaux Frères, Oregon.

such a move would have severe implications for the food security of millions of people. The low yields of organics would also necessitate the cultivation of larger areas of land, which would conflict with conservation attempts. Nothing is as straightforward as it first seems. Organics on a large scale would be not just an expensive luxury but also, to a degree, an immoral one. However, in the case of wine, organics is an expensive luxury that many winegrowers can afford because their crop is valuable enough, and it is not a staple food on which people depend for their survival. Lower yields in viticulture may mean less wine, but often they translate into better wine. Wine grapes therefore differ somewhat from most crops.

Interestingly, while organics has widespread consumer recognition and people are prepared to pay more for organic groceries, organic wine does not currently attract a price premium in most markets. It is presumably for this reason that relatively few wineries are certified organic. Many growers work in ways that are effectively organic, but they don't bother with certification because it has little benefit for them, and they may wish to have the option of using systemic fungicides, for example, if they have to deal with a particular problem.

CASE STUDY   CONO SUR, CHILE

Chilean producer Cono Sur, part of the large Concha y Toro group, has moved a significant portion of its vineyards to certified organic status. Currently, it has 266 hectares of

(continued)

(*continued*)

certified organic vineyards, which represent more than a quarter of its production. "In 1998 we decided to implement the green and clean plan," explains winemaker Adolfo Hurtado, "using integrated vineyard management and avoiding the use of synthetic products. We felt more confident in 2000 and moved to organics." The Cono Sur vineyards are certified organic by the German company BCS (www.bcs-oeko.com) and also have ISOs 9001 and 14001.

"I believe in organics, and every year we put more acres into organics," says Hurtado. "But organic production is not easy; you are more limited." He estimates that organic production costs about 30 percent more for vineyard management than standard agriculture. "If you receive a big rainfall 20 days before harvest, you have just two options with organics [to protect against the bunch rot caused by the fungus *Botrytis*]," he explains: "*Trichoderma* [a fungus used for biological control of *Botrytis*], or BC-100 (which is made from grape seed extracts), both of which are very expensive." The most difficult aspect of organic farming from his perspective, however, is nitrogen supply to the vines. Conventional farming uses synthetic fertilizers to provide missing macro and micro nutrients, but in organics composting is needed. Cono Sur has a novel way of producing organic nitrogen for its vines that involves composting all the skins, seeds, and stalks, adding a bacterial inoculum, and then stirring the pile up periodically to prevent the temperature exceeding 75°C. The compost produced is then put in 15 kg bags, which are placed in small ponds to macerate. The resulting nutrient-rich compost "tea" is then delivered to the vines through the drip irrigation system. The bags are later emptied and distributed throughout the vineyard to add organic material to the soil. Two analyses are done each year: soil analysis in spring and petiole analysis in the middle of summer. These analyses show whether there are any nutrient deficiencies, which can be corrected by a combination of the compost teas and organic foliar nutrients.

Before turning to organics, Cono Sur used to spray sixteen times a season. "In autumn, we'd make a schedule for all the sprays," recalls Hurtado, "whether or not you'd have the disease." On average, only two sprays are now used each year with the new regime. In its organic farming, Cono Sur works with a consultant named Carlos Pino from the Catholic University in Maule.

CERTIFICATION

Certification is important for organic farming, and a large range of certifying bodies exist. One website (www.organic.com.au/certify/) lists 385 organizations worldwide that offer organic certification. Most organic certifying bodies are registered with their country's government department responsible for agriculture. In the European Union

(EU), the technical definition for organic wine is "wine made with organically grown grapes," because only a fruit, vegetable, or other crop can be defined as organic. The term *organic wine* therefore cannot officially be used on the label. In the EU, the rules for organic production are detailed in Council Regulation (EC) No. 834/2007, Organic Production, which came into force in January 2009. However, these rules appear not to mention wine and its labeling. The regulation states, "Certain non-organic products and substances are needed in order to ensure the production of certain processed organic food and feed. The harmonization of wine processing rules on Community level will require more time. Therefore the mentioned products should be excluded for wine processing until, in a subsequent procedure, specific rules are laid down."

In the United States, the regulations are particularly confusing. In a 2009 document from the U.S. Alcohol and Tobacco Tax and Trade Bureau (TTB) in the United States, the guidelines for labeling organic wine are spelled out (http://ttb.gov/pdf/wine .pdf). If wine is labeled "100 percent organic," it must be from 100 percent organic fruit and must be made with the help of only organic processing aids. No added sulfites are allowed. If a wine is labeled "organic," then it must contain 95 percent organically grown fruit and may not contain added sulfites (the wine may contain up to 10 ppm sulfites that are a product of fermentation). "Wine made with organic grapes" must contain at least 70 percent organically grown grapes. Such wine may contain added sulfites.

BIODYNAMICS

Most scientists just don't get on with biodynamics. While some biodynamic practices make good sense and can be explained scientifically, such as the use of cover crops and emphasis on soil health, other elements of biodynamic practice are quite odd. For example, the biodynamic calendar has astrological elements to it, some of the preparations (concoctions of plant and animal matter, often fermented, that are applied to soils, vines, and compost) are rather strange, and the dynamization of the preparations by stirring them in certain ways seems a bit pointless. Also, the theoretical background to biodynamics was apparently received by Austrian polymath Rudolf Steiner while he was in a trance.

Indeed, it would be easy to dismiss biodynamics were it not for the fact that some of the world's great wine estates are farmed biodynamically, and frequently their wines have improved since they began farming this way. When you look at the calibre of some of the wine estates employing biodynamics, and when you visit growers, walk through vineyards, and hear their stories, you'd have to be extremely stubborn not to take biodynamics seriously.

That is not to say that uncritical acceptance of everything claimed by practitioners of biodynamics is called for. Rather, even the scientifically trained should be curious about what is going on here. What is it about biodynamic farming that is having these demonstrable positive effects in the vineyard? Even if it is simply better, more attentive farming, it would be useful to know this.

Whatever you may feel about the principles and practice of biodynamics, there are good grounds for suggesting that this is one of the most positive developments for fine wine over the past couple of decades. As increasing numbers of producers have begun working this way, they've frequently begun making more interesting wine. That has to be a good thing. We can't think of many biodynamic growers whose wines have become more spoofy and superficial since they started working this way, although no doubt there are many biodynamic practitioners who make poor or faulty wines. And the influence of biodynamics has extended far beyond the relatively small vineyard area that is now farmed this way: the prominent stories of biodynamic growers that have been repeated through wine media have undoubtedly had an influence on growers who haven't chosen to farm this way by making them think more carefully about what they do in their vineyards.

We do have one objection to biodynamic growers: the way some of them criticize those who choose not to farm this way. It is a mischaracterization to cast conventional agriculture as poisoning the environment, and it is mistaken to propose that it isn't possible to make terroir-driven, compelling fine wines without biodynamics. Bad old conventional viticulture, with its overreliance on calendar spray schedules and simplistic chemical solutions for viticultural problems, was harmful to the environment. But we have to be careful about judging the past by the standards of today. As various television dramas from the 1970s show, police in the United States and the United Kingdom had different standards for questioning suspects then than they do now. Likewise, farming has come a long way since the 1970s, with the rise of integrated pest-management approaches that take into account the complexity of natural ecosystems. But biodynamics is an expensive way to farm, as is organics. Unless we want to preserve wine only for the wealthy, not all wines in the world can be made in this manner, and producers who take an evangelistic approach need to question their position when it comes to supporting elitism.

Let's unpack biodynamics a little by exploring what someone farming conventionally would have to do to make the switch.

First, we point out that biodynamics isn't just an agricultural protocol; it is a different way of thinking that involves seeing the farm as a whole system, with a complex series of connectedness between the various components. One of the recurrent themes of biodynamics is the emphasis on life and life forces, although these are, by their nature, somewhat indefinable.

Accounts of biodynamics devote much attention to the various preparations, perhaps a little too much from the perspective of those who actually farm this way. This is probably because of the fantastic nature of many of these preparations. They seem almost deliberately bizarre. Their exact compositions are listed in Table 5.1.

One of the reasons that many people hire biodynamic consultants to aid them in their transition to this way of working is that the preparations can be used as a tool kit. Growers can adapt them to their own situation and use them to correct imbalances they see in

TABLE 5.1 Various Biodynamic Preparations and Their Intended Uses

Preparation	Contents	Mode of application
500	Cow manure fermented in a cow horn, which is then buried and overwinters in the soil	Sprayed on the soil typically at a rate of 60 g/ha in 34 litres of water
501	Ground quartz (silica) mixed with rainwater and packed in a cow's horn, buried in spring and then dug up in autumn	Sprayed on the crop plants
502	Flower heads of yarrow fermented in a stag's bladder	Applied to compost along with preparations 503–507 to control the breakdown of the manures and compost, helping make trace elements more available to the plant
503	Flower heads of chamomile fermented in the soil	Applied to compost
504	Stinging nettle tea	Applied to compost; also sometimes sprayed on weak or low-vigour vines
505	Oak bark fermented in the skull of a domestic animal	Applied to compost
506	Flower heads of dandelion fermented in cow mesentery	Applied to compost
507	Juice from valerian flowers	Applied to compost
508	Tea prepared from the horsetail plant (*Equisetum*)	Used as a spray to counter fungal diseases

NOTE: All these preparations are diluted and then activated or energized by a special stirring process known as "dynamization."

their vineyard or to promote vine health in certain ways. This takes a degree of practice and some level of intuition. Critics might suggest that it's all made up on the spot.

Health is a priority in biodynamics. Whereas conventional viticulture might focus on combating diseases or pests (dealing with problems), the focus in biodynamics is stimulating the health of the vine so that diseases don't become a problem. Still, biodynamic growers are allowed to use copper and sulfur as fungicides. Uncharitable critics would suggest that biodynamics, like much of alternative medicine, has limited efficacy, so when there is a real problem, you are forced to turn to scientific solutions. The vine is genetically susceptible to the imported fungal diseases powdery and downy mildew. American vines, having evolved with these diseases, have developed resistance, but

Vitis vinifera (the Eurasian grape vine) lacks these genes and is susceptible, hence the need for a chemical solution. Advocates of biodynamics claim that this use is acceptable because these are traditional chemicals, and some argue that the reason biodynamics is unable to afford protection to vines against these diseases is the way in which vines are grown in a monoculture. In defence of biodynamics, many report that once they switch to this way of growing, their vines tend to be much healthier and need less treatment than when they were farmed conventionally.

One phenomenon that seems to support the efficacy of biodynamics is that of "rescued" vineyards. Of course, these accounts are anecdotal and are delivered by advocates, but there is little reason to suppose that they are lying (although it is possible that there may be a little exaggeration). Anne-Claude Leflaive of Domaine Leflaive reports that their plot in Bienvenues-Bâtard-Montrachet was rescued by biodynamics. In 1990 the then thirty-year-old vines were in bad health, and they were advised to replant. The leaves were chlorotic, and the wood was small; the vines had been yielding badly. The new team of Pierre Morey and Anne-Claude decided to do an experiment on these "lost" vines. They stopped using herbicides, opened up the soil, and employed the biodynamic preparations. "We were the first to be astonished by the response of the vines to the new treatment," she recalls. "Now these vines are the oldest of the domaine, over fifty years old."

In the Napa Valley, leaf roll virus is a problem that has led many vineyards to need replanting before they are twenty years old. Ivo Jeramaz of Grgich Hills recalls how a fifty-year-old vineyard in Yountville that now yields his best Cabernet Sauvignon came within a whisker of being yanked out of the ground. "We had very low yields, and the vineyard couldn't ripen properly," recalls Jeramaz. "We'd be lucky to get to 22 Brix (a measure of sugar levels), and the grapes were pink." Instead of replanting, Jeramaz cultivated the vineyard in accordance with biodynamic principles. The results were that the heavily virus-infested vineyard suddenly sprang back to life. "After three years the vineyard had rebounded dramatically, and it now makes our most expensive Cabernet. There are fewer red leaves, and the vineyard wants to go to 30 Brix." Barry Wiss of Trinchero Napa Valley reports a similar experience in its 23-acre Chicken Ranch vineyard in Rutherford. The Cabernet Sauvignon vines in this vineyard had a bad leaf roll virus problem that was cured within a few years by farming with biodynamics.

CERTIFYING BIODYNAMICS

Demeter is the leading certifying body for biodynamic products worldwide, including wine. Use of the Demeter trademark incurs a fee of 2 percent of revenues from selling products with the trademark (usually up to a certain ceiling; for wine, this applies to the value of the grapes used to make the wine), a membership fee, and the cost of an inspection. In the United States, Demeter has trademarked the term *biodynamic*. In Europe, biodynamic winegrowers have an alternative certifying body: Biodyvin, a French organization that currently has 52 members.

Of course, biodynamics covers just what occurs in the vineyard, not what takes place in the cellar. Oregon winemaker Jason Lett (Eyrie) jokes that biodynamic winegrowers in the New World are frequently "like fairies in the vineyard but orcs in the cellar." In response to these sorts of criticisms, Demeter issued some guidelines for biodynamic wine production in 2008.

STANDARDS FOR DEMETER / BIODYNAMIC WINE

THE FOLLOWING ARE NOT PERMITTED:

- The use of genetically modified microorganisms
- Potassium hexacyanoferrate
- Ascorbic acid, sorbic acid
- PVPP (Polyvinylpolypyrrolidone)
- Diammonium phosphate
- Isinglass (Sturgeon swim bladder), blood and gelatine

ORIGIN OF FRUIT

Aim 100% Demeter certified fruit
Standard 100% Demeter certified fruit

HARVEST

Aim Hand harvesting
Standard Machine harvesting permitted. Pomace to be returned to the vineyard

CELLAR MACHINERY

Aim Maximum use of gravity
Standard Pumps that develop high shear or centrifugal forces, e.g., centrifugal pumps are not permitted in new installations or when replacing machinery

TANKS

Aim Natural materials
Standard Concrete, Wooden barrels, Porcelain, Steel tanks, Stoneware, Clay amphora, all permitted

PHYSICAL MEASURES WITH THE PRODUCT

Aim Forbidden
Standard Heating of the red wine mash to a maximum of 35° C allowed. Use of heating and cooling to steer fermentation is permitted. No pasteurisation

ENRICHMENT WITH SUGAR (CHAPTALISATION)

Addition of sugar / Addition of concentrated mash
Aim No addition of sugar
Standard Addition of sugar to increase the alcohol content by a maximum of 1.5% by volume is permitted. Demeter sugar or grape juice concentrate, if unavailable certified organic sugar, if derogation permitted.

Alteration of the juice, liquid in the mash (concentration)
Aim Forbidden
Standard Concentration of the entire must is not allowed. Alcohol reduction by technical methods is prohibited. Addition of water to the mash/must is forbidden, while by the Demeter International standards is permitted.

ALCOHOLIC FERMENTATION

Fermentation technique
Standard Heating to speed up fermentation permitted, no pasteurisation

Yeast
Aim Indigenous yeast only
Standard Indigenous yeast, pied de cuve (Demeter or organic), Demeter or organic yeast, GMO-free commercial yeast.

Yeast nutrients
Aim Demeter yeast hulls
Standard Demeter / organic yeast hulls: other yeast nutrients need approval

BIOLOGICAL ACID REDUCTION

Aim Indigenous Malolactic Bacteria only
Standard Lactic acid bacteria, free of GMO

PRESERVATION WITH SULPHUR

SO_2 total [mg/l] at bottling
Aim SO_2 to be restricted to the absolute minimum
Standard < 5g/l residual sugar   > 5g/l residual sugar

   white mg/l SO_2 140   white mg/l SO_2 180
   red mg/l SO_2 110   red mg/l SO_2 140

Sweet wines
   grapes with Botrytis mg/l SO_2 360
   grapes without Botrytis mg/l SO_2 250

TARTAR STABILISATION

Aim Only cold stabilisation, natural tartrate from Biodynamic / Demeter wine production

Standard Cold treatment, natural tartrate from Biodynamic / Demeter or organic wine production

FINING AGENTS

Organic

Aim No organic fining agents derived from animals.

Standard Egg white from Demeter / organic eggs; Demeter milk and milk products, if unavailable organic; Casein

Non-organic

Aim Not admitted

Standard Bentonite (non-detectible levels of dioxin and arsenic), activated charcoal, Copper sulphate, aeration

FILTRATION

Organic

Aim Allowable materials not defined

Standard Cellulose, textile (unbleached / chlorine free)

Non-organic

Aim Bentonite (non-detectible levels of dioxin and arsenic), Diatomaceous earth

Standard Diatomaceous earth, bentonite (non-detectable levels of dioxin and arsenic), perlite

ACIDITY REGULATION

Aim Not admitted

Standard Potassium bicarbonate $KHCO_3$, $CaCO_3$, Tartaric acid (E334) permitted

BOTTLING AIDS

Aim Not admitted

Standard CO_2, N2

BIODYNAMICS AND SCIENCE

What does science have to say about biodynamics? Most scientists ignore biodynamics because in their eyes the claims made are so outlandish and are couched in such non-scientific terms that it simply isn't worthwhile to address them. "Organic farming owes its origins in part to the development of biodynamic farming by Steiner," acknowledges leading plant biologist Tony Trewavas in a review published in the journal *Crop Protection* in 2004. "However, this form of farming with its belief in cosmic forces has no place in any scientific discussion and is considered occult in character."

Trewavas's statement sums up the attitude of many scientists towards biodynamics. A few scientists, however, are intrigued by the testimonials of growers. Intelligent, competent, honest winegrowers are seeing benefits in their vineyards that have an effect on their wines. Is this simply some sort of placebo effect, whereby the practice of biodynamics encourages people to work more diligently because they have bought into a philosophy that acts as some kind of motivational tool? Or are some or all of the claims of biodynamics, odd as they sound, explainable in scientific terms? To answer these questions, a number of trials comparing biodynamics with other methods of farming have been attempted. We will come to these in a moment.

Most biodynamic growers have little interest in scientific trials. While many of them take a wait-and-see approach before committing their vineyards to biodynamics, they are often sufficiently convinced by their experience not to require firm data to back it up. Generally they will adopt the entire suite of biodynamic tools and practices rather than pick and choose which elements to implement. This means that very few people have the motivation to conduct scientifically credible trials examining the effects of the different elements of biodynamic farming.

Those who oppose biodynamics can't see any plausible way in which these practices could work, so they also lack the motivation to investigate further. There are two further obstacles to rigorous research on biodynamics. First, because biodynamics sees the whole farm as a single "organism," the idea of separate, adjacent plots being farmed by different methods, in a trial-type scenario, doesn't really fit. A second difficulty is persuading research funding agencies to pay for these studies should the will be there to do them in the first place. John Reganold, a scientist at Washington State University (Pullman) who is one of the leading authorities on organic agriculture, told me that some of his research proposals have been vetoed by funding agencies because they have contained the word *biodynamics*. "Many scientists won't even look at biodynamics," he reports.

Biodyvin has commissioned a series of studies of the effects of biodynamics, but these studies, on a variety of topics, have not been published in peer-reviewed journals (the usual method of communicating scientific results). Instead, they are published on Biodyvin's website (www.biodyvin.com). While Biodyvin's attempts to examine the efficacy of the various treatments are commendable, its studies would gain scientific credibility if they were published in peer-reviewed scientific journals.

The key challenge for research on biodynamics is to show that the use of biodynamic preparations and the timing of their application has greater efficacy than organic farming. While in theory biodynamics is quite different from organics—for example, the notion that the farm is a whole "living" system, and the putative existence of life forces that influence plant growth—in practice, it looks much like organic farming with

FIGURE 5.3
Horn manure, a biodynamic preparation.

some extra elements added. The notion of encouraging soil health through the use of composts and the benefits of no-till agriculture have a sound scientific basis. Does biodynamics give a grower anything more than the application of organics would? This is the central question.

ACADEMIC STUDIES

There have been a few academic studies of biodynamics, and some of these have found their way into the scientific literature. In 1993 John Reganold and colleagues compared the performance of biodynamic and conventional farms in New Zealand, and published a report in the leading scientific journal *Science*. They found that the biodynamic farms had significantly higher soil quality, with more organic matter content and microbial activity, but this result doesn't show greater efficacy of biodynamics than of organics. In 1995 Reganold published a review of the various studies that had examined biodynamics and had met basic standards for scientific credibility. The conclusion was that biodynamic systems had better soil quality, lower crop yields, and equal or greater net returns per hectare than their conventional counterparts. Again, these gains could have been achieved by the organic, scientifically plausible component of biodynamics.

Lynne Carpenter-Boggs, a student of Reganold's, looked at the effects of biodynamic preparations on compost development. In an experimental setting, biodynamically treated composts showed higher temperatures, faster maturation, and more nitrate than composts that had received a placebo inoculation. However, these results were not published in a peer-reviewed journal. In a paper she published in *Soil Science Society of*

America Journal with Reganold in 2000, they found that organically and biodynamically managed soils had similar microbial status and were more biotically active than soils conventionally farmed (that is, they had more life in them), but that while organic management enhanced soil biological activity, the additional use of the biodynamic preparations did not significantly affect the soil biotic parameters tested.

In May 2002 the results of a twenty-one-year study comparing organic and biodynamic farming with conventional agriculture were published, also in *Science*. A group of Swiss researchers, led by Paul Mäder of the Research Institute of Organic Agriculture, showed that while biodynamic farming resulted in slightly lower yields, it outperformed conventional and organic systems in almost every other case. The biodynamic plots showed higher biodiversity and greater numbers of soil microbes and more efficient resource use by this microbial community.

"This appears to be the sort of detailed, long-baseline work we are after," state Douglass Smith and Jesús Barquín in an article addressing the credibility of biodynamics in the *World of Fine Wine*. "But buried in the supporting material, only available online, is the methodology behind the study. There we find that the biodynamic and organic farms began with composts prepared differently. Certain chemicals were added to the organic fields that were not added to the biodynamic ones. And these were only the 'main differences.' What were the others? We aren't told." They conclude that the results obtained from Mäder's experiment may simply be due to differences in the original composts or in the chemical additions to the organic plots.

Perhaps the most interesting study, however, is the research conducted by Jennifer Reeves for her MSc thesis in 2003 (this work was published in 2005 in the *American Journal of Enology and Viticulture*). Titled "Effects of Biodynamic Preparations on Soil, Winegrape and Compost Quality on a California Vineyard," the thesis was supervised by Reganold and looked at the same vineyard over a seven-year period (1996–2003). Two treatments were compared in this 4.9-hectare vineyard (1 hectare equals 2.47 acres): organics and exactly the same management but with added biodynamic preparations. The biodynamic field sprays (cow dung buried in a cow horn for a season, silica buried in cow horns, and barrel compost) were not shown to have any effect on soil quality, and analyses of the grapes showed surprisingly few differences (over the seven years of the study, the biodynamic treatments resulted in significantly higher tannins in 2002 and Brix in 2003, but these were the only significant differences). Nutrient analyses of leaf tissue, clusters per vine, yield per vine, cluster weight, and berry weight showed no differences.

BENEFITS BEYOND ORGANICS?

Overall, the few studies that have been carried out seem to provide little support for the efficacy of biodynamics beyond the benefits of organic farming. But we need to bear in mind that (1) biodynamics is very difficult to study in a trial environment because there are so many variables to look at; and (2) there have been precious few scientifically credible studies devoted to this topic.

Some of the spray preparations unique to biodynamics could be having an effect that is scientifically explainable. For example, they could be acting as microbial inocula, seeding the vineyard with tiny but significant levels of microbes that could then colonize the soil and vines. Or some of the tea sprays could be enhancing the vine's resistance to disease by inducing systemic acquired resistance.

Besides, it would be foolish to discount the placebo effect of such treatments if growers who adopt the philosophical system of biodynamics are developing a deeper relationship with their vineyard and are working more diligently because of this. It's too soon to conclude that biodynamics has no scientific basis, but the evidence so far does seem to suggest that certain elements of it (such as the ones it shares with organics) are likely to be more efficacious than the more esoteric components.

"What we see when looking over the biodynamic landscape is a vista of starry eyes and good intentions mixed with quasi-religious hocus-pocus, good salesmanship and plain scientific illiteracy," conclude Smith and Barquín in their article presenting objections to biodynamics. "It is the esoteric, occult aspects that give biodynamics its originality and raison d'être. Get rid of the esoterica, and it is not clear that any point remains for the small industry of consultants, conferences, press articles, books or fanciful homeopathic dilutions."

ORGANICS AND BIODYNAMICS IN BURGUNDY

Burgundy is one of the wine regions where organic farming, particularly biodynamics, has made the greatest impact. Some extremely high-profile producers have championed the cause of natural approaches in the vineyard, and their example has encouraged their neighbours to try them, too. As a result, even many growers who haven't switched have changed the way they operate, working in a more sustainable fashion.

The architecture of the Burgundy vineyards goes some way towards explaining why this has happened. The region is dominated by the concept of terroir. It is the vineyard that matters here, and with the exception of the *monopoles* (the small number of vineyards owned by just one grower), each vineyard is shared by many growers. Thus it is fairly easy to look at what your neighbour is doing, and the results of organic or biodynamic regimes are clear for all to see. Altogether, there are some 4,000 growers in the whole of Burgundy, farming 25,000 hectares. Philippe Drouhin of Joseph Drouhin reckons that of these there are some 40 serious biodynamic estates, and altogether 50 or 60 who are at least experimenting with biodynamics. While this number is currently growing, a sense of perspective is still called for.

A CONVERSATION WITH MONTY WALDIN

JAMIE GOODE and SAM HARROP

Monty Waldin is a wine journalist who has been committed to biodynamics for some years and now spends a good deal of his time consulting on the topic. In the United Kingdom he made the headlines for a reality television program on Channel 4 that followed his yearlong project to make wine using biodynamic principles in France's Roussillon region. He has also written books on organic and biodynamic wine. Therefore, he has a broad perspective on the topic, and we asked him some questions about his views on naturalness and biodynamics.

What are the roots of biodynamics? "It's the oldest 'organic' agriculture movement, dating from 1924, and it came about when a group of central European farmers felt that the industrialization of agriculture had rendered their soils less healthy, their seeds less fertile, their crops less nourishing, and their own health less certain. The idea was that bad farming had produced bad food, and the bad food had produced bad farmers. And so on." What about the preparations? "As a way of improving both the substance of our agriculture/food cycle—better soils, healthier crops—and to give the soils/crops the power to nourish our spirit, biodynamic sprays made from minerals, manure, and medicinal plants were devised to go directly on the crops and on the soil via biodynamic compost," explains Waldin.

"Unfortunately, economic and geopolitical instability would hold back the emerging biodynamic and organic agriculture movements, firstly because post-1945 agriculture was geared to maximum production to cope with austerity; and bomb-making technology developed during the war threw up some useful sidelines in chemical fertilizers, fungicides, pesticides, and weed killers," he continues. "It might be too simplistic to say bad farming won the day—but it did. By the mid-1990s only a few hundred of France's vineyards were organic, and only a handful were biodynamic."

We also asked him about the impact of biodynamics in the winery: does this approach continue from the vineyard to affect what goes on in the cellar? "Biodynamic farmers use nine plant-, mineral-, and cow-manure-based preparations. Six of these go in the compost and thus ultimately out onto the soil, and the remaining three are sprayed directly on the vines or vineyard. None are intended for direct use in the winery or to be added to the wine." But Waldin thinks that biodynamics has its impact in the cellar through adherence to a special calendar. "Because biodynamic growers recognise that forces as well as substances are important, they try to take account of the position of the sun, moon, planets, and stars when performing key vineyard tasks such as winter pruning or even the date for picking the grapes. In the winery key tasks—such as racking the wine off its sediment and bottling—can also be timed according to lunar and other celestial cycles, so yes, there can be a carry through in biodynamic practice from the vineyard to the winery."

But is there a benefit to biodynamics beyond what can be achieved by organics plus composting? "A good organic wine grower may well have better grapes come harvest than a bad biodynamic one," says Waldin. "A good conventional grower may have better grapes than a bad organic grower. But a good biodynamic grower has, I think, the match-winning approach for every situation. I always say organic growers take care of what is beneath their feet (the soil), but biodynamic growers also take care and account of what is going on above their heads by trying to work with celestial cycles."

Are there elements of biodynamics that people can adopt and see benefit from without taking on board the whole package of treatments and timings? "I think the most easily achieved and easily understood biodynamic goal is self-sufficiency. Don't take out of the ground what you are not prepared to or are unable to put back. Ideally a biodynamic winegrower will find space on the vineyard for some farm animals, with cows preferred. The reason is that while a cow needs a couple of acres (one hectare) to live off, her manure can, once composted (hopefully with the six biodynamic compost preparations) fertilize around double that. That's a pretty powerful tool if you want your vineyard to stay healthy, fertile, and alive."

How did Waldin first get into biodynamics? "I used to make compost as a kid with my dad for our vegetable garden, so I was always into the idea that the best veggies come from worm-rich soils, and compost is the best tool to encourage worms. When I got into wine as a teenager, I was always predisposed to organic wines. In 1993 I visited my first biodynamic wine grower, Paul Barre of Châteaux La Grave/La Fleur Cailleau in Fronsac, Bordeaux. A top Bordeaux winemaker had given me Barre's number and told me to 'go see him, as he's doing something which may interest you.' It was only after I had tasted Barre's wine that I asked him how he'd managed to make something so distinctive. He took me to the vineyards and asked me what I saw. I replied that I could see vines whose leaves had a very natural colour and sheen and soils which were friable and smelt of the earth. I could dig my hands in. Most of the Bordeaux vineyards I had visited up to that point had soils which resembled cement, due mainly to heavy use of weed killers and chemical fertilizer pellets, and produced wines which needed a lot of winemaking (yeast, enzymes, exaggeratedly hot macerations). Barre didn't have the greatest vineyard sites, but he was producing distinctive wine that really tasted of its origins. Why was it other Bordeaux estates with much better vineyard sites than Barre were producing banal wines that all seemed to taste as if made to a

(*continued*)

template? I decided biodynamics was a good vineyard tool—and I haven't found anything since that has made me change my mind."

Is biodynamics practical for larger companies? "Absolutely," replies Waldin. "And why shouldn't it be? Most wine critics in the UK and beyond would consider Chile's Alvaro Espinoza as among the best if not the best winemaker in Chile. What's nice about Alvaro is he spends his time largely in the vineyards rather than the winery. 'It's the vineyards, stupid.'

"One of Alvaro's clients, the Concha y Toro side-shoot Emiliana Orgánico, now has 600 hectares (1,500 acres) of certified biodynamic vineyards spread across Chile's four main winegrowing valleys. This is biodynamics on a massive scale— around five times bigger than anything in Europe. Each vineyard has its own composting programme. Farm animals and habitat breaks ('beetle banks') are major features on each site to make boring monocultural vineyards more polycultural, more diverse, more interesting, and more inherently healthy ('prevention rather than cure'). Medicinal plants like chamomile and stinging nettle are grown amongst the vines to be used as vine teas / liquid manures. The staff have bought into the biodynamic philosophy because their jobs have become more varied—instead of having to wear protective masks to spray weed killers, employees are asked to visit local fields to collect and then sow seeds of local plants in the vineyard to help the vineyard become part of the landscape. A vineyard which is part of the landscape, or the habitat, is less likely to be attacked by that habitat's pathogens. Biodynamics does work on a large scale if, like Alvaro, you do it properly."

What about biodynamics in vineyards where the grower owns only a small section, such as the isolated blocks of vines owned by growers in the top vineyards of the Mosel? "One main principle for biodynamic farmers is their farm becomes as self-sufficient as possible. Obviously, in regions like the Mosel, Champagne, Burgundy, and Alsace, winegrowers will have vineyards in noncontiguous plots spreading over a dozen villages. This does, in theory, make attaining the biodynamic ideal harder. In reality, when a winegrower converts his plot to biodynamics but is surrounded by other growers who weedkill, for example, the biodynamic grower must lean over the metaphorical garden fence and ask his neighbours if they might possibly not use weed killers on the last few vine rows touching the biodynamic plot. The biodynamic grower won't always get a polite response, but what we are increasingly seeing is that while initially the presence of biodynamic vineyards may arouse contempt or suspicion, in time it's the conventional growers who are reaching out and asking questions about how biodynamics works because they can see that biodynamic soils are less likely to compact or erode, that the vines produce better-

FIGURE 5.4
A tractor cultivating under the vine rows at biodynamic winery Beaux Frères, Oregon.

quality grapes (if slightly lower yields), and the vineyard becomes a nicer place to work in. It sounds utopian, but if you speak to growers in Alsace, Burgundy, and Champagne, for example, who are converting to biodynamics, an overwhelming majority say that they converted to biodynamics because they could see that biodynamics actually worked in vineyards owned by both winegrower friends and rivals."

If a top Bordeaux property owner came to you and asked about implementing biodynamics, where would you start them off? "There are three main reasons why no top Bordeaux châteaux have embraced biodynamics successfully. First, Bordeaux is very corporate, and shareholders view organics/biodynamics as a big risk especially, which brings me to second of the three reasons, because Bordeaux's wet / humid Atlantic climate makes organic/biodynamic a tricky proposition unless you are prepared to sacrifice 10 percent to 15 percent volume (yields). The third issue is vineyards can be very large in size, which gives you no margin for error as a biodynamic farmer. However, having spent many years working in Bordeaux, I'd say that if a top château wanted to get into biodynamics, I would essentially follow the template of how I approached working with a classed growth style "château" in Germany.

(continued)

"The German owners are aristocratic and the vineyards are huge (100 hectares / 250 acres)—which means to get biodynamics to work can be a logistical nightmare. My first year there I basically said: let's get the basic winegrowing right and, if we can, we can add some biodynamics in when and if we have time. This builds confidence in the vineyard crews who are always, always, always behind on day-to-day vineyard tasks (tractors break down, staff get ill / injured, etc.). By 'getting the basic winegrowing right,' what I meant was: is each and every one of our vineyard plots pruned and trellised in the correct way? If not, how can we get better quality grapes? Does our Pinot Noir (Spätburgunder) work best when grown on single canes (guyot pruning) or on cordons (spur pruning), for example?

"Does our soil management (ploughing weeds away or encouraging our own choice of weeds—cover crops like clovers and grasses) make sense? In badly drained vineyards are we leaving every row grassed / cover cropped, the idea being the grass cover soaks up all that excess water from the bad drainage? If that water is not being soaked up, we're going to get big grapes (high yields, no flavour) whose thin grape skins are an easy target for vine pests and diseases. And if we are fighting pests and disease when we don't need to be, other vineyards are going to get neglected, and they're going to produce worse grapes than they should, and we are in a vicious circle, chasing our tails.

"Stage two was showing how pruning by the moon costs zero euros and can help maximise quality from the best or 'grand cru' vineyards while making our least good vineyards at least perform to the very best of their ability.

"Stage three was making sure every time we used organic / biodynamic-approved antifungus disease sprays (like Bordeaux mixture and sulfur), we blended in some herb teas (mainly stinging nettle and/or common horsetail) to make the sprays less aggressive and more effective. The teas cost a few euros per hectare, and by allowing vineyard crews to use two-in-one sprays I was (a) adding nothing to their workload (or burning extra tractor diesel) and (b) building their knowledge/confidence base. Tractor drivers are seen as the lowest of the low, but in fact without them 99 percent of vineyards could not function. If the tractor crews buy into the biodynamic approach, you have a much better chance of biodynamics being a success.

"And stage four was, having won some credibility, to explain about manure and cows' horns and so on. When the vineyard crews filled the horns and six months later dug up the same horns and could see the 'biodynamic' effect for themselves, they seemed to say, 'OK, it works. Biodynamics feels a nice and safe thing to do.' When they saw the effect biodynamic compost had on opening up the most compact vineyard soils, they were completely sold on the idea. Why? Because it made their jobs of ploughing or mowing vineyards much easier. And they had more fun too."

Dominique Lafon, of Domaine des Comtes Lafon, is one of the great producers of white Burgundy. Under his stewardship, his family's celebrated domaine shifted from conventional viticulture towards organics and then to biodynamics. He is the fourth generation to have stewardship of this domaine, which began when his great-grandfather married a woman from Meursault who had some vineyards. "In those days you didn't make money with vineyards," says Dominique. "He was a wealthy collector who wanted wine to drink with his friends."

Fourteen different wines are made from 14 hectares, one-third Pinot Noir, two-thirds Chardonnay, mostly in Volnay. The majority of his vines are Chardonnay in Meursault, with a little bit of Montrachet. When Dominique's father René arrived at the domaine in 1956, it was a hard time for Burgundy. He was an engineer who ran the estate by sharecropping. Under this system people worked in the vineyards and were allowed to keep half the crop for themselves in exchange for their labour, with the domaine receiving the other half. It wasn't until the early 1980s that the contracts were terminated and the Lafon family took back control of all its vineyards.

Dominique arrived in 1987 after studying enology, including spells in Oregon and California. In the 1980s farming practices varied. There were nine different people taking care of the vineyards (including Pierre Morey, who now has his own domaine, as well as working for Domaine Leflaive), and all had different methods of cultivation. Weed killers and chemical fertilizers were being used.

Dominique reveals how at this time a group of growers, all of his generation, felt that there should be a change (including Jacques Seysses, Étienne Grivot, Pascal Marchand, Patrick Bize, Emmanuel Giboulot, Christophe Roumier, and Jean-Claude Rateau). Together they moved in the direction of cleaner agriculture. "I started with the chemicals when I took over," he reveals. "There were all these merchants selling us products. They worked, but then they tell you they have a stronger product." He was concerned that he might be poisoning his family. "The more you try to fight nature, the more resistance emerges, and you need to fight more and more. It has no end."

In 1989 Dominique became interested in organic cultivation. "It took three years to change," he recalls. "I realized I should change in 1989, and by 1992 we were organic. I then visited some growers who had started using biodynamic techniques, and their vineyards looked better." Dominique experimented with biodynamics in 1995 on 1 hectare and then moved to applying it on 3 hectares. "The vineyards looked healthier," he recalls. "It worked well."

But can biodynamics be applied on a large scale? "We decided to go for the whole estate. For me, biodynamics is just applying a few products: horn manure, horn silica, and some plant extracts (such as nettles and horsetail)." Dominique reckons that for 14 hectares, applying biodynamics involved one hundred hours more work per year. "It takes you to what is happening in your environment around the vines: you understand what is going on around your vines. The sun, the moon, the stars; there are planetary influences."

He also thinks that the vineyards look different. "When I started the experiment, visually it was impressive. The vineyard had miserable crops, but it grew better and we got more crops." Dominique reports that there is a transition period, and that the most difficult part is changing from chemical agriculture to organic agriculture. "The vineyards cultivated with fertilizers are like those Tour de France guys," he jokes. "It is quite a hard transition. When you start ploughing the vineyards you cut out the superficial roots. You have to get the soils started again to feed the vines. BD500 [one of the biodynamic preparations] helps a lot in getting deeper roots." He points out that it's actually easier if you don't go from conventional viticulture to organics and then to biodynamics, but go straight from conventional to biodynamics.

Is there anything in the cellar that is done differently now that Dominique has changed to biodynamics? "Not that much," he replies. With Pinot Noir he doesn't need to extract as much. "Pushy extraction was in fashion in the 1990s, but Pinot Noir has to be elegant, and I don't want too much extraction."

Burgundy expert Jasper Morris MW, who has twenty-five years' experience with Lafon wines, has seen a change in how these wines have tasted since the switch to biodynamics. He cites three main differences: "First, there is enhanced purity. Second, there is greater minerality. Third, precise vineyard definition is clearer and more focused."

"Each wine becomes more typical of each vineyard," agrees Dominique. "It is very satisfying."

CASE STUDY   AUBERT DE VILLANE DOMAINE DE LA ROMANÉE CONTI

Domaine de la Romanée Conti, commonly referred to simply as DRC, is one of the world's most famous and highly respected wine domaines. All its vineyards are now run biodynamically. Co-owner Aubert de Villane says that being organic is very important and has had an effect on the quality of the wines. "Twenty years ago I would have said that organics doesn't bring something to the quality of the wine; it is just good for the soil and for people," explains Aubert. "But today I'd say the contrary. Being organic for years in the vineyard brings a plus to quality—it brings finesse. You reach a certain finesse of maturity with organics that you don't reach as effectively with other methods."

The domaine has been organic for twenty-five years, and part biodynamic for a while. With the 2008 vintage it went fully biodynamic. Yet Aubert thinks the big quality gain is achieved by switching from conventional farming to organics, not by moving from organics to biodynamics. "We chose to go fully biodynamic because it was complicated to have just one part of the vineyard in biodynamics. Frankly, I don't see a superiority in the quality of the wine. A lot of people have gone directly from conventional viticulture to biodynamics and they see what we saw going from conventional to organics."

"What interests us in biodynamics is the use of plants to try to reduce products such as copper which aren't sustainable. We want to verify what some people who have used it for a while say: that there is a development of very deep roots which allows the vine to fight better by itself against diseases."

CASE STUDY   ANNE-CLAUDE LEFLAIVE, DOMAINE LEFLAIVE

Anne-Claude Leflaive (Domaine Leflaive), however, thinks that biodynamics brings an extra level of quality over the gain obtained from switching to organics. She is fortunate to have sufficient vineyard holdings to be able to run trials of conventional, organic, and biodynamic farming.

Domaine Leflaive needs little introduction to wine lovers. It has been described as Burgundy's greatest white wine domaine, and while this is a pretty strong claim, it is a justifiable one. The domaine is a family estate that was initially created by Anne-Claude's grandfather Joseph, who was born in Puligny-Montrachet but left to become an engineer. At one stage he had a factory in St-Étienne and was part of the team that made the first French submarine, but things went badly, and bankruptcy followed.

Not deterred by this misfortune, he returned to Puligny-Montrachet in 1905. This was just after the phylloxera crisis, and so land was pretty cheap. "No one believed any more in the vines," says Anne-Claude, "so he bought 25 hectares for virtually nothing." Joseph certainly believed, though: he thought that these vines had value, and he set about building the domaine. Of his five children, four, including Anne-Claude's father Vincent, became involved in the domaine. After Joseph died in 1953, Vincent, along with his brother Jo, were responsible for its development. Together, they established the reputation of the domaine as one of the best in Burgundy.

In 1990, Jo was ninety, and it was time for the next generation to take the reins. Anne-Claude and her cousin Olivier Leflaive took over, and this arrangement continued for four years. However, Olivier was also running a *négociant* business, and in 1994 the shareholders (made up of some thirty family members) decided that they wanted just one person running things—Anne-Claude. Therefore, the businesses were separated. "It was a hard task for me," she recalls, "but also a challenge." She

(continued)

(*continued*)

decided to change the way the vines were cultivated, moving to a more natural approach. "I asked the people who had been working there for twenty-five years to change the way they worked: forget weed killer, fertilizer, and phytosanitary products. I thought it was important to put the soil in good health, and I was convinced that something should change, but I didn't know what."

"I think that in your life, if you really want something, heaven helps you and you find people in front of you to help you," Anne-Claude says philosophically. It was at this stage that she met biodynamic consultant François Brochet and soil expert Claude Bourguignon, both of whom would lead her towards the biodynamic winegrowing that she now practices.

For several years Anne-Claude experimented, doing direct comparisons between biodynamics and organics on the same blocks of vines. Together with her right-hand man Pierre Morey and the rest of the team, she made the final decision to shift all viticulture to biodynamics in 1997. "I didn't want to just take the decision myself," she recalls. "I asked the team to make the decision, and fortunately they decided to go for biodynamics. They saw it was better for the soil, the health of the vines, and the wines. For seven years we had tasted the wines blind, and most of the time the biodynamic wines showed more complexity and purity."

Biodynamics proved to be particularly effective in 2004, a difficult vintage for most growers. "It was wet and cold, which was very good for oidium [a fungal disease], which was present everywhere," recalls Anne-Claude. "Biodynamics helped our harvest in 2004 to be incredibly healthy. I was shocked by the health of the grapes around us: most were black, attacked by oidium, especially for the winegrowers still working with chemicals."

CASE STUDY   PHILIPPE DROUHIN, JOSEPH DROUHIN

In 1986, aged twenty-five, Philippe Drouhin decided to join the family company. "My father told me it all starts in the vineyard and that I didn't know anything about vineyards, so I needed to go back to school." So Philippe studied viticulture and enology in Dijon and Beaune.

During his studies he was struck by warnings from teachers about the use of fungicides, such as not to use them more than twice a year because of the risk of resistance developing, and the existence of sixty-day exclusion periods because of residues that would otherwise prevent the yeasts from functioning normally. Another issue was the use of miticide sprays in the 1960s that killed some mites that were natural predators of other mites that are a problem today. "The negative impact of new chemicals made me wonder whether there was a safer way," Philippe recalls. He remembers that when he asked his teachers about the likely effects on the soil of a cocktail of chemicals sprayed on vines, no one had any idea.

"So I decided to look for an alternative way," he recalls. "Looking back, I found that people had used just sulfur and copper sulfate for a long time. I looked at organic and biodynamic vineyards at harvest and thought that I could do this." But Philippe realized that because he was only in his mid-twenties, he couldn't tell everyone in the company what to do. His father, who had been overseeing vineyard operations since 1957, agreed to allow Philippe to begin changing things, with the proviso that he go slowly at first. "So I began with a few vineyards and progressively converted them to organics," he recalls. "Everything in the Côte d'Or was converted by 1997, and Chablis was converted two or three years later."

Philippe soon made the acquaintance of other growers in the Côtes de Beaune interested in biodynamics. They formed a study group and invited a teacher to come and instruct them—agriculture expert Pierre Masson of Biodynamie Services. Philippe started with biodynamics in the Côte d'Or, and when Philippe felt confident, he extended the approach to Chablis. Now everything in the Drouhin estate is organic and biodynamic. "I did this for technical reasons, because I think it is better for the soils and the wine," says Philippe. "It's also much safer. We know copper [one of the permitted fungicides in biodynamics] is not good for the soils, but at least we know what it is." He emphasizes that the switch was not made for commercial reasons. "At the time I started, it was counterproductive to say that you were organic. Recently, it has been commercially useful for people to follow the consumer trend for green things, so many estates are starting to pretend that they are organic or 'part organic.' I didn't want to be in that category, so in August 2006 I asked for certification for all the estates, with Ecocert [a body that certifies organic agriculture]."

Drouhin belongs to an organization called G.E.S.T. (Groupement d'étude et suivi des terroirs, which translates as group for the study and following of terroirs). There are over one hundred members, including some of the most famous names in the region. 'We were not happy with how INRA (Institut National de la Recherche Agronomique) viewed how the soil functions, so we built our own knowledge base," says Philippe. A key figure in this organization is Yves Hérody, a pedogeologist from the Jura who consults worldwide. "He has a vision of how soils function. We formed this group to learn about soils and also to form an entity that would make compost for us. Part of this company also makes the biodynamic preparations."

In Burgundy, very few vineyards are under the sole control of a single producer. In the most famous vineyards, it is common for some growers to have just a few rows of vines. So is it possible to do biodynamics on just a fraction of a vineyard? "The neighbours in some vineyards have some influence on us," admits Philippe. "It would not be honest to

(continued)

(continued)

say I know how much influence they have. As soon as we have a fair number of rows, then we have enough effect that it is worth doing."

One question Philippe is keen to investigate is how much biodynamics can help reduce interventions in the vineyard. "It may be that we can enhance the resistance of the vines," he speculates. "Last year [2008] we had responsibility for a new vineyard in Chablis. We already had a parcel in Vaillons 100 metres away that was run biodynamically. This new vineyard was previously conventionally farmed, and in it we had a burst of downy mildew even though we used the same regime in both vineyards. It was obvious that there was less self-defence in that vineyard."

Currently, Drouhin is experimenting in the winter with deep ploughing versus cover cropping. "We think deep ploughing may not be the best answer, even though it is traditional," says Philippe. He says that it is difficult to fine-tune cover cropping during the growing season, and that it is necessary to manage each vineyard depending on its characteristics.

One interesting anecdote concerned the practice of burying cows' horns in the vineyards with the biodynamic preparation BD500, which contains dung from a lactating cow. Cows' horns differ from bulls' horns in that they have a series of rings (calving rings) in them. Some students from Dijon made the mistake of burying some bulls' horns as well as cows' horns, and when they dug them up, the contents of the bulls' horns were stinky, but the cows' horns were lovely, like humus.

On average, Philippe uses 3 kg of copper per hectare (kg/ha) each year. The law allows 6 kg/ha per year, based on a five-year average. According to Claude Bourgignon, a soil scientist, the soils can absorb 3 kg/ha per year. "This used to be sprayed in a single go in the 1950s," comments Philippe.

CASE STUDY   JEREMY SEYSSES, DOMAINE DUJAC

Dujac stopped using herbicides in the early 1990s. "For me, this is the most important thing," says Jeremy Seysses, son of Jacques Seysses (who founded the domaine) and now in charge. "My gut feeling is that 90 percent of the change came from working the soils and stopping herbicides. It led to an introduction of a degree of biodiversity in what otherwise is intensive monoculture." He admits that moving in this direction generates significantly more work. "We have an extra tractor and tractor driver," he reveals. Jeremy reckons that by the time you get to implementing biodynamics, you are usually better at working in the vineyards, spotting mildew patches on leaves and oidium-affected berries. "The people who are poster children for biodynamics are in the vineyards a lot and are good growers." Jeremy began with organics and biodynamics on some of the Grand Cru vineyards and in 2009 moved all vineyards under Dujac's control to this form of viticulture. Dujac cultivates 15.5 hectares in all and has a permanent team of seven, plus seasonal workers to do such jobs as debudding, shoot thinning, and green harvest. He says that they are very thorough in their shoot thinning and leaf pulling because this is a prophylactic measure to get good air flow through the fruit zone and canopy and thus reduce the risk of fungal disease.

BIODYNAMICS IN THE NEW WORLD

CASE STUDY   JAMES MILLTON, MILLTON VINEYARDS, GISBORNE, NEW ZEALAND

Gisborne is a slightly anonymous region. It is quite damp and is not known as a fine wine zone; instead, most of the vineyards here are geared up to make large volumes for the big producers. A lot of sparkling wine grapes come from here. This is why it's especially remarkable that James Millton makes such good wines, using biodynamics, in a place where you'd expect the disease pressure to be high. "We take lots of risks by not using herbicide and fungicide," says James.

"I've been doing biodynamics now for twenty-three years," says James, who started Millton Vineyard in 1984, when he was twenty-eight. His wife Annie's father had developed vineyards on his Opou estate in Gisborne, and so when James and Annie decided that they wanted to establish their own winery, this was the obvious place to start. It's fascinating that they have managed to make such interesting wines from a region that no one thinks much of. "Gisborne, with its clay soils, is acknowledged as making wines with full, fat fruit," says James, "but I'm looking for minerality." He's surprised that other New Zealand winemakers have so little interest in Gisborne. "I'm confused about why people don't want to lean over the fence and have a look," he says. But there's lots of interest from outside New Zealand, and people from all over the world come to Millton to see what is going on.

The estate now consists of four separate vineyards in the Gisborne region, which James describes as "consistently inconsistent." "We get vintage variation," he adds, "and I think that's good thing." Opou, a 7.7-hectare vineyard, was planted in 1969 and then replanted in 1983. Young vines are being interplanted with old, and the idea is that if a row of new vines is planted between the old ones, then the spacing will be better—originally it was 3 m × 1.8 m (2,500 vines per hectare), and the goal is to get it to 1.5 × 1 m (6,000 vines per hectare). Te Arai vineyard is near this: it's 2.8 hectares, and within it are two single-vineyard plots, named Samuel (Viognier) and Monique (Chenin) after James and Annie's children. Riverpoint is a 6.8-hectare vineyard growing Chardonnay

(continued)

(continued)

FIGURE 5.5

James Milton preparing a biodynamic preparation (BD501) to spray on his vines in Gisborne, New Zealand.

and Viognier, while the jewel in Millton's crown is the spectacular Naboth's Vineyard, a steep hillside vineyard that first produced in 1993. This site has been developed to include five separate parcels, which together make up the Clos de Ste. Anne estate. Altogether there are now 30 acres here (approximately 15 hectares), which takes the total Millton vineyard holdings to about 30 hectares.

Until a few years ago James used to collect manure from a biodynamic farm, but then he decided to buy his own cows. He started with six calves and has now had three lots of calves with these cows, which make his manure. James enjoys having the herd. "They rationalize my feelings," he says. "They know when I'm cross and when I'm happy. Since they've been here, the whole vineyard has changed. It seems to have a spring warmth to it, and the distraction they provide is quite positive." The manure the cows produce is used to make compost as well as some of the preparations.

During our visit, we mixed and sprayed one of the preparations, BD501. This is a silica (ground quartz) preparation that is buried in a cow's horn for six months. The horn is dug up, the contents are mixed with water, and the mixture is sprayed on the vines. Early on a beautiful morning, with the sun poking through the trees, James added a small amount of the white powder preparation to a barrel of water. The liquid was pumped through a Heath Robinson–esque device that stirred the mixture one way and then another as it flowed through, thus "dynamizing" the preparation, making it ready for spraying on the foliage of the vines.

Later that morning we dug up some cows' horns. A few vines had been marked high up in Naboth's Vineyard. James and his team dug until they hit the cache of horns that had been buried there a few months earlier. Inside each of these horns was the preparation BD500. This is cow manure from lactating cows that is placed in the horns for a subsoil sojourn. The resulting preparation is a smooth, claylike paste that is then diluted and sprayed onto the vineyard soil to encourage microbial growth.

CASE STUDY   FELTON ROAD, CENTRAL OTAGO

Nigel Greening, of leading Central Otago producer Felton Road, describes biodynamics as "Harry Potter grows grapes," admitting that it is quite strange. "But it is not really as wacky as it sounds when you get down to it." Among Felton Road's vineyard holdings are 30 hectares of hill country, which quickly gets taken over by thorns. Neighbours use helicopters to spray herbicide, but Greening's solution was to use a herd of goats from the Kalahari Desert. "We have less of a problem than the guys who use helicopters," he reveals. "The goats eat the thornbushes, and we eat the goats. You can get nature to solve your problems." Greening isn't a fan of Sustainable Winegrowing New Zealand (see chapter 6), the official body that promotes and certifies sustainable winegrowing. "They set the bar too low," he said. Felton Road resigned from it because of these perceived low standards.

CASE STUDY   BRICK HOUSE, OREGON

With its gently rolling hills, Oregon wine country is beautiful, and it's hard not to be just a little bit envious of Doug and Melissa Tunnel's Brick House estate. As it is for many, winegrowing is a second career for Doug. He established Brick House in 1990 after working as a foreign correspondent for CBS. His first plantings were 10 acres of Pinot Noir on their own roots, followed in 1992 by some Chardonnay. While he was working in France, Doug developed an affection for Gamay, and so—unusually for Oregon—he now has 3.5 acres of Gamay Noir.

Brick House is in a new subappellation of the Willamette Valley called Ribbon Ridge AVA (American Viticultural Area). This is part of the Chehalem Mountains, another appellation that Doug could use. From here you can see the Dundee Hills to the south. Doug's neighbours include Adelsheim and Bergstrom. Doug's postings at CBS included

(continued)

(continued)

Lebanon, London, Bonn, Paris, and Miami. "In the course of living in the Middle East and Europe I came to love wine," he recalls. "In 1988 I was living in Paris and spent all my vacation time in a vineyard." Then Doug heard that the Drouhin family was buying 120 acres in Yamhill County, Oregon. He had grown up in Oregon, about five miles from where he is now living, so he put the word out to his family that he would be interested in buying an old farm in the area.

In 1989 an old friend of the family alerted him to a property, and Doug bought it the same day. The transition from journalism to farming turned out to be easy. "I bought my first tractor and loved driving it," says Doug. "It was a great release and very soothing after my previous life.'" He had lived for seven years in Beirut during the war, so he was ready for the peaceful life. "It's not for everyone," he admits. "A lot of people would go nuts out here, but Melissa and I really enjoy it."

From the beginning, in May 1990, he wanted to grow grapes without any synthetic chemicals, and had his vineyard certified organic right away. In 2001, however, he started to take an interest in biodynamics in order to get away from the need to use copper (which is permitted as a fungicide in both organics and biodynamics). He chatted with his organic certifier, who put him in touch with a friend who did Demeter certification. Soon after, Doug and Michael Etzel (owner of another Oregon estate, Beaux Frères) met with this certifier for lunch. The first practical move towards biodynamics was to build a compost pile. A group of around ten winegrowers took a class in 2002. Doug slowly began building his piles and started using preparations. He began working with his Chardonnay and then expanded biodynamics to his Dijon block of Pinot Noir. It seemed to be working, and since 2005 Brick House has been Demeter-certified biodynamic.

"I believe in certification," says Doug. "It is good for people to step up if they are making the claim and take responsibility to prove it." He adds, "The story is not over: I am still a student; I am still reading and studying. I feel a lot of times I am not doing enough." The application of biodynamics does seem to be having a significant effect. "I wouldn't do it except that I'm beginning to see real results. If I look at the wines from 2002 and 2003, five years later I am really pleased with them. I can't make the claim that it's because of biodynamics, but I am motivated."

We took a look around the vineyards. Doug has a special machine for tilling called a spader, which comes from Italy. Many people use rotor tillers with blades that take out weeds, but over time these can create a till pan (a layer of hard, compacted soil), and water doesn't percolate through it. The rotor tillers also pulverise the soil, and because the soil at Brick House is sedimentary, it is prone to turning into sand. The spader has paddles that poke and move the ground, leaving no pan that prevents water from percolating. For his compost heaps he uses a mixture of three parts manure from an organic dairy and one part residue from fermentation (seeds, stems), covered by organic straw.

Beaux Frères is one of the most talked-about Oregon wineries, in part because it is co-owned by Robert M. Parker, Jr., the famous wine critic. The story began in 1986 when Michael Etzel identified a pig farm in Ribbon Vale as a promising vineyard site and went into partnership with Parker, his brother-in-law, with the goal of producing world-class Pinot Noir. The first grapes were harvested in 1990, and in 1991 a third partner, Robert Roy, joined to help make the venture financially viable and to help them build a winery.

There are now two vineyards, the 23-acre Beaux Frères Vineyard and the 10-acre upper terrace planted in 2000, which produce around 105 tons a year. Both are farmed biodynamically. In addition, another 20 tons of grapes are brought in to supplement the estate fruit.

The Beaux Frères Vineyard was originally planted in 1988 with Pommard and Wadenswil clones of Pinot Noir on their own roots (phylloxera was not discovered in Oregon until 1989, and there are still many ungrafted vineyards in the state, some of which are showing signs of succumbing). The upper terrace is planted with a range of Pinot clones, and this is the vineyard we visited.

We first stopped to look at one of the three compost heaps. These heaps need a thousand gallons of water every couple of weeks to help them function, and Michael uses an old fire truck to water them. The aim is to get the internal temperatures up to 140–160°F.

In the vineyard, vine spacing is 4 × 6 feet, and no irrigation is used. The biodynamic preparation BD501 (horn silica) is sprayed three times a season. Cover cropping is employed, and a diverse range of plants is used so that something is in flower all the time, which is great for the insect life.

We also had a look at Michael's barrel compost: just a handful of this is used in five gallons of water for each acre. It's made from cow manure, treated with the usual preparations and some egg shells, and fermented in a pit for a few months.

"Biodynamic farming with all the soil aeration helps refine the tannins, to give you the highest-quality tannins that carry the delicate fruit from midpalate to finish," says Michael. "This illustrates to me the benefits of farming biodynamically."

After we tasted the wines, we went off to lunch with Philippe Armenier, who is Michael's biodynamic consultant. Originally from Provence, Armenier is the former owner of Domaine Marcoux in Châteauneuf-du-Pape. Twenty years ago his wife gave him a book on Steiner. He was bored with farming conventionally and was seeing a decline in the soil on his property. He joined up with François Brochet, who was just starting his consulting business in 1989, to make his first biodynamic wines. In 2001 he came to California and now consults for a range of producers in California, Oregon, and Washington State, with more than 1,500 acres under his supervision.

Ted Lemon of Littorai spent the first four years of his career, in the early 1980s, farming conventionally in Burgundy. "But people were beginning to question chemical use," he recalls. He also worked in Oregon and New Zealand, and by the mid-1990s he began to be convinced that "Western" farming with its reliance on fertilizers just doesn't work. "I thought about it and chose the path of biodynamics," he says. Lemon felt that organic farming was substitution farming that was still following the Western agricultural model. He began to adopt biodynamics in his vineyards in 1998. Also, all the vineyards he rents are farmed biodynamically. "I'm not motivated by certification," he reveals. "It doesn't matter to us. Our label and our name are our certification."

Lemon outlines four principles of biodynamics:

1. The farm should be seen as a self-contained individuality. A farm that is entirely self-sustaining is the goal. This is a very important concept.

2. The material world is nothing more than condensed spirit. Suddenly we are farming spirit rather than material.

3. The idea behind the preparations is that by putting them in the ground you are enlivening them with spiritual forces. This enhances the spiritual dimension of your farm.

4. This enhanced wine gives humanity the force to confront the challenges of our lives.

Henschke is a fifth-generation winery, and the sixth generation is now coming to the fore. The vineyards date back to the 1860s, almost as far as Australian viticulture itself. The first family vines were planted in 1861 in Keyneton by Johann Christian Henschke, an immigrant from Silesia. The winery is currently run by the dynamic winemaker and viticulturalist pairing of husband and wife Stephen and Prue Henschke. After trying organics, Prue and Stephen have decided to go fully organic, including the adoption of some biodynamic practices. They explained what this blend of sustainability looks like in practice.

Hill of Grace is the most famous vineyard. It's a 9-hectare block with five soil types, including the celebrated grandfather vines dating back 120 years. Mount Edelstone is another old vineyard of the Henschkes, planted in 1912 and consisting of 16.5 hectares. It's quite high vigour, with deep red brown earth over gravel. The trellis style here has been changed from the traditional single-wire umbrella to Scott Henry (a split canopy system) to cope better with the vigour, and the vineyard is planted east to west so that the face of the vine rows gets the northern sun.

One of the problems facing organic growers has been the control of under-row weeds, which is achieved in conventional vineyards by the use of herbicides. The Henschkes have switched under-vine weed control in their vineyards from herbicides to pine oil in the winter; in the summer they use an under-vine ploughing device that takes out weeds without damaging the vines. In addition, in some of the vineyard blocks a permanent sward is left in the vineyard with straw mulch under the vines, deterring weed growth and helping maintain soil moisture.

The Henschkes practice a schedule of organic sprays that include *Bacillus thuringiensis*, copper and sulfur (which they are moving away from), bicarbonate (Ecocarb), and canola oil (for control of powdery mildew). The following are some of the other sustainable/organic/biodynamic practices they are putting into place:

- The Keyneton home vineyards use recycled water from winery effluent dams. Stalks and skins are recycled in a compost pad.

- Regeneration patches have been planted with native vegetation. "We're trying to cover up what our forefathers removed," explains Prue. Part of the organic schedule is that 5 percent of landholding is returned to native vegetation, but Prue says that her target is 20 percent. There are native cypress pines in the vineyards.

- Soil is protected with native plant swards, such as wallaby grass (*Danthonia* sp.) and saltbush, which encourage beneficial insects. Mulch is used to conserve the moisture in the soil.

- They are moving away from wooden fence posts in the vineyard because of problems with contamination of the soil by chromated copper arsenate (CCA). Plastic is being used instead.

- Composting is being done by the biodynamic process, with different layers. One of the growers Henschke uses has a dairy, which is a source of manure. BD500 is spread as a soil conditioner. Prue doesn't have to make her own biodynamic preparations. "We can just send away for BD500 and it is delivered in three days," she says.

"We're looking for management systems that help the health of the soils, and help them retain moisture," explains Prue. "The soil components are manufactured by the microbes in the soil: they need food and the right conditions." She adds that "for me it is not marketing—it is survival."

"We are combining organics and biodynamics to give an integrated system," she explains. This fusion of sustainable wine growing, organics, and selected biodynamic

(*continued*)

(continued)

practices seems an enlightened, rational approach, although purist followers of biodynamics would probably frown on it.

Stephen Henschke emphasizes this point. "We are looking at biodynamics from a scientific point of view," he says. "We look at soil microbes, beneficial insects, and so on, rather than seeing it as a religion."

Not only the vineyards are old: the winery also dates back to the 1860s. The Henschkes employ traditional and "natural" winemaking practices. The reds are fermented in open-top fermenters with the cap submerged by boards. The submerged cap gives gentle extraction of softer, silkier tannins. However, cultured yeasts are used, which biodynamic practitioners would find worrisome (they consider cultured yeasts unacceptable because the natural yeast populations in the vineyard are thought to be part of terroir). Towards the end of fermentation the reds are transferred warm to American and French oak barrels, where they remain for some time (two years in the case of Hill of Grace).

CRITICISMS OF BIODYNAMICS

While the biodynamics renaissance offers the most visible solution to the problems of high-input chemical-laden viticulture, it has detractors. First, to adopt biodynamics as a package requires the grower to accept a philosophical system that is at odds, in many places, with scientific understanding. For many university-trained winegrowers, adopting biodynamics would necessitate an extremely difficult cultural shift. Most wouldn't contemplate it, and despite its high visibility in the wine world, it seems that it will remain a niche.

A second criticism is that biodynamics doesn't always have the effects it claims. Growers struggle with it in wet vintages or find it hard to apply successfully in regions that are consistently damp. To counter disease, almost all biodynamics practitioners have to supplement their preparations with the chemical solutions copper sulfate and elemental sulfur, a move that is justified on the grounds that these are natural chemicals.

One winemaker I spoke to was extremely sceptical about the efficacy of biodynamics and referred to the effects of this system on the property of one of his colleagues. "I've seen his vineyard," he reported, "and the weeds are higher than the vines!" But his major criticism was that in regions where biodynamics is becoming well established, covert pressure may be placed on other leading producers and cause some to join the system for the sake of appearances. Of course, this problem is not unique to biodynamics: where there is some prestige associated with any particular form of vineyard management, far more will claim to practice the desired regime than actually do.

One of the major problems with biodynamics is that it is distracting people's attention from scientifically based sustainable viticulture, based on integrated farm management. This is the focus of the next chapter, which looks at sustainable wine growing.

6

SUSTAINABLE WINEGROWING

Vineyards are the worst monoculture in the world.

JOSH BERGSTRÖM, OREGON WINEGROWER

Sustainability is a buzzword at the moment: everyone seems to be using it. But it's also a word in search of a meaning because most people can't define exactly what they mean by *sustainable*. One attempt to illustrate the notion is graphic, with three circles representing the environment, social issues, and profitability. Where these three circles intersect, we have sustainability. It's also a controversial notion. For some, sustainability is a cop-out, a sort of toothless sop for people's green consciences without forcing them to do anything too radical. For others, it is a moral imperative.

In this chapter we argue that properly certified sustainable winegrowing is the best way of reducing the environmental impact of the wine trade because it is a way of working that is feasible for all, from the smallest producer to the largest multinational wine brand. As the epigraph of this chapter indicates, vineyards are typically a monoculture and thus are susceptible to diseases and pests; their chemical control has typically led to environmental degradation. In addition, it should be pointed out that organic or biodynamic winegrowing is not always totally sustainable.

In the introduction we discussed how naturalness is a sort of continuum. Nothing about wine is totally natural; nowhere on earth will you find a small lake of Shiraz or a bubbling brook of Chablis. The act of planting a vineyard is a manipulation that takes the grapevine from its natural environment and growth habit. Almost all vines are now grafted onto phylloxera-resistant rootstock. And some chemical intervention is needed in vineyards, because there are very few places where it is possible to get acceptable crops of grapes from *Vitis vinifera*, the grapevine, without any inputs at all. The chief problems

FIGURE 6.1
Buckwheat (*Fagopyrum esculentum*), grown as a cover crop to attract beneficial insects to the vineyard.

facing a grower who wants to work as naturally as possible are three fungal diseases: oidium (powdery mildew), downy mildew, and botrytis. The first two of these are the worst because *V. vinifera* lacks resistance to them, and it is impossible to control them without using some preventive measures, which means spraying vineyards with some form of chemical. Even organic and biodynamic growers need to resort to chemical sprays (albeit the "traditional" chemicals sulfur and copper) to protect against these fungal diseases, although the number of biological solutions is growing. Then, if you are unlucky, and depending on where you are working, insect pests can cause problems, and sometimes a degree of intervention is needed to prevent damage beyond an acceptable level. Then there is weed control, which can be done either chemically or manually. Finally, there is fertilization. Grapevines are well adapted to impoverished soils because in their native environment (as woodland climbers) their roots have to compete for nutrients and water with already-established root systems of the plants they are using for support. But each year vines do take nutrients from the vineyard soil that at some point will need replenishing. These nutrients and trace elements can be returned to the soil in ways that are more natural (such as composting or using specific cover crops) or less natural (chemical fertilizers).

The goal for winegrowers who want to work naturally is to produce healthy grapes with the minimum level of intervention. This means trying to culture vines in a way that minimizes pest and disease problems, targeting any interventions as specifically as possible, and seeking the most natural solutions to any problems that do arise. This chapter explores how winegrowers worldwide are turning to sustainable viticulture protocols to help them achieve this goal.

It is widely recognized in conservation circles that if you want to make people take an interest in preserving wildlife diversity, then the most effective way to do it is to make it pay. People protect things that they value. Of course, everyone likes the *idea* of conservation, but when push comes to shove, few are willing to put their hands in their pockets and pay the bill. However, give people an economic incentive, and they'll go out of their way to make it happen. This may sound overly cynical, but it's the way people work. For example, if a wildlife reserve or a special habitat becomes an important tourist draw that helps the local economy, then that habitat or reserve will be effectively protected.

In some ways, the issue of sustainable winegrowing is similar. People will generally switch to organics or biodynamics because they believe in it, and because they have a strong personal conviction that it is the right thing to do. But sustainability risks being a rather nebulous, ill-defined concept that few growers will be willing to adopt if it means a reduction of crop yield or quality or an increase in operating expenses. Persuading the average grower to switch to sustainable farming requires an assurance that there is something tangible to be gained other than simply a warm feeling from doing the right thing.

In July 2008 the focus of the annual International Pinot Noir Celebration (IPNC) in McMinnville, Oregon, was "Sustainability without Sacrifice." This clever title highlights what is surely the way forward for sustainable winegrowing. While it is true that all of us have a moral imperative not to leave the land to our children in a worse state than when we received it, growers will be much more interested in becoming sustainable if they realize that no sacrifice (in either quality or financial commitment) is needed to achieve this state.

Shouldn't we all be switching to organics and biodynamics anyway? Although many practitioners will probably disagree, organic and biodynamic farming will likely remain the preserve of relatively small, high-end wineries. It is unlikely that a substantial proportion of the world's vineyard area will ever be farmed in these ways. So while they attract attention in discussions of the greening of wine, they won't significantly lessen the environmental impact of vineyards worldwide. Sustainable winegrowing, however, promises to make a huge impact because it can be adopted by all growers, large or small. Entire appellations or even national wine industries could potentially be farmed by sustainable methods. As with successful conservation efforts, the way to make sustainable winegrowing happen isn't to appeal to people's better natures, but rather to show them that it can pay. This is a pragmatic viewpoint. Of course, everyone *should* work sustainably. Recognizing the way most people work, though, how can we make them choose sustainability? Only by changing the incentive structure so that they'll actually want to work this way.

THE DEFINITION OF SUSTAINABILITY AND THE IMPORTANCE OF CERTIFICATION

Some very exciting examples of sustainability are currently in practice in the wine world on different scales—from individual producers to whole appellations, regions, and efforts that involve whole countries. But first, we need a definition of sustainable winegrowing. There's a danger, of course, that the term *sustainability* will be used too frequently and that it could simply become marketing jargon that is thrown around ("greenwashing"), while little will actually change in the way in which vineyards are run. But the good news is that vineyards in many parts of the world are now being farmed in a more natural way.

So what is sustainability as it applies to wine? It is working in a way that maintains the quality of the vineyard land (so there is no degradation of soil structure, fertility, or the water table) and minimizes any chemical inputs. Growers who choose to work sustainably may also decide to lessen their carbon footprint by reducing the emission of greenhouse gases, which have been implicated in global climate change. (This topic is covered in depth in Chapter 12.)

Sustainable growers will therefore choose to move away from current practices such as calendar spraying of agrochemicals and the systematic use of herbicides. They will likely move towards integrated pest-management (IPM) practices and the use of biological control methods. They will take an interest in soil fertility and may choose to adopt composting, manual tillage, or the use of cover crops. They may go further and embrace biodynamics or organics. We'll cover the practical aspects of sustainable farming later in this chapter.

It's all very well for growers to claim that they are working sustainably, but if this is to mean anything to consumers, then some form of certification is needed. Without certification, anyone would be able to call himself or herself "sustainable," even if he or she weren't making the required changes to practices. With certification, there is a chance that winegrowers will reap some benefit if consumers become sufficiently aware of the issues that they are prepared to pay a premium for wine that has been grown and made in a sustainable, more natural way.

SUSTAINABILITY IN ACTION

NEW ZEALAND: A SUSTAINABLE WINE COUNTRY?

New Zealand's wine industry has led the way in its emphasis on sustainability. The clever use of the slogan "Riches of a clean, green land" has helped communicate the measures being taken in sustainable winegrowing to consumers, which is an important element of this sort of strategy. In some ways, New Zealand has had to grapple with issues of agricultural sustainability earlier than many other countries because of the legacy of intensive agricultural models that have left New Zealand anything but a "clean, green" land. Since its beginnings in 1995, Sustainable Winegrowing New Zealand (SWNZ; www.nzwine .com/swnz/) has gradually enlisted growing numbers of producers in its program, to the extent that it is a realistic prospect that before very long the entire New Zealand wine industry will be able to declare itself sustainable.

Some critics suggest that SWNZ sets the bar too low: in trying to get everyone to join, they have made it too easy to belong. But there's no doubting the impact that the program is having on the image of New Zealand wine. Because so many producers are participating, the whole SWNZ has a visibility and consumer awareness that will raise the value of joining. This is one way of making adopting sustainable practices pay. Also, it's much easier to tighten up the membership criteria when you have people on board and involve them in the discussions about progressing with sustainability. It is likely that a broad coalition of growers like this will have much more impact than wineries going it alone and sending out press releases about what they are doing. Because SWNZ is scientifically based, it is unlikely to alienate anyone as biodynamics, with its metaphysical aspects, sometimes does.

Steve Smith of Craggy Range is one of the producers who claim that SWNZ has been beneficial. "I think the program and philosophy have been hugely successful in changing attitudes away from what I call synthetic and technical agrichemical applications to a much more holistic approach," he says. He cites five major benefits:

1. There is almost no residual herbicide use now.
2. Insecticide use is greatly reduced.
3. The vineyard floor is a multispecies sward and is rarely cultivated, bringing great benefits for biodiversity and improved soil health.
4. Significant investment in organic-based research into botrytis control has made it possible to achieve control organically, largely with products that have been developed from this philosophy. Also, there is significant encouragement to use much softer synthetic chemicals, particularly insecticides.
5. Greatly improved canopy management, which has also provided much better grape quality due to a better canopy microclimate.

"It has changed a mind-set significantly to a stage where it is possible to produce grapes on a commercial scale with nil agrichemical residues," Smith claims. "I have no doubt that this would not have happened without that program. It has made producers realize that growing organically in some areas is not that difficult. For example, Central Otago has stated a goal of being a 100 percent organic grapes region." He adds, "The sustainability program now needs to take another step if we are to continue to lead, with a goal of developing highly researched organic compounds that combined with the right vine management can allow the country a very high percentage of organic production."

FIGURE 6.2
Sustainable Winegrowing New Zealand sign at Carrick, Central Otago.

Clive Dougall, winemaker at the biodynamic winery Seresin, applauds this scheme, even though he thinks that it does not go far enough. "The best thing about it is that it makes people think about what they are doing," he says, "and if that is what they need to open their minds, then it is a success."

Overall, while SWNZ is not strict enough for some, it seems that this inclusive strategy, with the barrier not set too high, is a very effective way of helping growers in their sustainability journey.

SOUTH AFRICA: STEPS TOWARDS SUSTAINABILITY

Since 2000, South African wine producers have been able to demonstrate their sustainability by being certified by an organization called Integrated Production of Wine (IPW). IPW's voluntary environmental sustainability scheme consists of a set of guidelines detailing good agricultural practices related to grape production, as well as guidelines covering winemaking and bottling. Compliance with these guidelines is assessed through a self-evaluation questionnaire and is then independently audited through spot checks. Certification is overseen by the Wine and Spirit Board.

The guidelines operate on a score-sheet basis; producers who adopt environmentally friendly practices score more points. They need to reach a certain threshold score to be certified. Below are some examples of the guidelines issued to producers (these are available in full from the IPW website, www.ipw.co.za).

One person from the farm or cellar must attend an IPW training course. Each farm must have a conservation plan for natural areas and an environmental management plan for cultivated areas (the website provides information about how to do this). There is also an exhaustive list of environmental guidelines. For example, new vineyard blocks are to have wildlife corridors in them, and producers are encouraged to think of implementing these in existing vineyards where possible. The use of cover crops is encouraged to reduce the use of herbicides and to lessen the risk of erosion. If preemergence herbicides are used, a record has to be kept together with sufficient justification for their use. Fertilizers must be used only to replace what has been taken out during the growing season; records of plant and soil analyses need to be kept to show that this was the case. For disease control, IPM tactics must be applied. Only registered chemicals are permitted, if indeed chemical use is found to be necessary at all. Growers are given guidelines on how to monitor various vineyard pests, including the use of pheromone traps, and on the appropriate control measures depending on the pest population level. In the winery, waste management is a strong focus, but the guidelines also cover greenhouse gas emissions and steps to reduce them.

Along with IPW certification, South Africa also has the Biodiversity and Wine Initiative (BWI; website: www.bwi.co.za), which is a partnership between the wine industry and the conservation sector. The BWI aims to prevent further loss of native habitat in critical sites, to increase the total area set aside as natural habitat in contractual protected areas, and to promote changes in farming practices that enhance the suitability of vineyards as a habitat for biodiversity while reducing farming practices that have negative impacts on biodiversity, both in the vineyards and in surrounding natural habitat. Producers who want to join need to commit to managing areas of native habitat in certain ways compatible with promoting biodiversity. As of March 2011, 167 members were managing 127,266 hectares, which is slightly more than the actual vineyard area in the Cape winelands. The BWI works in partnership with the IPW.

OREGON: COMMUNICATING SUSTAINABILITY TO CONSUMERS

In regard to sustainability and its certification, Oregon is an example worth studying in some detail. The wine industry there has a number of certification programs, but many people have recognized that this can be a bit confusing for consumers. For starters, there are Low-Input Viticulture and Enology (LIVE), Oregon Tilth Certified Organic, Demeter Certified Biodynamic, and Salmon Safe. Because of this potential confusion and also the difficulty of communicating such a complex message, the Oregon Wine Board is currently in the process of bringing all these programs under a single banner: Oregon Certified Sustainable Wine (OCSW, www.ocsw.org). OCSW doesn't aim to add another form of certification in order to supplant the others, but instead looks to create a single sustainability brand that can then be communicated to consumers by means of a logo on the bottle, with supporting educational material. In order to use the OCSW logo, wineries must be certified by one of the existing bodies and must meet some further basic requirements. For example, the wine must be made from 97 percent certified

grapes, all of which were grown in Oregon. The licensing fees are US$0.01 per bottle up to 600,000 bottles and $0.005 for the rest, plus a $250 audit fee.

LIVE is the leading certification body for sustainability in Oregon. Ted Casteel, one of the owners of the Bethel Heights winery in the Eola-Amity Hills AVA in the Willamette Valley, was one of the founders of LIVE, which was established in 1999. The Casteels were part of the first wave of Oregon wine producers and began their winery in the late 1970s. "The Willamette Valley is a diverse ecosystem with 200 different horticultural crops and no insect pests," Casteel explains. "Bethel Heights was 90 percent colonized by [beneficial] mycorrhizal fungi. In the first seven or eight years the only thing we needed to do was to spray for powdery mildew, but in the early 1990s the industry changed. More people came here. There used to be 17 wineries; now there are over 350. Over time a lot of rather foolish people joined our ranks who didn't understand about sustainability." So Ted decided that it would be a good idea to form a sustainability group for the industry, and LIVE was the result. "The goal remains to have a group that will certify the whole industry," he adds.

Casteel explains that LIVE has four tenets:

1. The gradual reduction and elimination of out-of-farm inputs.
2. Biodiversity: the way you avoid insecticides is not to have a monoculture. We encourage flowering plants in and around vineyards, and the use of ecological compensation areas (ECAs).
3. The notion of the whole farm as an ecosystem that interacts with itself.

4. "We are trying to certify the entire industry," says Casteel. "Certification is an important part of sustainability: it gives growers a sense of rigour and discipline and encourages record keeping and monitoring for pests."

Certification requires two years of farming under LIVE guidelines. Third-party inspections are used as part of the certification process, which costs US$100 for an application and then $175 a year for up to 20 acres and an extra $2 per acre beyond that. The inspection fee is $300 yearly for the first two years and then every third year, with the specific year chosen on a random basis.

LIVE has what they call a "yellow list" of approved chemicals, and a grower who wants to use something that is not on the list can apply for a variant. This application goes to a technical committee for approval, and LIVE works with the grower to try to find a sustainable solution to the problem. A grower can apply for a variant only once every three years, and a grower who uses a nonapproved chemical loses certification for a year.

LIVE currently certifies 7,626 acres of vineyards, which represents around half the Oregon wine industry. Two hundred and thirty seven vineyards are enrolled, 219 in Oregon and 18 in Washington. That's an impressive achievement.

CHILE: DEVELOPING A SUSTAINABLE PROTOCOL
FOR THE WINE INDUSTRY

Caliterra is a winery in Chile's Colchagua Valley that was founded as a joint venture of Eduardo Chadwick and Robert Mondavi in 1996. In 2004 Chadwick brought Mondavi's share back when Mondavi was sold to Constellation, and he decided to change strategy. "We thought about organics," explains chief winemaker Sergio Cuadra, "but we wanted a broader approach to winegrowing and winemaking. We thought that sustainability as a concept was the best option we had." There was a problem, though: the sustainable approach wasn't certifiable. Therefore, Caliterra contacted Professor Yerko Moreno of the University of Talca about creating a protocol for sustainability in Chile.

Moreno lived in Oregon for five years and has taken a keen interest in the development of the LIVE certification of sustainability in Oregon. He thinks that the situation in Chile is very similar to what happened in Oregon several years ago when growers began to think about ways of working sustainably but weren't satisfied with organics and biodynamics. In Oregon the growers approached a researcher, Carmo Candolfi-Vasconcelos, for help establishing the scheme; this approach has been mirrored by Caliterra approaching Moreno. Moreno outlined how Caliterra and the University of Talca were devising a sustainable protocol, which they hope will be adopted by much of the Chilean wine industry.

"We have used many ideas from the LIVE system," Moreno explained, "which is based on the International Organization for Biological and Integrated Control of Noxious Animals and Plants (IOBC) guidelines and the key aspects covered by the Organisation

Internationale de le Vigne et du Vin (OIV) sustainability guidelines." While these guidelines are useful, they don't give details, and so Moreno and his colleagues need to consider the particular growing conditions in the different Chilean wine regions. A unique feature of this Chilean protocol is that other information is gathered from guidelines for social responsibility. Thus the protocol not only covers the environment but also deals with social issues. "This is very important," says Moreno, "but it is not considered in organics and biodynamics." Moreno also stresses that the system must be profitable. "If you go broke, there is one less environmental warrior in the system." He adds, "If you do it because of marketing, it is going to be a mess."

The Talca team consists of five people in the university and five people from Caliterra (two winemakers, two viticulturalists, and an agronomist), and the project has now been going since 2009. The first goal is to develop version 1.0, which has three chapters: a green chapter (viticulture), a red chapter (in the winery), and an orange chapter (social). When version 1.0 is complete, it will be opened up to companies that specialize in certification with a view to giving one of them a contract for third-party certification of sustainability in Chile.

One example of the sort of approach the sustainable protocol will take concerns irrigation. Many vineyard managers irrigate whenever they want; others monitor water status of vines and soils. "We promote and give a better score if you have three monitoring methods and use them," says Moreno. "You have to justify everything you do, and record keeping is a key aspect of our system."

Another example is the use of herbicides. "For years and years people have been using residual herbicides," says Moreno. "We tell people that if you stop using them, you will see the benefit in one season. Already the winery owners have realized that they have to be looser in managing their vineyards. They used to look neat with vines only, but now we start to see different plant species and biodiversity." Growers get points for biodiversity in their vineyards.

Cover crops are also encouraged, but Moreno points out that there are some pitfalls for the unwary. "You seed them and think that all this biodiversity is great, but you can find that they are hosting pests," he warns. "Nature is not easy to understand. We need to find out which cover crops work best for each vineyard."

Moreno and his colleagues have been working on using precision viticulture approaches to manage vineyards more effectively. These approaches use aerial imagery to identify differences in vigour in the vineyard. Using software, this sort of imagery can identify separate management blocks, which can then be managed differentially to increase quality. For example, some parts of the vineyard might be ripening later than others, perhaps because there are differences in soils in those particular blocks. Rather than wait for these blocks to catch up, they could be picked separately, while the earlier-ripening blocks could be picked at peak ripeness. Another example is particular sections of the vineyard that are susceptible to disease or certain pests. Action could be taken just on these blocks, rather than on the level of the whole vineyard.

Biological control approaches for pests are one of the cornerstones of sustainable viticulture. Moreno cites the ladybird *Cryptolaemus montrouzieri* as a promising biological control agent for mealybugs. Mealybugs can be a big problem for vineyards because they are vectors of leaf roll virus. However, this form of biological control hasn't been tried yet because it will work only when there is a big enough infestation of mealybugs to support the ladybird predator. Red spider mites are a problem, and they can be controlled biologically by predatory mites such as *Phytoseiulus persimilis*. Alternatively, they can be controlled by spraying oil. For nematode problems, biological nematicides exist, as well as rootstocks that are resistant to nematodes. "We have learned to monitor things and determine thresholds for taking action," says Moreno. He stresses the importance of information. "If you don't have information, you are blind, and you just have to use the calendar," he asserts, referring to the old-style practice of calendar spraying.

The hope is that the protocol produced by Moreno and his colleagues will be taken up by wineries across Chile and provide a solid certified sustainable basis for the whole industry.

SUSTAINABLE VITICULTURE IN THE DOURO: THE FLADGATE PARTNERSHIP'S INITIATIVES

The Douro Valley in northern Portugal is one of the world's most spectacular wine regions. Around two-thirds of its vineyards (28,000 hectares out of a total of 39,000) are planted on hillsides with a gradient of over 30 percent. The main block of these vineyards, on the banks of the river Douro, has been designated as a UNESCO World Heritage Site.

In 2009 the prestigious Banco Espírito Santo Biodiversity Prize was awarded to the Fladgate Partnership for its project "A New Model for Viticulture in the Douro Region." This annual prize is sponsored by BES in partnership with the Centre for Research in Biodiversity and Genetic Resources (CIBIO) and recognizes innovative projects in the fields of research, conservation, and management of biodiversity in Portugal.

The Fladgate Partnership owns over 500 hectares of vineyards in the Douro, from which it produces Port from three historic Port houses: Taylor, Fonseca, and Croft. Over the last ten years it has invested 27 million euros in the Douro valley, and recent work has focused on replanting the steeply sloped vineyards in a more sustainable way.

In the past, the only way to plant these slopes was to construct walled terraces. The walls, built of stone, were necessary to support the earth and prevent erosion. In the 1970s and 1980s a new method of planting became more popular: using bulldozers to carve out from the schist reasonably wide terraces, called patamares, on which two rows of vines are planted.

There are two problems with these patamares. First, the earth banks are unsupported, and so winter rains are liable to cause erosion. Second, the only way to control weed growth is the use of herbicides because the proximity of the inner row of vines to the earth bank means that mechanical cultivation isn't possible.

FIGURE 6.4
New-style terracing at Croft's Quinta da Roeda. It is built at a special angle to encourage runoff and can be managed without herbicides.

The Fladgate Partnership has pioneered a new model for planting based on a single narrow terrace that supports just one row of vines. These terraces are constructed using laser-guided earthmoving equipment that allows the terraces to be inclined at precisely 3° to the horizontal. This 3° inclination strikes a balance between rainwater runoff and its penetration into the soil, avoiding topsoil erosion.

The single row of vines allows mechanical control of weed growth, which means that herbicide use in the vineyard can be eliminated. Cover cropping is also used on the surface of the terrace, with vegetation remaining between November and late spring, when it is mowed as the vines grow to prevent competition for water and nutrients and to act as a natural mulch. This also adds organic material back to the soil.

Other components of the model include planting olive trees along the vineyard boundaries and the conservation of indigenous vegetation on slopes too steep to cultivate. In addition, care is taken to plant the right vine varieties in the right place to help prevent diseases and avoid pests. The Fladgate initiative is not part of any certification program, but initiatives such as this, if applied more widely, have great promise to ensure the sustainability of the spectacular Douro vineyards.

AT THE WINERY LEVEL IN AUSTRALIA: YALUMBA

Yalumba, Australia's oldest family-owned winery, is proud of its efforts in the field of sustainability. A staff member, Dr. Cecil Camilleri (senior technical manager for environmental matters), is in charge of Yalumba's Environment Management System, a systematic approach to managing the impact of the winery on the environment. This system has five elements, including a commitment to reduce greenhouse gas emissions and to manage waste more effectively, but the most relevant here is Yalumba's Vitis land stewardship program, which takes an integrated approach and aims to reduce the use of pesticides and fertilizers, encourage biodiversity, preserve and even enhance soil fertility and structure, and set aside land for conservation purposes. While Yalumba's efforts are not externally certified, there is no doubt that it is making a genuine commitment to sustainability, and that these efforts are not just window dressing.

SUSTAINABLE GROWING IN PRACTICE

Scientifically based sustainable viticulture goes under a variety of names. *Integrated pest management* (IPM) is the most widely used term, along with the broader term *integrated farm management* (IFM), which encompasses not just pest and disease control but also soil health and plant nutrition. In France, which is leading the way in the application of these practices in viticulture, *lutte raisonée* (which translates best as the "rational fight") and *viticulture raisonée* are the corresponding terms.

IPM represents a paradigm shift in agriculture: previously the prevailing attitude was one of blitzing all pests with chemicals, leaving just the crop species, perfect and unblemished. Farmers intervened to prevent any crop loss to disease or pests. This approach was based on a simplistic understanding of nature and a failure to recognize the complex network of relationships that exist in most ecosystems. Thus science wasn't the problem; it was bad science that led agriculture in this direction.

However, there has recently been a sea change in attitudes, partly because such practices simply don't work when pests develop resistance, and also because farmers are increasingly realizing that the only morally acceptable way of farming is in a sustainable way that doesn't involve the next generations picking up the tab for our bad practices.

Natural ecosystems have evolved with checks and balances to produce a stable system, a bit like a cease-fire arrangement. Biology is incredibly rich and complex and consists of numerous interactions among the various players in the system. Farming creates an artificial ecosystem where just one species is grown at high density, resulting in ideal conditions for suitably equipped insect, fungal, and nematode pests, as well as weed species. The simplistic twentieth-century response was for chemists to develop an arsenal of sprays targeting these problem species, but this approach created a more serious problem of pests with resistance to the fungicides and pesticides employed by farmers, and the sprays also killed the natural enemies of these pest species that before had kept their population numbers under a degree of control. In addition, the widespread use of agrochemicals has in some cases led to degradation of soil quality.

IPM rests on a thorough scientific knowledge of the biology of pest, weed, and disease organisms in the context of the larger ecosystem. Practitioners use this knowledge to monitor populations of potential problem organisms and anticipate when they will reach damaging levels. In essence, IPM is about reconciling rather disparate aims: farmers want to reduce crop losses while at the same time reducing environmental degradation and avoiding buildup of pest resistance. Farmers who use IPM are making choices based on a broad perspective that takes into account the whole ecosystem rather than just part of it.

Data and knowledge are both keys for IPM because they can help reduce the number of chemical inputs by predicting when certain pests or diseases are likely to be a problem. Any spray programs can be scheduled intelligently and applied only when they are really needed. This climatic monitoring is inexpensive to implement and is likely to actually save money because sprays and the labour required to administer them are costly. An example of this monitoring in action is the work at Glen Carlou in South Africa's Paarl region. The viticultural team uses in-vineyard environmental data gathering, which is linked to a computer in the winery running a software package called Plant-PLUS. This software allows the team to predict the incidence of pests and diseases and apply control only when and where it is needed. The system combines data collected from the various parts of the vineyard with weather forecast data to indicate when control might be necessary. The viticulturalist can manually add further data on the growth phase of the vines. As a result, minimal chemical inputs are used, and this system paid for itself from these savings in just one season.

Biological control is another foundation of IPM. If you have a pest problem, introduce the natural enemies of this pest—be they predators or diseases—and let them control it. Many IPM strategies rely on the identification of natural enemies of pest arthropods. These are also known as "beneficials." Natural enemies might be predators, who eat the problem species, or parasitoids, which are insect parasites. An example of a parasitoid is parasitic wasps: these might lay eggs in a problem caterpillar that produce larvae that then grow inside the caterpillar, using it as a food source and killing it in the process. A twist on the biological control theme is to use pheromones to cause sexual confusion in the pest species. This is already widely practiced in vineyards to control the serious pest species Eudemis (*Lobesia botrana*) and Cochylis (*Eupoecilia ambiguella*), which are moths whose larvae damage developing grape clusters. Small brown plastic capsules are hung on wires in the vineyards at regular intervals, releasing pheromones that attract the male moths and thus prevent them from finding and mating with females. This biological control is around three times more expensive than chemical control but is widely practiced.

There is serious science behind biological control, and an organization coordinates efforts worldwide: the IOBC (www.unipa.it/iobc/), which is split into six regional groups. A nice example of biological control in vineyards is the use of flowering buckwheat, *Fagopyrum esculentum*, as a cover crop that acts as a habitat for the wasp *Dolichogenidea tasmanica*, a common parasitoid of leaf roller larvae, a serious pest of grapevines (see figure 6.1).

Biopesticides are a new development that may prove important in the future. These are pesticides that use specific microbes as the active agents. Examples are *Trichoderma*

FIGURE 6.5
Cover crop at the Calvert Vineyard, Central Otago, New Zealand.

harzianum, a fungal enemy of another fungus, *Botrytis cinerea*, that causes bunch rot on grapes, and *Ampelomyces quisqualis*, an antagonist of powdery mildew. Some are already being used in vineyards.

If parasitoids or predators of pests are introduced into a vineyard, they need somewhere to live, and vines might not be an ideal home. In addition, clean-cultivated vineyards are barren during the dormant season and provide no hiding place for overwintering insects. This is where ecological compensation areas or zones (ECAs or ECZs) come in handy. These are patches of ground given over to specific patterns of vegetation, such as scrubland, woods, or hedgerows that can act as refuge areas for natural enemies of problem species. This sort of biodiversity can offset some of the negative effects of monoculture. It is likely that the efficacy of these compensation areas can be enhanced by the use of cover crops or by allowing some vegetation to grow between vine rows. These compensation zones are not a panacea for all vineyard problems: there is a risk that growing certain types of vegetation near vineyards could encourage the presence of insect species that turn out to be a problem, either directly as pests themselves or indirectly by acting as transmission agents of viral or bacterial diseases. Knowledge and experimentation are needed to fine-tune the use of ECAs for specific wine regions because no broad-brush solutions can be applied everywhere.

One researcher who is trying to implement ECAs in French vineyards is Marteen Van Helden, who works for the École Nationale d'Ingénieurs des Travaux Agricoles (ENITA) in Bordeaux. His research concerns developing the science behind ECAs so they can be used as an IPM tool in vineyards. "Viticulture is particularly interesting for IPM," explains Van Helden, "because there is very little risk of increasing the pressures of diseases or pests on the vines: this is not the same with other crops." Vineyard insect

FIGURE 6.6
Cover crop growing between the rows at Gladstone Vineyard, Wairarapa,
New Zealand.

pests are usually a problem late in the summer; the idea is that in vineyards in early summer there will be a buildup of natural enemies on the hedgerows that eat pest species there and then move to the vines later. "Our experiments have been ongoing for five years now," says Van Helden. "We don't have solid results, but a lot of farmers are interested."

As well as his work in Bordeaux, Van Helden is involved in a project that will see trials of ECAs across a whole appellation, Saumur Champigny in the Loire. "We want to see whether we can re-create functional biodiversity in an existing situation," says Van Helden. "We want to see what we can adapt; we don't want to redo the landscape entirely." The project will be interesting because it will help explore which sorts of landscape elements are most significant for encouraging viable natural enemy populations. Hedgerows are a vital component of this type of project because they act as refuges and are also linking elements and corridors, but alone, they might not be enough. Some natural enemies prefer larger natural sites such as patches of scrub or woodland. The hedges can act as "roads" directed towards the vineyards. In the vineyard, small landscape elements such as undergrowth provide important refuge areas. In the Saumur Champigny experiment, Van Helden will be advising growers what sorts of plants might be useful for ECAs and vineyard undergrowth. Farmers might find space for these around their plots or might plant hedgerows in or at the boundaries of their vineyards. He estimates that the cost of planting a hedge is around four to five euros per metre, and some soil preparation, mulching, and a year or two of follow-up are also involved. There are possibilities for funding hedge planting through the local chamber of agriculture or local governments.

IPM is also gaining support in Champagne and has been championed by the Comité Interprofessionnel du Vin de Champagne (CIVC), which provides technical support and advice to growers in the region. It claims that Champagne is the first wine region in the world to run environmentally friendly programs at the scale of the region. IPM in Champagne goes under the name *viticulture raisonnée*, and since 2001 the CIVC has issued a *guide pratique* for growers. The technical services of the CIVC have actually been working on *viticulture raisonnée* for a decade; it has found that it doesn't need to enforce it because growers are embracing it readily. The CIVC has weather stations throughout the region and provides growers with alerts and advice. This sort of project is extremely encouraging, mainly because with its high participation and official sanction, it is likely to have a widespread effect on entire vineyard regions and is relevant to all types of producers, from boutique wineries to industrial giants.

Perhaps the greatest appeal of IPM/IFM is that it is scalable, applicable to the largest producers as well as smaller ones, and can pay for itself within a short time. One large company that has successfully implemented the approach is Yvon Mau, a big player in the Bordeaux region, responsible for 5 to 10 percent of its production. Christophe Mangeard, agronomist and enologist with Yvon Mau, told us about its use of *viticulture raisonnée*. In recent years it has organized some of its best suppliers into a producers' club whose members have now all been certified in *agriculture raisonnée* by the Department of Agriculture. This involves seventeen estates and 60,000 hectolitres of wine. "We did this because we think it is the best way forward for the future of agriculture," says Mangeard, "and particularly viticulture, which uses lots of chemical inputs." He adds, "Organic winegrowing is not efficient enough in terms of quality of product and environmental protection of soils and biodiversity. Integrated farming succeeds in preserving the environment and the economic balance of properties. We launched this program because of this: it gives good results in terms of the environment, costs, and quality of product."

How much does implementing IFM cost? "Not so much," says Mangeard. "We have one technician taking care of the producers. This is necessary because otherwise the producers might not do it, as it requires effort." The producers need to do things differently in order to conform to the regulations, but there are considerable savings to be made in agrochemicals. Currently, there is no premium attached to wines that have been made by *viticulture raisonée*. "The market doesn't ask for this at the moment," says Mangeard, "so we have to do it for free. But we think this may change in the future: we feel there's an increasing demand by consumers for products that respect the environment."

Mangeard thinks that *viticulture raisonée* has the potential to be used by almost all producers. "The regulations are not elitist, but they aren't too easy either: it's possible for any producer to do it with effort," he maintains.

With the technician in charge of this program, Stephan Becquet, we visited three of the contracted producers for Yvon Mau. His job is to advise the 11 private cellars and 6 cave cooperatives that are part of this producers' club. Yvon Mau buys its wine the year before it is made. "This helps me to make what changes I want in the vineyard and during vinification," explains Becquet. The producers get a premium for following the guidelines and also premiums for the tasting, pruning, and phytosanitary program. Becquet says that in Bordeaux the problem in the past has been that people have been using too much product: salesmen of phytosanitary products have been devising the spraying program, and the result has been too much applied, often at the wrong time. Becquet stresses the importance of adapting the phytosanitary program for the year: in a vintage with less disease pressure it is best to use a contact product; in a more difficult year systemic fungicide is needed.

As an example, these are some of the outcomes of the partnership between one of these growers, Château Lavison of Entre-Deux-Mers, and Yvon Mau.

CASE STUDY   CHÂTEAU LAVISON, ENTRE-DEUX-MERS

Lavison is a thirteenth-century château that is currently run by the energetic Alexandra Martet, the third generation of the Martet family to own this property. It has 55 hectares of vines and in the last few years has dramatically reduced vineyard inputs. "Before, there wasn't much concern for the environment," says Martet. "Everyone treated all the time. Now we take the money we used to spend on antibotrytis treatments and use it for staff costs to work on the vines." The work that is done is cutting out rot and removing leaves to ventilate the canopy.

1.   Objective: to improve the health of the grapes while reducing the use of sprays and chemicals in the vineyard. The methods used are the following:
     · Adapted pruning to ensure a better spread of grape bunches
     · Improved canopy management to allow better air circulation
     · Manual thinning and removal of leaves
     · Transition from single-guyot to double-guyot training
     · Reduced fertilisation

The results? Zero antibotrytis treatments in 2007 as against two in 1999, and a reduction of 30 to 50 percent in copper treatments (2.1 and 1.5 kg/ha in 2006 and 2005 respectively, compared with 3.0 kg/ha in 1999).

2.   Objective: to improve the soil and the microbiological life within it. The methods used are the following :

- Reducing the width of the weeded area under each row to reduce the total amount of weed killer used
- Use of wide, low-pressure tyres, leading to less compacted soils
- No use of weed killers between 31 August and 1 April of the following year

The results? A reduction of 40 percent in the amount of weed killer used. Lavison stopped using Diuron and Gramoxone long before they were officially banned. There is less erosion and rutting because of the wider strip of grass between rows.

3. Objective: to recycle as many materials as possible and to avoid accidental pollution. The methods used are the following:
   - Sorting of all waste
   - Using local recycling schemes

The results? Ninety-eight percent of all waste and empty packaging are recovered and recycled. Oils and diesel no longer leak into the soil.

4. Objective: to develop a more diverse and balanced ecosystem in the vineyard. The methods used are the following:
   - Reduced use of chemicals, both antifungals and fertilisers
   - Using products that are less noxious to the environment and reducing the doses
   - Limiting the number of tractor passages through the vineyard, for instance, by allowing grass to grow between the rows rather than ploughing
   - Planting of hedges and building of wildflower ditches and ponds

The results? Ladybirds and other insects reappear, and predators that prey on parasites of the vine are attracted.

What makes the Lavison case study interesting is that this producer works on tight margins, selling inexpensive wine in a difficult market. A property such as Lavison could not swallow the costs associated with switching to organics or biodynamics, but sustainable growing is a realistic option. Lavison is a member of Linking Environment and Farming (LEAF; www.leafuk.org). This organization was established in 1991 to try to bridge the growing gap between consumers and farmers who were keen to develop a system of farming that was realistic and achievable by the majority of farmers. On the basis of work in Germany that had been carried out since 1986, LEAF aimed to develop and promote IFM. It is part of the European Initiative for Sustainable Development in Agriculture (EISA; www.sustainable-agriculture.org), an umbrella organization for LEAF and similar bodies in six European countries. In addition to certifying farms with its LEAF mark, LEAF also acts as an educational body that helps make both farmers and consumers aware of IFM.

In March 2008 a small survey of pesticide residues in wine found some disturbing results (http://www.pan-europe.info/Resources/Briefings/Message_in_a_bottle_Results
.pdf). The study, coordinated by the Pesticide Action Network (PAN) (Europe) in collabo-
ration with Greenpeace Germany, Global 2000 (Friends of the Earth Austria), and Mou-
vement pour le Droit et le Respect des Générations Futures (MDRGF) (France), found
that every bottle of wine tested that was made from conventionally farmed grapes contained pesticide residues. In this study, 34 bottles of conventional wine were tested by independent contract laboratories. All contained at least 1 pesticide residue. The average
number of residues per bottle was 4, and the highest number of residues found in a single bottle was 10. Altogether, 24 different pesticides were identified. In contrast, 6 bottles
of organic wine were tested, and just 1 contained detectable pesticide residues. While this
is a small sample, the results are quite striking. "I was surprised that we found so many
pesticides," says Elliott Cannell, a spokesperson for PAN (Europe). "The concentrations
are low, but there are lots of pesticides."

Traditionally, elemental sulfur and Bordeaux mixture, which contains copper, have
been used as fungicides in vineyards. Because they are contact products, they need to
be reapplied frequently during the growing season and are washed off by rain. Consequently, in recent decades they have largely been replaced by systemic fungicides that
offer more effective protection. Because vines are highly disease susceptible, in the EU
grapes account for 3 percent of all cropland but are responsible for 15 percent of synthetic pesticide applications.

According to PAN's Cannell, the motivation behind its study wasn't to bash the wine
industry. "Half of all food that is tested contains pesticides," says Cannell. "It is not a
problem that applies only to wine." While the EU actively monitors pesticide use, its focus
is on the maximum residue limits (MRLs) on crops, and it doesn't legislate about levels in
processed foods and drinks made from these crops. "There are maximum residue limits
for grapes," says Cannell, "but wine doesn't have these limits."

Alarming as they sound, are these results something the wine industry should be
concerned about, beyond the damage that is done to the image of wine by the sorts of
headlines that PAN's press releases generated? Yes and no seems to be the rather vague
answer. In the wine industry's favour are two points. First, while pesticide residues are
something we'd rather not have in our wines at all, the levels found in these wines
were extremely low. Second, these pesticides seem to be quite a safe group of chemicals,
and it is likely that the levels found in the study present no threats to human health
at all.

One problem with this sort of discussion is that it is hard for the trade and consumers to interpret the results of studies of this kind in their proper context. It is not easy
for a nonscientist to come to grips with the issue of levels and concentrations of pesticides that constitute a risk. The levels quoted in the PAN results were given in micro-

grams per litre (mg/L). One mg is one millionth of a gram, and a litre of wine weighs about 1 kg, so these results are in the realm of parts per billion. In Table 6.1 these levels are put in the context of the regulations for pesticide use; in most cases they are well below the MRLs, which themselves are set at a conservative level.

One issue that people don't always understand is that of safe levels of exposure. Many substances are harmless at normal levels of exposure, but with repeated exposure at high concentrations they can be carcinogenic or toxic in other ways. Let's give a hypothetical example. It could be that the active ingredient in sunscreen, at one hundred times the concentration found in commercial preparations, can cause cancer when it is rubbed on the ears of laboratory rats every day for a year. Does this mean that sunscreen is carcinogenic? No. There is a dose that has no observable adverse effects, and to avoid using sunscreen because of worries about health could end up putting you at risk. It is entirely possible that for many compounds there is a threshold for carcinogenesis: at a certain level a harmless substance crosses this threshold and becomes harmful.

Understandably, Peter Watson of Dow Chemical Company dislikes the way in which PAN announced its study findings. "NGOs [nongovernmental organizations] tend to use tactics that are not necessarily based around fact in order to generate the publicity that they are seeking," he states. "There exists a set of guidelines and rules about what is acceptable in terms of residues," says Watson, "and these limits shouldn't be exceeded. Sometimes they are, but the excess is small and these levels have large safety margins."

"The headlines [generated by the PAN study] were that there is illegal, unauthorized, and unsafe use of pesticides in wine," says Stuart Rutherford of the European Crop Protection Association (ECPA). "Their actual results were that out of 123 samples, 99.6 percent contained detectable residues, but only 4.8 percent of samples were above the MRLs."

Watson describes how EU regulation of pesticides has evolved. "In the past, each of the member states operated national systems of regulation, and the Commission tried to harmonize these," he explains. "They've now gone one step further with the publication of MRL regulations, which are themselves based on EFSA (European Food Safety Authority) regulations." Rutherford amplifies on this. "Two bits of legislation are currently under review," he explains. "First is the residue legislation which came into force in October 2008, and then there is the framework legislation governing the authorization of pesticides. This is currently undergoing amendment; essentially, it is all done." Cannell's interpretation of the new authorization legislation is that "as a result, some of the most hazardous pesticides will no longer be authorized for use. For example, carbendazim, which is classified as a reprotoxin and mutagen." But Rutherford thinks this is premature, and that it is too soon to predict which products, if any, will be placed on a pesticide blacklist.

What does PAN think should be done about pesticide use in wine? "We wouldn't advocate organics as the only solution," says Cannell, "but we can replace the most hazardous pesticides with safer alternatives. Where we have a fungicide that is a carcinogen and one that isn't, can't we use the safer one?" His logic seems self-evident, but the

TABLE 6.1 The Major Agrochemicals Mentioned in the PAN Report

Name	Description	LD50	MRL	Other notes
Azoxystrobin	Systemic, broad-spectrum fungicide methoxyacrylate compound used as a preventive and curative systemic fungicide.	LD50 >5,000 mg/kg for rats.	MRL in grapes = 10 ppm (JFCRF),	Unlikely to be a carcinogen. Degraded rapidly under agricultural field conditions with a soil half-life of less than 2 weeks; sensitive to photolysis.
Dimethomorph	A morpholine fungicide that acts systemically, this is a cinnamic acid derivative that is only slightly toxic to mammals. It inhibits the formation of fungal cell walls; mammals don't have these.	Mouse = 3,900 mg/kg; rat = 5,000 mg/kg.		Reported as not likely to be a human carcinogen
Carbendazim	A systemic benzimidazole fungicide that has low toxicity and is rapidly excreted. Inhibits beta tubulin synthesis (microtubules), but fortunately doesn't work on mammals.	LD50 >15,000 mg/kg for rats and mice.		Acceptable daily intake of 0–0.03 mg/kg body weight was set by WHO/FAO joint meeting on pesticide residues (JMPR) in 1995. Toxic to earthworms.

Cyprodinil	An anilinopyrimidine fungicide.		MRL in grapes = 5 ppm (JFCRF).	Acceptable daily intake = 0.03 mg/kg bodyweight per day (EU). residue tolerance (EPA) = 2 ppm. Residues unlikely to represent a public health concern (JMPR).
Iprodione	A dicarboximide fungicide.	LD50 >4,400 mg/kg for rats (EPA); LD50 >2,000 mg/kg bodyweight for rats (EU).	MRL = 25 ppb (JFCRF).	Rapidly eliminated from the body and breaks down quickly in the soil.
Procymidone	A dicarboximide fungicide.	LD50 >5,000 mg/kg for mice and rats.		
Pyrimethanil	An anilinopyrimidine fungicide.	LD50 = 4,150 mg/kg for rats.	European MRL = 3 mg/kg on wine grapes; U.S. MRL = 5 mg/kg.	ADI (acceptable daily intake) = 0.17 mg/kg body-weight. Not acutely toxic (EPA).

NOTE: The LD_{50} values quoted are the levels of these chemicals that cause half of the animals tested to die: this is an indication of the toxicity of the product, although of course our concern about pesticide toxicity relates to end points some way short of death. MRL refers to maximum residue limit. These figures are all in mg/kg (this is the same as parts per million, ppm). Bear in mind that the average person weighs around 70 kg, and that 1 mg = 1,000 μg (the unit quoted in the PAN report).

SOURCE: Table of MRLs in food from the Japan Food Chemical Residues Foundation (JFCRF): For grapes[EW1] http://www.m5.wsoo1.squarestart.ne.jp/foundation/fooddtl.php?f_inq=10800

FIGURE 6.7
A bee feeding on lucerne, a cover crop used in vineyards.

assumption here is that many of the current pesticide products are unnecessary. How-ever, farmers need a range of products with different mechanisms of action because the use of any fungicide poses a risk of development of resistance. The way to prevent re-sistance is to rotate fungicide applications, using products with different mechanisms of action. Take away too many pesticide options from farmers, and there is a real risk that the fungal pests that are a major problem for viticulture will become resistant.

"The current situation is sustainable," says Watson. "We provide growers with tools, and the regulatory authorities ensure that these tools are appropriate to the job, with a margin of safety." He adds that grapes are only one of many potential sources of pesticide intakes for humans, and that risk assessment is done on this basis: that all of our intake sources contain the maximum allowed pesticide levels. We don't understand enough about how pesticides interact with health," counters Cannell. "We have to be precautionary."

Many farmers are now implementing IPM solutions. "I'm quite happy to promote IPM as an approach," says Cannell. "I don't see how you can justify being a farmer and not following IPM." This seems to make sense: even if pesticide use at current levels is safe when the regulations are adhered to, grape growers could save money by using fewer products in their vineyards, as well as feel better about the way they are working.

The PAN study focuses on wines from a number of different countries. "We were quite keen not to target one country," explains Cannell. "We see the problem in all wines." But he adds, "Wines from the EU are less likely to have higher levels of pesticides because Europe has stricter regulations on what pesticides can be used. There are more hazardous pesticides that are legal for use outside the EU."

Cannell is pleased that the new EU regulations promise to be more rigorous. "If the EU wants to lead the world, we shouldn't shy away from being proud to have tougher regulations," he states. But Phil Newton of the ECPA is concerned that these new regulations may affect agricultural productivity. "The new legislations haven't been explored," says Newton. "There has been no impact study on productivity and prices, so we are heading into uncharted waters."

But for Cannell, the take-home message is a straightforward one. "If there's a choice between hazardous and nonhazardous pesticides, go for the less hazardous. Grape farmers have to control fungi, but with around five hundred different active substances, we can easily avoid the worst."

Biodynamics and organics currently may have centre stage as the most visible and high-profile green ways of winegrowing. But perhaps more important for the majority of winegrowers worldwide is sustainable winegrowing, which draws heavily on IPM in its various forms. With its potential for cost saving, its efficacy, and its green credentials, sustainability could be the future of winegrowing the natural way. Increasingly, wine regions worldwide are looking to implement certification of sustainability, which is needed to prevent it from being seen as a nice idea with no real substance. As certification schemes are applied more widely in the industry, there is a real chance that consumers will begin to recognize sustainable farming in much the same way in which they currently recognize organics. This would be an important breakthrough. Certified sustainable promises to be an exciting way forward for winegrowers worldwide.

7

WHEN WINEMAKERS INTERVENE
Chemical and Physical Manipulation

We consider the best wine is one that can be aged without any preservative;
nothing must be mixed with it which might obscure its natural taste. For the most
excellent wine is one which has given pleasure by its own natural qualities.

COLUMELLA, *ON AGRICULTURE*, BOOK 12

Even the most fundamentalist supporters of the philosophy of terroir—and the role of natural winemaking in seeing that this terroir is expressed in the final wine—would agree that the winemaker has a responsibility to watch over the wine as it develops and to intervene where necessary to ensure that the wine reflects the true potential of its site. To put this another way, doing nothing and watching a wine spoil because of some avoidable fault results in that wine failing to express its terroir. The human aspect is therefore important in any definition of terroir or typicity, because without human effort there is no wine, and without wine there is no expression of terroir. Any review of naturalness in wine must therefore look closely at the corresponding philosophy and actions or interventions of the winemaker. That's what we are aiming to do in this chapter.

A consistent theme of this book is that one of the things that separate wine from other alcoholic drinks is that it isn't a manufactured product. The agricultural components of beer or whisky or gin, for example, are starting points in a manufacturing process in which most of the flavour and quality depend on the execution of this process. Changes in style are largely brought about by differing manufacturing techniques and different ingredients. Although the quality of the raw materials is important, the characteristics of the final beverage aren't anywhere nearly as much influenced by the properties of the starting materials as they are with wine. You can make bad wine with good grapes, but you can't make good wine with bad grapes. And even the most skilled winemaker cannot make a great wine without a great vineyard to work from.

It is perhaps for this reason that the issue of what is added to wine during its production is so controversial. The outcry prompted by the revelation a few years ago that some South African winemakers had added methoxypyrazines to give their Sauvignon Blancs the grassy zip that their New Zealand counterparts achieved naturally was justified: while some may argue that methoxypyrazines occur naturally in grapes anyway, these additions were illegal, and permitting the addition of flavourings to wine would be perilous indeed for an industry that counts "naturalness" as one of its selling points, even if the flavourings were present in grapes and were in fact isolated from grapes.

Winemakers can intervene either chemically or physically. A common belief is that excessive intervention, in whatever form, tends to lead to wine that lacks a sense of place and a unique identity. For some time now, opinion formers have been voicing concerns over the emergence of so-called industrial wine styles. While such views may be warranted, most critics of these industrial wines fail to recognize three important factors that stem from commercial realities:

1. The greater the volume of wine, the greater the need for winemaker intervention to maximize quality and value for the consumer. There simply isn't any market for funky or strangely flavoured wines in the commercial end of the marketplace.

2. Larger volumes mean increased technical and financial risks that justify a need for an increased level of intervention to protect a valuable asset. While higher-risk, low-intervention strategies are reasonable for smaller wineries dealing with smaller lots of wine, they are hard to justify in large commercial settings.

3. There is an equally dynamic movement in the premium end of the market away from intervention, and many of the wines produced by this philosophy also run the risk of being homogeneous in style. That is, natural wines can end up all tasting rather similar, no matter where they come from. We will return to this topic when we discuss wine faults and natural winemaking in more detail.

So what should be added to wine? In this chapter we will consider common additions during winemaking and discuss what shouldn't be added to wine. Along the way we'll ponder whether the rules need to be different for different sorts of wines, how much consumers should be informed about what is added to wine, and whether there is such a thing as "fake" wine.

CHEMICAL INTERVENTION

Because additives are one of the major inputs in the winemaking process, any discussion of the topic of natural wine must first consider this group. Additives in various shapes and forms have been used in the production of wine for thousands of years. Resin use as a preservative for wine can be traced back to 5400 BC, according to Patrick

McGovern, who has studied ancient wine in detail. He suggests that tree resins were first added because people guessed that if they could heal a wound in bark, they could prevent the deterioration of wine. Other ancient additions include pepper, wormwood, saffron, capers, and other herbs and spices, some for their preservative properties, some to cover up the taste of deteriorating wine, and others just to excite the taste buds. Only the very best wines would have been drunk without flavor additions, although it was almost universal practice to dilute wine with water. Sulfur dioxide, a wine preservative now almost universally used, was first introduced by the Romans. Wine additives can be classified as either ingredients (where they remain in the wine) or wine-processing aids (where they don't).

SULFUR DIOXIDE

You can make wine with no additions at all, but there is one almost universally added chemical without which commercial wine as we know it would be pretty much impossible. That chemical is sulfur dioxide (SO_2), usually referred to on wine labels as "sulfites," which we can think of as the molecular guardian of wine. (Here we introduce the use of SO_2 briefly; we will discuss this subject in greater depth in the chapter on the natural wine movement.) SO_2 is a very interesting chemical entity whose usefulness in winemaking was discovered serendipitously through the practice of burning sulfur wicks in barrels to sanitize them. The residue of SO_2 produced by this process was found to protect the wine and extend its useful life.

With a seasonal product such as wine, extending its life in such a way would have been important. Until the seventeenth century, glass bottles were far too expensive to be used for wine. The bottle and cork combination that we take for granted today allows us to store wine quite safely for long periods through the almost complete exclusion of oxygen. Before bottles were in common use, wine would have been shipped in barrels (or some other similar type of container), and the length of time it could stay fresh would have helped determine its potential marketplace. Indeed, this was one of the reasons for the evolution of fortified wine styles: Sherry and Port are made in regions with high summer temperatures a good distance away from their primary markets, and a slug of brandy greatly aids stability. The addition of brandy to Port early in the fermentation process would ensure that even extremely rustic attempts at winemaking would result in Port that tasted pretty good and was fairly stable. This also explains why the advent of the railway spelt the end of the relatively large vineyard area surrounding Paris. Suddenly it became feasible to slake the thirst of Parisians with wines from the south of France, which could now make the journey quickly and cheaply, and the vineyards near Paris could no longer compete because their wines were more expensive and less tasty.

What does SO_2 do? First, it acts as a microbicide. It is especially toxic to bacteria, and for this reason it is often added at the time of crushing at a dose high enough to kill the microbes naturally present in grape juice, but not high enough to delay the onset of

FIGURE 7.1
A microoxygenation control panel.

fermentation. Then, after a short period, the juice is usually inoculated with cultured yeast to initiate fermentation with a microbial population that the winemaker controls. Second, SO_2 counters the effects of oxidation, protecting wines from the harmful effects of oxygen during maturation in barrel or tank and then after bottling. Notice that we haven't described SO_2 as an antioxidant: this is because it isn't, exactly. This is somewhat technical, and we shouldn't get bogged down by too much detail, but the reaction of SO_2 with oxygen is actually quite slow. When wine is exposed to air, the oxygen will first react with other components of the wine, and then the SO_2 will bind with those oxidation products.

Typically, SO_2 is added at three stages in the winemaking process: first, at crushing (or, with machine-harvested fruit, in the field just after the grapes have been picked), as we have discussed; second, after malolactic fermentation (the second, bacterial fermentation that takes place in many wines) has finished (in red wines, and in whites that are to undergo malolactic fermentation—in those where this isn't desired or possible, SO_2 will be added after alcoholic fermentation is complete). This is important because after malolactic fermentation red wines risk developing *Brettanomyces* (a spoilage yeast), and SO_2 at a sufficient level slows the growth of this rogue yeast. Sometimes, additions are also made during the process of wine maturation, for example when barrels are racked. Finally, there is an addition at bottling to ensure that the wine stays fresh during its trip from winery to consumer.

These are all reasons that SO_2 is an almost universal addition to wine. Are there any reasons it shouldn't be added? And what happens if you don't add sufficient or any SO_2? These are good questions.

First, if you don't add any SO_2, your wine becomes microbiologically unstable. You risk the growth of rogue yeasts and bacteria that can create off flavours. You also risk refermentation in the bottle, a process that creates a fizzy wine, which consumers may find off-putting. Second, your wine is at risk of oxidation. Note, however, that these are simply risks. We have tasted many wines made without addition of SO_2 that were really good. Some were a bit funky, admittedly, but they were still attractive and interesting. Many weren't funky at all. We haven't tasted many SO_2-free wines that have been disgusting or completely spoiled, but we admit that we have been doing some selective sampling. It's unlikely that vilely bad wines would make it to the marketplace or be shown to journalists.

There are three potential reasons to take the risk of working without SO_2. The first is the philosophical position that wine should be as natural as possible, with nothing at all added. So, irrespective of whether such wines might taste better, advocates of this position simply refuse to make these additions because this is the way they believe wine should be made. The second is that wines made without SO_2 might taste better. Some people argue that SO_2 additions take something away from the purity of the wine. Certainly, some wines made without SO_2 have wonderful aromatic purity and beautiful texture. We discuss this topic in depth when we look at the natural wine movement in Chapter 8. Finally, some people do without SO_2 for health reasons, because they believe that this chemical can cause adverse reactions in some people. From the medical literature, it is clear that asthmatics can have adverse reactions to high levels of SO_2. However, the levels used in wine are regulated and are usually quite low. There doesn't seem to be a strong health objection to the use of SO_2 below legal maximum levels in wine.

SUGAR

One of the most common additions to wine in both the Old and the New Worlds is sugar. Specifically, sugar is added to wine in three rather different ways. The first is chaptalization, where sugar is added before fermentation to raise the alcoholic strength of wine. Then there's the use of *liqueur d'expédition* in the *dosage*, the wine that is used to top up Champagne just after disgorgement (getting rid of the dead yeast cells from the bottle fermentation that adds the bubbles) before the final cork is applied, and attempts to do away with this. Finally, there is the more controversial use of grape juice concentrate or rectified sugar to sweeten otherwise dry wines at the end of the winemaking process to make them more appealing to consumers. In fact, controversy surrounds all three practices, although with Champagne it is the nonuse of postfermentation sugar that is causing the stir, rather than its inclusion, which is the thorny issue in sweetening table wines.

Chaptalization　In the more northerly vineyard regions of the Northern Hemisphere, summers aren't quite warm enough for sugar levels in grapes to reach the point where target levels of alcohol are achieved in the wine. As a consequence, it is a long-standing and quite legal practice to add sugar to grape must to bump up the potential alcohol levels a little. Even in the prestigious Burgundy and Bordeaux regions winemakers will be seen shoving large bags of sugar into their tanks in what seems like quite an un-natural addition to the wine. This practice is known as chaptalization, named after Jean-Antoine Chaptal, an eighteenth-century French chemist who was one of the initial supporters of the technique.

In the European Union there are rules governing how much sugar is allowed and which regions are allowed to use it (generally those that are more northerly). In different climatic zones the degree of chaptalization permitted varies. In the coolest areas, alcohol levels can be bumped up by as much as 4.5 percent; in warmer regions such as Beaujo-lais, the permitted enrichment is 2 percent. No region is allowed to add sugar and acid to the same wine, because this would allow unscrupulous producers to stretch their wines by adding water along with the sugar and acid.

In warm climates the problem is quite the opposite: harvested grapes have such high levels of sugar that the final wines are simply too alcoholic. The problem of high alcohol levels and what can be done about them is addressed in Chapter 9.

Chaptalization is quite interesting because of the effects it can have on the wine ma-trix, affecting the perception of other aromas and flavours. We are aware of a number of New World producers who pick a little earlier and then chaptalize precisely because they like the effect this has on their wine. Some Old World producers who don't need to prac-tice chaptalization (they get their grapes ripe enough to do without this) still choose to do it for this reason. The slow addition of sugar at various stages in fermentation prolongs the fermentation period and is said to add texture to the wine. In most New World re-gions, however, this practice is illegal, so these producers are technically breaking the law.

Dosage Champagne is unique. Although sparkling wines are made in just about every wine-producing country, there's something distinctive about the Champagne region and its climate that means that it is rare to find a fizz from outside the region that can show the same sort of elegance and flavour profile. The cool climate and chalk soils of Cham-pagne yield grapes that, at harvest time, have high acid levels and relatively low sugar levels but are just about physiologically ripe. It is possible to achieve the same high acidity and low sugar by picking grapes from other, warmer regions early, but usually wines from such regions won't be properly ripe and will have off-putting green herbal flavours.

Fermenting these Champagne grapes results in light, acidic *vins clairs* with around 10 percent alcohol. A good *vin clair* isn't balanced on its own (it's too acidic to taste nice), and it isn't terribly strongly flavoured. After the *vin clair* has been aged for an appropri-ate time, yeast and sugar are added, which cause a second fermentation stage, leading to the bubbles that make Champagne fizzy. Through a process called riddling, the sedi-ment of dead yeast cells is concentrated towards the neck of the bottle, from where it is removed as a plug. The bottle is then topped up in the final stage of the winemaking process, which is the addition of *liqueur d'expédition*, a sweet, syrupy substance usually derived from grapes, which typically adds 7 to 10 g of residual sugar, commonly called the *dosage*. This liqueur adds flavour as well as sweetness. Champagne houses take a great deal of care with their liqueurs for this reason, and maturation in oak barrels, which themselves can add flavor, is not unusual. Champagnes with this sort of *dosage* will be described as Brut, and this category accounts for the vast majority of Champagne sold. Yet despite containing this much sugar, these wines taste dry.

This is because our perception of sweetness is altered by acidity. The two counter each other like riders on a seesaw. The high acidity of Champagne is tempered by the sugar such that the final wine seems dry and balanced. "The acid structure of Champagne is such that it requires a *dosage* for balance," says Champagne expert Tom Stevenson. If the *dosage* stage were omitted, most Champagnes would simply taste excessively dry, acidic, and quite unpleasant. But with a growing category of wines, variously labeled alternatively non-*dosage* wines, Brut Zero, Zero *Dosage*, Ultra Brut, or Brut Nature, this is precisely what is being done. This is Champagne's version of natural wine. Indeed, if we wanted to pick a fight, we could argue that of all wine styles, Champagne is the most manufactured: less is required on the part of the grower to produce grapes with distinctive characteristics that carry over to the wine, and most Champagne vineyards have absolutely heroic yields.

Proponents of non-*dosage* wines do indeed argue that these wines are more natural. They maintain that *dosage* is in effect a corrective measure, and if the grapes were grown properly in the first place, it wouldn't be needed. "If you do a good job in the vineyard to harvest ripe and balanced grapes, you just need low or no *dosage* to appreciate the real wine that you make," says Pierre Larmandier of Champagne Larmandier Bernier, a small producer specializing in non-*dosage* wines. "We have nothing to hide: we are confident in our grapes and proud of them, so we want to show the wine for what it is." Larmandier adds, "*Dosage* is like makeup: it can help or hide. But it is a question of style: we prefer the natural and pure style of true wines."

Another producer keen on the non-*dosage* style is Benoît Tarlant of Champagne Tarlant. "My father began to do Brut Zero twenty years ago," he says, "so it is not a new thing." Tarlant is so convinced by non-*dosage* wines that he is committing his efforts to it. "Ten years ago it represented 5 to 10 percent of our production; now it is around 60 percent of it." He adds that it is still a very small segment in Champagne.

What are the keys to success with this style? "The first key is the people," says Tarlant. "It's really a goal for me to achieve this style of Champagne wine. I make every possible effort at all production steps to do it. We have to be ready for risks, we have to like to play with acidity. The next step is picking mature grapes (not just by alcohol level, but also physiologically), respectful pressing, and then natural vinification, in which we follow the wines rather than forcing them. One particular key is we work half in tanks, half in barrels. If vineyard origin is well selected, barrel fermentation can open more taste sensations. A blend of the three grapes (Chardonnay, Pinot Noir, and Pinot Meunier) helps to get a better balance, but that's a point of view. We also blend with a good proportion of reserve wine (between 30 percent and 50 percent), which has been also aged in barrels. We also allow respectful aging in the bottle."

There are critics, however. "Zero *dosage* has become a cause in itself like the hair shirt or bed of nails," says Australian wine scientist and sparkling wine expert Brian Croser. "It is mostly unpleasant, but satisfies the 'dryer is more sophisticated' perception of some consumers, encouraged by the marketers." "It's a very tiny niche market," adds Tom Stevenson. "I doubt that in total non-*dosage* wines represent even as much as 0.05 percent of sales." Stevenson adds, "Personally, I'm not a fan of the style because it seldom works."

Who is right? The tension between high acidity and a bit of sweetness is likely to be an important element in the Champagnes that we know and love. But by and large, these Champagnes are the work of the skilled *chefs du caves* (chief winemakers) who taste and then blend to achieve a desired goal. While non-*dosage* Champagnes may have a claim to being more natural, those with some *dosage* are the more complete and compelling wines in the best cases.

Grape Juice Concentrate   If *dosage* is a normal, accepted part of creating Champagnes, why is adding sweetness such a controversial issue with still wines? One of the reasons that the issue of grape juice concentrate is currently a hot topic is the enormous success of the Australian brand Yellowtail in the U.S. market. From a standing start a few years ago, it exploded onto the scene by virtue of its clever packaging and astutely made wines, which seduced sweeter-toothed American consumers with a dollop of residual sugar from a postfermentation addition of grape juice concentrate, the level of which changes with vintage but is usually around 8 grams per litre (g/L). Yellowtail quickly leapfrogged other established Australian brands such as Lindemans and Rosemount, which had been experiencing success in the United States, and is now the best-selling Australian wine in America.

One of the few people willing to speak to us on the subject was Justin Knock MW, who was a winemaker with Foster's EMEA (now Treasury Wine Estates), the corporate organization responsible for a range of Australian brands, including Rosemount, Lindemans, Wolf Blass, and Penfolds. We asked him about the use of grape juice concentrate. "It's pretty widely used in the Australian wine industry in commercial wines, mainly for palate modification postferment as you might imagine," says Knock. "Most producers use it, but it's used more by some (Yellowtail, McGuigan, and Hardys) than others (Jacobs Creek, Yalumba, McWilliams). Even within our own portfolio it's more readily used on entry-level Lindemans and to some extent entry-level Rosemount but not in Penfolds or Wolf Blass."

"Grape juice concentrate is a very common additive in red, white, and rosé wines in the branded commodity market," agrees Brian Croser. "The clear separation of expectations of commodity wine from those for fine wine allows the use of all tricks in the food production repertoire to 'improve' commodity wine to make it more consumer palatable at the lowest price. This would include the addition of 'sugar to taste.' Better it be product of the vine than of cane or beet, although that's probably not that important for commodity wine." Croser adds that "the use of grape juice concentrate is targeted at the commodity wine market perhaps with allowance for different national tolerances/preferences for sugar, i.e., more in the U.S."

While the use of grape juice concentrate has been uncontroversial for inexpensive sweeter white wines in Germany (where it is known as *Süssreserve*), it is increasingly being used around the world for red wines. The extra dollop of sugar adds a little sweetness, but it also rounds the palate and masks any harshness or greenness that might be present from the use of inferior fruit. "Obviously, grape juice concentrate is expensive, so we don't use it just to make ourselves feel better," says Knock. "From long experience the modification of palate texture from hard and dry to rounder and softer is the benefit. I would postulate that following the massive planting boom of the 1990s (that brought a lot of young, mainly red vineyards into production), the use of grape concentrate increased to deal with the relatively thin, green, and hard wines these vineyards produced. I'd like to think that its use has dropped in recent years as these vineyards have matured, but following the success of obviously sweetened styles such as Yellowtail, it's an unlikely hope."

Grape juice concentrate is made by vacuum evaporators; this equipment is expensive, but large companies will make concentrate themselves in order to guarantee quality, while smaller producers buy it. "It's certainly not only the domain of the major producers," says Knock, "though they obviously have the infrastructure for handling reasonable volumes of a product that can be relatively difficult to handle in terms of cost and microbial stability." Knock adds that for commercial wines, he sees adjustments to residual sugar as part of the fining process. "Modification is done on the basis of bench blending and tasting in conjunction with any tannin/egg/milk/isinglass/copper fining in the hours or day preceding bottling."

Of course, it is possible to achieve residual sugar by arresting fermentation, for example, by chilling the wine down and then stabilizing it through a mix of chemical and mechanical means, but this is rare for commodity wines. "It should be noted that barring stuck or sluggish fermentation, all wines are fermented to dryness," says Knock. "We do not practice arrested fermentation, and I'd be amazed if anyone else did. It's far too difficult to control at the levels we are discussing (anywhere from 2 to 10 g/L), and subsequent risks with malevolent strains of bacteria and yeast relating to malolactic fermentation and *Brettanomyces*, for example, further preclude early use."

"For fine wine the addition of sugar is interfering with the natural balance achieved in the grape by the influence of site (terroir) and of management and is a wound to the naturalness of the wine and its site expression," says Croser. "That is antithetical to the intellectual concept of fine wine that distinguishes it from most other products, which is its intrinsic interest as the product of a site and which supports fine wine as the most expensive food we consume made from the most expensive pieces of agricultural land on the globe."

It should be added that it is not always grape juice concentrate that is added. In New Zealand it was common practice to use sugar at blending to balance out Marlborough Sauvignon Blanc, although this practice has stopped (as of the 2009 vintage) because of

EU requirements concerning imported wines. Concentrate or simply unfermented grape juice is now being used.

ACIDIFICATION

In warmer wine regions it's common at harvest time for acid levels in the grapes to have fallen to such low levels that some sort of correction is required in the winery. There's a strong correlation between pH of the must and microbial stability. In Australia the realization of this by Penfolds winemaker Ray Beckwith in the 1950s was one of the factors contributing to the revival of Australian table wines: suddenly they became much less susceptible to microbial spoilage. Australian red wines now are routinely acidified to a pH of around 3.6. Legally, winemakers may add a range of different acids, but in practice tartaric acid is almost universally used if some acid correction is needed because it is the cheapest option. Some commentators are critical of the tendency automatically to adjust the pH of wine to predetermined levels. While this practice certainly helps ensure product consistency (there is no room at the bottom end of the market for "funky" wines), it results in a certain degree of uniformity in wines from warm climates. In some cases, significant acid adjustment is needed because of a choice to pick late: in this instance, there's often a discontinuity between the very sweet fruit profile with soft tannins and the sharp acidity in red wines. Also, as acid-adjusted wines age, the acidity can sometimes stick out a bit as the primary fruit recedes. Some people think that they can spot when wines have been acidified by their flavour profile.

But there are good reasons that acid is added, aside from simply the flavour of the wine. Reducing pH is one of the most effective ways to combat *Brettanomyces* and other spoilage organisms, not only because sulfur dioxide is more effective at lower pH, but also because more of it is in the free, active form. At a pH of 4 you'd need astronomically high levels of total sulfur dioxide to protect a red wine against *Brettanomyces* development.

Citric acid is sometimes added to white wine just before bottling; if the wine in the tank needs adjustment, you can't use tartaric. Citric acid is also supposed to make the wine taste a bit fresher and zippier. Citric acid isn't added to red wines before fermentation because it can create problems with volatile acidity. A few winegrowers add malic acid, and this appears to be a growing trend. But malic acid is unstable because bacteria can metabolize it, as occurs during malolactic fermentation. Lactic acid is also a legal additive in winemaking in certain regions. Illegal, but by no means uncommon, is the addition of sulfuric acid to wines. Talk to those in the know and they will claim that winemakers in warm-climate regions are using phospohoric acid to reduce pH without greatly lifting the TA.

For more serious wines, acidification should be seen as a strategy of last resort. If at all possible, it is much better for grapes to be picked when they have sufficient levels of natural acidity. We feel that picking late and routinely adding large doses of tartaric acid can result in rather homogeneous-tasting wines.

YEASTS

Until relatively recently, wine was the product of a fermentation process that started spontaneously and was carried out by the "natural" yeasts present in the vineyard and winery. But over the past few decades the use of cultured strains of yeast to inoculate the must has become widespread. Yeast is a topic so vital to the theme of this book that a separate chapter is devoted to it (Chapter 9).

FINING AGENTS

Fining is an established part of winemaking. For red wines, it involves the use of protein-aceous agents to remove unwanted tannins from the wine. Tannins are very sticky molecules; they bind with proteins and fall out of solution. Commonly used agents include egg whites, isinglass, and polyvinylpolypyrrolidone (PVPP). Tannins themselves are also used as fining agents. White tannins are used in white winemaking where the grapes have experienced some fungal infection. The tannins bind to and inactivate the laccase enzyme, which otherwise would oxidize the must. These products are expensive.

Egg whites are still quite widely used. They normally come in powdered form, as albumin, which is usually mixed with water and then added to the wine.

PVPP is an important commercial fining agent. Normally it is used with white wines, but it works well with reds too. It is useful for avoiding pinking in whites. If a white wine is too angular, you might do a fining trial with gelatin, isinglass or casein, or PVPP to see how these affect the wine. As with tannins, PVPP is also effective at cleaning up juice that has a percentage of botrytis infection. Isinglass has always been considered the best of all fining agents, taking the least from the wine, but we are not aware of any published studies comparing the exact effects of different fining agents on the perception of wine.

Yeast lees are also a form of fining agent. Inactive yeasts are not primarily fining agents; they take some things from the wine, but they also give things back, including the tripeptide glutathione, which is an antioxidant. These are extremely natural in the sense that they are yeasts that are then inactivated and added back to the wine.

With global warming and the movement to certain aromatic wine styles, pinking is likely to be more of a problem for white wines. Pinking is caused by oxidation of colourless proanthocyanins, which then discolour the wine and also affect its flavour and freshness. Both Sauvignon and Viognier are white varieties at high risk of pinking in a warm dry vintage, when the skins have much higher levels of phenolics. If this is a concern, it is possible to separate the pressings and then add PVPP to them before fermentation.

Fining is a common and uncontroversial process, but many high-end red wines are nevertheless marketed as being unfined, the notion being that fining removes something that is an important part of the wine. For high-end red wines, throwing some sort of deposit in the bottle is not seen as the problem it would be if it occurred with commercial wines.

Bentonite is used primarily with white wines (but also occasionally with reds) to remove proteins, which can become unstable in wine and form a haze when the temperature of the wine increases. In warm vintages protein problems can arise in reds and whites. In white wines protein hazes are obvious; they are less so in reds, which is why bentonite isn't used as commonly in reds. Most smaller wineries send wine off for analysis, and the results tell them how much bentonite to add in order to stabilize proteins. Relatively few wineries do trials on the fining agents they use, and we consider overfining to be a big problem because bentonite can remove beneficial aroma and flavour compounds. You can reduce input of any fining agents by doing trials to determine the amount that is just right.

Gelatin and casein are sometimes added to wine; these are more commonly used for juice fining. Egg white and isinglass are more commonly used on the finished wine.

If you don't extract excessively, this sort of fining is not as necessary. In a sense, the use of fining agents is a function of excessive input, or green phenolics. In red wines you could argue for the use of microoxygenation to avoid the use of fining.

NUTRIENTS

For healthy fermentation to take place, yeasts need an adequate supply of nutrients. The commonly encountered problem of reduction (see the chapter on wine faults) is frequently a result of inadequate must nutrition. When yeasts are stressed in a variety of ways, they can respond by producing volatile sulfur compounds such as sulfides, disulfides, and mercaptans (thiols). This process is collectively known as *reduction*. A lack of nitrogen in the must is probably the leading cause of reduction, so for this reason many winemakers do an analysis of yeast-assimilable [or available] nitrogen (YAN) in the must and correct it if there is a deficit. The most common nutrient addition is diammonium phosphate (DAP), but winemakers also use more complex nutrients such as Fermaid. In addition, dedicated yeast nutrients are also widely used. Interestingly, DAP additions can actually worsen the problem of reduction if they are made clumsily. Some winemakers call DAP "junk food for yeast." The yeasts happily consume it, their population swells excessively, and then they get very stressed and make lots of smelly sulfur compounds. Work on aromatic compounds in Sauvignon Blanc has shown that the aromatic impact of correcting YANs by using DAP is very different from that of the yeasts fermenting nitrogen from other sources already present in the must. If at all possible, winegrowers should sort out YANs in advance by work in the vineyard because the results seem to be much better than those from later correction in the winery.

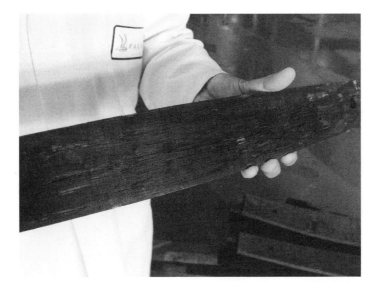

FIGURE 7.2
A barrel stave that has previously been bolted into a tank of red wine as an alternative oak source.

WATER

For obvious reasons, it's almost always illegal to add water to wine. Clearly, there's an economic benefit for producers of inexpensive wine where quality isn't the prime issue to stretch the wine in this way. Ironically, though, this ban penalizes winemakers aiming for quality who want to reduce the potential alcohol level of wines made from very ripe grapes. Still, many winemakers do admit to water additions for this very reason: they feel that it is the most "natural" way to reduce alcohol levels by 1 percent or so, rather than using techniques such as reverse osmosis on the finished wine. In California, water additions are fairly common in high-end wines, and the rules allow a surprisingly high amount of water to be added, for example, during routine winemaking additions. Indeed, a 2001 rule change effectively gave the green light to watering back wines to reduce alcohol in the state.

Regulations are tighter in Australia, but the practice still occurs. Water additions are very hard to police, but stable isotope analysis is a technique that can prove whether it has occurred, so while the risk of getting caught is small, it exists, if only in theory.

Winemakers need to take care that the water source they use in any water additions (even legal ones, such as the preparation of yeast or bacteria starter cultures, or mixing dry goods additions) is a good one. For example, it would be a bad idea to add chlorinated mains water to wine.

Immaculately labeled barrels of Pinot Noir at the Rippon Vineyard in Central Otago, New Zealand.

OAK CHIPS, STAVES, AND POWDER

Oak barrels, the traditional vessels for the *élevage* (a useful French term describing the upbringing of wine, after fermentation, to the point where it is ready to bottle) of wine, can impart flavour, especially when the barrels are small and new. Compounds such as oak lactones, which taste of vanilla and coconut, and grippy-tasting wood tannins (ellagitannins) are flavourings that wine can get from oak, and in the right context they are desirable as a sort of "seasoning." But oak barrels are expensive and hard to manage and also can increase the risk of *Brettanomyces*. For this reason, some producers do without oak, but they still want some of the flavour of oak. Hence they turn to oak substitutes, such as chips, staves (the planks that the barrels are made with), and even oak powder. These alternatives are prepared the same way as barrels, with the appropriate level of toasting, and then introduced into the wine in the tank. The results can be variable. One problem with this approach is that oak barrels do more than just add flavour compounds. They allow the developing wine to be exposed to a very small amount of oxygen in a way in which wine in a tank is not. This low-level oxygen exposure is important in the wine's development, and this is one of the reasons that many producers still use barrels that are many years old and have no more flavour compounds to release to the wine. Therefore, many producers couple the use of oak alternatives with the addition of very small amounts of oxygen to simulate the effect of barrels.

Some argue that there would be little wrong with oak alternatives if the quality of the oak used were as good as that used to make top barrels, and if the wood were properly seasoned. For really good barrels, the staves need to be seasoned outdoors for three years in a relatively damp climate, where the rain will help leach various undesirable compounds out of the oak. When the barrel is made, the oak is toasted to various degrees over a flame. Some winemakers take old barrels, shave the staves to expose new wood, and then reassemble the barrel. But the barrel is different from a new barrel because the freshly exposed oak is not properly seasoned. This could be why oak alternatives often produce disappointing results. Oak alternative technology has improved greatly in recent years but it still has some way to go before it can genuinely challenge well-seasoned, toasted, and well-made oak barrels in the quality of flavour it will impart into the wine. It would be great if wineries could do away with barrels, because they are very expensive and difficult to handle, but they can't. Even the most modern winery bedecked with shiny stainless steel will still have a barrel cellar that looks more like a museum than a vital part of a modern installation. But isn't there something a little reassuring about this? We do, however, find the position of some winemakers who consider oak alternatives unnatural due to their flavor impact to be odd, because barrels also have a flavor impact. We are not saying that they need to be converted to oak alternatives, but rather that they should open their mind to the use of these alternatives for commercial reasons, for those making more commercial wines.

OXYGEN

Oxygen is both a friend and a foe of wine. Most of the time, winemakers strive to protect wine from oxygen, but it is beneficial at some stages during the winemaking process, particularly for red wines. Some white wines, particularly fresh fruity styles, are made reductively: right from crushing the grapes, every effort is made to keep oxygen away. Other whites seem to benefit from juice oxidation: the juice is exposed to oxygen, and the phenolic compounds turn brown and are precipitated out before fermentation. If this were not to happen at this early stage, the wine could run the risk of turning an off-putting orange brown in maturation or in bottle and be more susceptible to oxidation. For most reds, oxygen exposure is encouraged during fermentation, with punch downs, pumpovers, and rack and return (various ways of manipulating the mixture of skins and juice) all being useful techniques to help provide the yeasts with oxygen to promote their growth. After fermentation, small amounts of oxygen can be helpful in modifying the tannic structure of the wine and fixing colour. The traditional means of allowing this positive oxygen exposure has been the use of barrels. Some winemakers are now experimenting with the use of microoxygenation to mimic this natural exposure of the wine to oxygen by delivering small doses of oxygen to wine in a tank through a ceramic diffuser. It is becoming clear that the interaction of oxygen and wine is a complicated but vitally important topic, and the evidence points to some wisdom in the traditional practice of *élevage* using oak for forming fine wines (see the sidebar titled Mastering the Art of *Élevage*).

MASTERING THE ART OF *ÉLEVAGE*

JAMIE GOODE and SAM HARROP

An interesting development in winemaking is the way in which many pioneering winegrowers are now exploring other means of *élevage* than simply stainless steel tanks and small oak barrels. It is fair to say that fine wine has been in a bit of a small oak rut. Might small oak not be the best way to conduct *élevage* for many wines? Too many winemakers just put their finest wines in the most expensive new oak they can obtain without thinking about alternatives. Particularly insidious is the prevalent trend for carrying out malolactic fermentation in the barrel. This may result in flattering young wines, but might it compromise the wine's definition and ability to age?

There's something mysterious about the process of wine's slow development, and wine science has relatively little to say about it. Oxygen clearly plays a role, but the way in which oxygen interacts with wine is not clear-cut. At one extreme, exposing wine to too much oxygen simply results in oxidation. At the other extreme, total exclusion of oxygen slows the development process of the wine; what is more, it alters the pattern of the wine's evolution. A different destination will be reached. During alcoholic fermentation, the must requires exposure to oxygen in reasonably large quantities and has the ability to soak up large doses fairly quickly. Racking, pumping over, punching down, and other such means of working the cap in red wines are ways of giving the actively dividing yeasts the oxygen they need to thrive. But once primary fermentation is over, wines need very little oxygen, although tiny amounts are beneficial. There's no scientific formula to calculate this amount. Indeed, we think that wine scientists cannot explain exactly why oxygen has the effect it does, other than its complex effects on tannins, involving the changing combinations of tannins and other molecules, as well as the changing degrees of polymerization of tannin chains that take place over time.

Barrels are favoured tools of *élevage* because, among other reasons, they allow very slow exposure to small quantities of oxygen. Larger barrels have a reduced ratio of surface area to volume, and thus the rate of oxygen exposure is proportionally lower. New oak allows a slightly higher rate of oxygen exposure than old. Topping up affects oxygen levels in the wine. Practices such as battonage also allow some extra oxygen exposure. What seems clear is that it is the rate of oxygen exposure, and not merely the net quantity of oxygen, that determines how the wine develops. Wine does not move along a single pathway of development that is determined by the total amount of absorbed oxygen; instead, it can take different paths at numerous "nodes" and arrive at different destinations for the same amount of absorbed oxygen, depending on the rate of exposure. This runs counter to the simplistic notion that each wine has a buffer capacity against oxidation that depends on its free sulfur dioxide concentration and its phenolic content.

The importance of the dose of oxygen is illustrated (indirectly) by the attempts by some winemakers to reduce the risk of reduction in screwcapped wines by bottling with air in the headspace rather than an inert gas. This single slug of oxygen produces some oxidative characters in the wine without reducing the risk of reduction. In contrast, wines seem to be able to cope better than you'd expect with very low levels of oxygen exposure over long periods. Take the example of very old wines, aged in cool cellars. Their free sulfur dioxide levels must be close to zero after a decade or two, but the wines don't simply oxidize from the continued low-level oxygen transmission that occurs through the cork. (Clearly, some old wines do oxidize and take on a rather anonymous "old-wine" character, having lost any sense of regional or varietal origin. But the best wines, well stored and with good corks, don't.)

So while oxygen clearly plays some role in the long aging of fine wine, that role isn't simply oxidation of the wine components. Something more complex is happening. Here's another anecdotal data point: it seems that magnums tend to age optimally, which suggests that the rate of oxygen transmission, which is presumably the same as with a cork in the neck of a standard bottle, is just about right when it is delivered to twice the volume of wine that is in a standard bottle.

This discussion is relevant to the practice of microoxygenation, which is a tool of *élevage* that has been widely adopted in the past couple of decades. The theory is that small amounts of oxygen, delivered through a diffuser at the bottom of a tank, replicate the slow exposure to oxygen experienced by wine in a barrel. But the quantities of oxygen delivered in this way are far greater than those to which a wine is exposed in a barrel because they are bubbles of gas, even if the total dose per volume of wine is calculated to be the same. While science doesn't yet offer an explanation, rate of exposure may change the actual reactions that take place. If microoxygenation plus the use of suitably weathered, high-quality oak staves in a tank could replicate the work of barrels, then they would be widely used for fine wines; the fact that they simply aren't, and that horrendously expensive barrels are still used, is good circumstantial evidence that rate of oxygen exposure matters a good deal. If wineries could rush *élevage*, they would, for very good commercial reasons.

Length of *élevage* may also be an important factor in producing more serious wines. As an example, J.-P. Fichet in Meursault, Burgundy, makes some stunning wines, almost all of which are from village-level vineyards, and they age beautifully. These wines spend a full eighteen months in barrels. This could be significant. Here's another odd observation. Mac Forbes is one of Australia's most

(continued)

interesting young winemakers. While Forbes was in Europe, he spent some time with Dirk Niepoort, trying to get a sense of elegance with Douro fruit. Niepoort's Charme was the inspiration for Forbes's EBL Pinot Noir, with its ultrashort maceration of just a few days. "It stayed orange for two years, and I was expecting to put it down the drain," he reports. But the wine picked up colour during its *élevage*. "It goes against what we think we know," Forbes adds. "Anyone who thinks they know all the answers is a long way from making interesting wine."

The size of the barrels matters. There seems to be a move away from small barrels towards larger ones among some winegrowers. In Italy, traditional winemaking has involved the use of lengthy periods in large botti. Is there a wisdom here that is disregarded in the rush to small, new oak barrels?

Proper *élevage* is irrelevant to those who champion the modern international style of red wines. For them, wine is about masses of sweet fruit character, bolstered by the spicy imprint of new oak barrels. But fine wine is not just about sweet fruit. There's nothing wrong with sweet fruit, but we'd argue that concentrated, sweetly fruited, spicily oaked red wines are not legitimate expressions of fine wine. They are not morally wrong; they are just not that interesting, and there's not much to be said about them beyond the immediate hedonic rush the sweet fruit gives. What proper *élevage* delivers is nonfruit complexity, and it sets the wine up for graceful development in the bottle.

"Surely there is more to winemaking than stainless steel and oak," says Duncan Savage of Cape Point Vineyards in South Africa. Savage, one of South Africa's most inspiring young winemakers, has recently become interested in using clay amphorae as tools for *élevage*. He didn't want to import them, so he contacted a local potter, Yogi de Beer, who is now throwing 600-litre pots for Savage. Savage describes this experimentation as a "cool journey." The first pots he tried were 120 litres (the potter he used had only a small kiln). They were earthenware and had been fired at low temperatures, so when Savage poured wine in, they leaked like sieves. The ones he's using now are stoneware clay made at high firing temperatures and are not lined. Savage currently has capacity for just 3,000 litres of wine in amphorae. He's trying reds and has done a long maceration of Grenache that has been allowed three months on skins.

Savage is following in the footsteps of winemakers like Josko Gravner from Friuli and Frank Cornelissen and Cos from Sicily, all of whom use amphorae in the upbringing (aging before bottling) of some of their wines. They find that Georgia is the only country that still has skilled craftsmen who can make large enough amphorae; clearly this is not a practical option for all wineries, however successful the big pots may be as tools of *élevage*. Another new development has been the emergence of the concrete "egg" tanks made by Nomblot in France. These are appearing in cellars all around the world. We've seen them in Oregon and South Africa, for example. Are these tanks merely affectations by biodynamically influenced wine-growers, or do they have a significant effect? Aside from metaphysical explanations of their efficacy, we've heard it suggested that their shape helps keep yeasts in suspension and eliminates the need for oxygen-introducing battonage.

When a wine is bottled, the final stage of *élevage* begins. This is where the issue of closure is very important, because wine is not locked in time but continues to change. Mystery surrounds the nature of this evolution, but at least, with the onset of alternative closures to natural cork, some data are beginning to emerge about the role of oxygen transmission after bottling in wine evolution. For fine wine, this bottle development is critical; empirical evidence suggests that a bottle, sealed with a decent cork (sadly, not a variable that can be controlled) and placed in a cool, dark cellar, achieves the optimum outcome.

In some ways, it's nice that wine isn't all about science, and that there's still a lot of room left for art. And the art of *élevage* is one of the mysterious keys to making profound, rather than merely impressive, wines.

ASCORBIC ACID

The use of ascorbic acid was formerly more widespread, but there has been a move away from it in recent years. It can be used as an antioxidant and also to combat pinking. If a must has been protected from oxygen, and then suddenly in the bottle it is exposed to oxygen for the first time, there can be colour changes. Ascorbic acid is more commonly used with aromatic styles of white wine.

SORBATE

Sorbate is widely added in Europe. It is often used when it isn't needed in wines where there is a small sugar addition before bottling; in the New World it isn't widely used. It is an antimicrobial that helps prevent refermentation in the bottle, and it is frequently used in sweet wines, but also in dry wines. It alters the flavour of the wine slightly and and has a negative impact on longevity of the wine.

INGREDIENT LISTING ON WINE LABELS

Whether ingredient listing on wine labels would be a good thing is a tricky question. On one level, ingredient listing signifies a healthy degree of openness and honesty with the consumer. On another, it could be alarming to consumers who consider wine to be natural, and for whom the argument that wine is pretty natural but does have a number of additions (but these additions don't add flavor) would be far too complex to grasp.

Some wineries and retailers have bravely attempted to do this. In the United Kingdom, the Co-op (a major supermarket) lists ingredients on all its own-label wines. Here's a typical example:

EXPLORERS VINEYARD SAUVIGNON BLANC

Ingredients

Grapes (Sauvignon Blanc), acidity regulator (potassium bicarbonate), preservative (potassium metabisulphite), copper sulphate

Made using: antioxidants (carbon dioxide, nitrogen), yeast, yeast nutrient (diammonium phosphate)

Cleared using: bentonite, filtration, pectinolytic enzymes

In the United States, Randall Grahm has listed ingredients on his Bonny Doon wines. Here's an example:

Ingredients: Grapes, Tartaric Acid, Sulfur Dioxide
In the winemaking process the following were utilized: untoasted wood chips, French oak barrels, cultured yeast, yeast nutrients, malolactic culture, copper sulfate

At the moment, the only legal requirement in most countries is to add "Contains sulfites" if the level is above 10 ppm. In practice, this means that all wines to which sulfur dioxide is added will have this on the label; also, some wines where none is added will exceed this level simply through the sulfur dioxide produced naturally during fermentation by the yeasts. One advantage of ingredient labeling would be that it could help consumers see exactly how interventionist the winemaker has been, and it could therefore encourage winemakers to mess with the wines less. But it could create some practical problems for small producers, who, while they might not make much wine, often supply dozens of export markets. For them, translating the back label copy with the list of all ingredients into several different languages and then fitting it all on one label would be a major headache.

COPPER

There's nothing new about adding copper to wine. Copper ions are oxidative (that is, they promote oxidation), and in the past it was common for barrels to have a copper or brass plate near the opening, or to have copper fittings, such that when wine was

FIGURE 7.4
Ingredient labeling on a U.K. supermarket wine.

racked (aerated by transfer out and then back into the barrel), copper from these plates or fittings would find its way into the wine. Some natural winemakers still practice this.

The goal of copper additions? To oxidize volatile sulfur compounds such as hydrogen sulfide or mercaptans, and thus eliminate their sensory impact, which is known by the term of reduction. This is discussed in greater depth in chapter 11. These days, it is more common for winemakers worried about reduction to add copper in the form of copper sulfate solution. Typically, a fining trial will be done to determine the minimum that should be added to eliminate any reductive characters. This sort of copper addition is controversial, in part because copper is a heavy metal, and thus toxic (although not at the levels found in almost all wines).

As with the debate as to whether oak alternatives are any more unnatural than oak barrels themselves, we see here a certain double standard. Surely if the winemaker feels the need to run their wines over copper fittings to eliminate certain "reductive" compounds derived from inadequate nutrients for the yeast during fermentation, they cannot have an issue with others choosing to follow the more scientific form of trials to determine the smallest necessary addition, and a subsequent addition in a controlled manner to avoid associated complications such as copper haze and/or oxidation.

But we should also add that copper use has increased significantly in recent years and a growing general understanding in the trade of certain sulfides and the detrimental aspect they can have on overall wine quality. In Australia, it is not unusual to find wine-makers practicing prophylactic copper additions just to be safe. Some refer to this as copper "fining," but others suggest that this implies that all the copper is removed during this process, which may not be the case, and addition may be a better term. With screw cap use becoming much more popular in recent years, there has been an increased risk of reductive characters forming in bottle if the wine has not been made and/or prepared before bottling in the right manner. Such steps include adequate fermentation management (namely inoculating with selected yeast strains and a sensible approach to nutrient addition if necessary), dissolved oxygen management at bottling (it is okay to have higher levels of dissolved oxygen at bottling with screw cap), free sulfur dioxide management (look to reduce additions of sulfur dioxide at bottling with screw cap), and choice of screw cap lining—to name just a few. Even then, it seems that the use of the tin/saran liner with screwcaps, and its incredibly low oxygen transmission rate, does carry with it risks that are hard to quantify. These are discussed more in chapter 11.

The sulfide aromas that can develop in bottle may not be picked up as a fault by the consumer, but there is a pretty good chance that their presence may not be appreciated by the majority of consumers, even if these consumers aren't able to make a positive identification of a fault in the wine. At low levels certain sulfides can mask fruit and deny the wine of its true "commercial" potential/appeal. When present in greater levels, sulfides can not only mask fruit but can dominate the aromatic profile, moving it into a more "mineral" vegetal spectrum most consumers (but not all) consider displeasing.

Copper is a curative approach and can be avoided/prevented with a more focused winemaking approach to reducing the levels of the precursors of these detrimental sulfide aromas. One essential step is controlling fermentations and keeping yeasts healthy. Natural winemakers who refuse to inoculate with commercial strains and choose not to adjust their nitrogen status of their must are running the risk of ending up with more sulfidic wines.

MANIPULATIONS

So far we have been looking at wine additions, that is, things that have actually been added to the wine. But there's another level of manipulation: physical interventions in the winery that have an impact on the flavour of the wine. These range from simple bulk movements to more elaborate techniques such as cross-flow filtration or ion exchange. Whether these interfere with the naturalness of a wine is a subject of some debate. We start from the premise that the more one physically intervenes with the wine the less natural it becomes. The most natural winemakers will move their wines twice: once after fermentation and then again on route to bottle, leaving the wine on its primary and/or secondary fermentation lees. This is a risky business if it is not monitored and managed properly! At the other end of the continuum, the most commercial winemakers can be forced to move their wine numerous times, for both technical and/

or economic reasons. We (along with most of the winemaking community) believe that the more you move a wine (irrespective of the nature of the physical interference that takes place), the more you take from your wine. Putting this another way, winemakers who minimize movement and physical intervention tend to make wines with more stuffing. But we're not saying that those who choose to limit movements will always be left with better wines, because not all stuffing is good. A certain level of intervention is necessary to maximize quality.

As an example of this, wines need a certain level of movement and a certain level of oxygen during the winemaking process. Little movement can result in an abundance of sulfides that ultimately mask the fruit expression and it can lack balance and harmony or even result in aromas that many consider faults. We know natural winemakers who consider the reductive state as critical to protecting the wine during its journey in bottle and that only when the fruit bursts through this mineral expression can the consumer enjoy the wine in all its glory. This is all very well and good if you are selling to a consumer who has the time and patience to wait for such an opportune moment, but as we know, the market doesn't really work like that.

Physical manipulation is necessary in all wineries, however natural they might consider themselves to be. We believe this all too basic concept is not only paramount to understanding how to make great wines, but also that it is all too often overlooked by those pushing the boundaries of naturalness. Those who refuse certain basic manipulations because it is against their "natural" philosophy run the risk of making faulty wines. It's true that such wines may well have a more impressive philosophical backbone, but as we know, this does not always mean that they are superior.

Here are a few common manipulations that wine is subjected to. This is not an exhaustive list, but such a list would fill a book in its own right.

REVERSE OSMOSIS

Reverse osmosis is a process that makes use of cross-flow filtration techniques either to concentrate wine or must or to selectively remove components such as alcohol or volatile acidity. It works on the basis of selective fractionation and is covered in more detail in Chapter 10.

EXTRACTION

Extraction refers to the process by which flavour compounds and pigments are separated from grape skins. It is mainly relevant to red wines because most whites see no or only limited skin contact. Deciding how to extract and for how long is a crucial issue in red winemaking, and decisions about how much skin contact to allow are important for whites. At the most basic level, there is the decision whether to destem and crush the grape bunches before fermentation or to use whole clusters, with the stems.

It's amazing that some wineries look as they must have many centuries ago, with stone lagares (shallow fermentation tanks) designed to permit foot treading. Lagares are still widely used in Portugal, and each September you can visit wineries in the Douro where extraction is being managed in the most traditional way possible, by teams of people treading the grapes in these shallow stone troughs. Never before have there been so many options to alter or manipulate the level and type of extraction you are looking for in your final wine. It's a complex topic and not one we want to spend too much time on, but here are a few factors to consider when thinking of extraction: enzyme use or not, fermentation vessel, fermentation temperature, pump-over techniques, plunging device, type of press, the press cycle, post-fermentation maceration period (if any), and temperature during maceration. Each manipulation has the aim of managing extraction from the skins.

PRESSING

After fermentation of red wines, the wine is drained (free run), and then the skins are pressed to yield the remainder of the wine (pressing). The method of pressing can be significant. In old times, the grape skins were pressed while they were in the lagare, but now they are shoveled into either a basket press (more traditional) or a pneumatic or cage press. The press fractions may be blended back to the wine or kept separate during the aging process. While in theory you can drink wine once the fermentation process is complete, in practice the wine is usually aged for at least a few months to let it come together.

ENZYMES

While enzymes are actually wine additions and rightly belong in the first part of this chapter, they are most commonly used to facilitate extraction from skins. Enzymes are used at different stages of winemaking. They have the potential to increase the aroma, mouthfeel and color extraction in the final wine and facilitate the clarification of the grape must. Pectinases, the most important enzymes for the wine industry, are used for economic reasons and help break down grape skins and thus assist in the release of pigments and flavour compounds. These are mostly used for yield reasons (the amount of juice that can be extracted during pressing). β-glucanase enzymes can help breakdown colloids and β-glucan present in grapes with some level of botrytis infection at harvest. These enzymes can improve the filterability of wines high in colloids. They can also be used on wine to accelerate autolysis adding to mouthfeel and complexity in the finished wine. The wine group Laffort declares that most commercial enzymes are a mixture of different enzymes which might contain pectin esterase, polygalacturonase, pectin lyase, hemicellulase and/or cellulase.

COUNTERCURRENT EXTRACTION

Countercurrent extraction is a method for extracting wine from marc, the waste product produced by pressing red wine solid material after fermentation. It relies on a cross-flow filtration technique to clarify and filter liquid extracted from the marc, reducing the amount of solid waste and improving the yield of wine. The idea is that the free-run juice should be taken away, and then the solids, instead of being pressed, go to the countercurrent extractor, which takes out wine water that is then used to extract further from the marc. The technique was first introduced in Australia in 2004; it is unclear whether many wineries are using it yet. Estimates are that this improves yields of wine by 100 litres per ton, a significant amount.

FLASH RELEASE

Flash release (also known as *flash détente*) is a technique for improving extraction from red wine skins during the fermentation process. Grapes are rapidly heated by steam and then cooled rapidly in a vacuum. Typical conditions might be 95°C for six minutes, before vacuum treatment at 30 mbar. This bursts the skin cells, releasing all kinds of compounds and also inhibiting the activity of any oxidative enzymes such as laccase, thereby protecting the must. This technique is expensive, but it is popular for more commercial wines. Studies show that wines made in this way have higher levels of polyphenols.

FILTRATION

Filtration is a widely practiced manipulation of wine and can occur at a range of levels, from very coarse to very fine (sterile, which filters out bacteria and yeasts). Filtration is not necessary for all wines. Those that have had a long maturation process will typically be clear and bright without the need for further treatment. Traditional filtration techniques involve forcing the wine through the filtration medium, which is typically made from diatomaceous earth (a soft, silica-based rock made of fossil diatoms, also known as diatomite or kieselguhr). Cellulose pads are also used in some cases, and for fine filtration of an already pretty clear wine a membrane with pores of specific diameter may be used (but care must be taken because these can easily clog). A more modern filtration technique is cross-flow filtration, where the wine runs parallel to the filtration membrane and is cleared by a process of osmosis. This technique is gaining in popularity because it is gentler and quicker than traditional methods.

Filtration needs some discussion here because it is one of the most controversial topics in the discussion of natural wine. Some years ago, the notion became widely established in the fine wine scene that filtration strips flavor from wines. The likes of wine merchant Kermit Lynch (in his wonderfully readable book *Adventures on the Wine Route*) and critic Robert Parker, Jr. began to champion those winemakers who took the risk of bottling wines unfiltered because these wines had more flavor and character. The simple story was that filtration was reserved for the commercial winemaking concerns where risk management rather than optimal flavor was the goal. But we feel this is an overly simplistic story.

We have seen trials of varying degrees of filtration before bottling of some Châteauneuf-du-Pape wines. After six months of bottling, the winning wine in sensory appraisal was the wine that went through 0.45 micron filtration. Of course, some of the wine's texture may be lost in the short term, but much of it comes back after time in bottle. And in time, the filtered wines show purer flavours than the unfiltered wines. This could well be because of the microbial activity taking place in the unfiltered wines.

We think that it is wrong to think of filtration as solely an evil force in the wine world. It can in some cases lead to a more true expression of terroir in wines by eliminating microbes that can be the cause of faults. Especially with climate change and the trends toward riper wines with higher residual sugar levels and higher pH levels, filtration can be seen as a necessary tool to ensure integrity of wines that may well be shipped across the world to target markets.

Because filtration is another intervention in the life of a wine, it can legitimately be viewed as a negative factor. It is true that badly carried out, filtration can result in a loss of quality, for example, through the introduction of oxygen into the wine. So it is important that it is carried out well. With poor management, the wine can be damaged badly by filtration. Too often, wines are filtered too many times because of poor preparation of the wine, for example fining not being done properly before filtration. Integrity testing is important during filtration to check that the filter is working properly. In addition, many producers, we suspect, do filter but claim they don't.

TARTRATE STABILITY

Whites and reds should be tartrate stabilized to avoid crystals forming at a later stage in bottle. Reds don't need as much because their tartaric acid is lower, and the tartrates tend to fall out naturally in the longer *élevage*. Also, because there are more phenolics, there are more natural nucleation sites for tartrates in red wines.

One can also add metatartaric acid to avoid the need for cold stabilization. You could argue that this is not as natural because it involves an addition to the wine; however, cold stabilization uses a lot of power. For whites you need to reduce the temperature below zero (around −2°C) for an extended period that can take weeks. Typically, bentonite is added at the same time, and then one racks off (separates liquid from solid residue) the bentonite and tartrate lees at the same time. The wine must be moved with care when it is cold because gases are more soluble at lower temperatures. During cold stabilization some acidity is lost; the amount depends on the amount of potassium. This is because potassium combines with tartaric acid to produce potassium bitartrate, which comes out of solution, thus reducing acidity. The more potassium in the juice, the more the acidity lost. Citric acid may need to be added to high-potassium juice at this stage to adjust the acidity. What is the problem with having a few crystals of tartaric acid in the bottle? If you can communicate effectively with your customers, then tartrate stabilization is not necessary. It takes from the wine, and there can be oxygen pickup that can affect the wine's quality. It is also expensive. A new development is the use of carboxymethyl cellulose (also known as cellulose gum) to make wine tartrate stable. Cream of tartar can be added when cold stabilizing to speed up the formation of crystals and the stabilization process. Tartrate stability can also be achieved with electrodialysis technology that uses a lot less energy that the traditional cold treatment approach. It also results in less wine loss. It does however, use more water in the process which is another consideration to make in view of efforts towards sustainability.

PUMPING

During winemaking, it is necessary to move wine. The number of times wine has to be moved varies, and ideally, the fewer moves the better, because any time wine is moved there is the potential for oxygen pick-up and damage to the structure of the wine. During fermentation itself, oxygen pick-up is no bad thing: yeasts need oxygen, and oxygen helps build structure in red wines because of its interaction with wine polyphenols, including tannins. But later on, during wine maturation, oxygen pick-up usually results in a loss of quality—particularly so for white wines.

One of the considerations in moving wine is the physical impact this can have on the wine itself. If red wine is moved clumsily during fermentation, when skins and seeds are still present, this can result in the over-extraction of elements from these skins and seeds. For example, crushed seeds can release bitter-tasting tannins. For this reason, many wineries are constructed so that the key movements can take place via gravity. Wineries like this are known as gravity-flow wineries, and are typically on many levels with the fermentation facilities at the top, and then the barrel hall at the bottom, usually underground where temperature is controlled naturally. But in most wineries, pumps will have to be used to move the wine.

Winemaker Justin Knock MW explained the pros and cons of the various pumps that are used in wineries.

"1. Monos (the standard quarterhorse pumps). These are the workhorse of many wineries, the equivalent of a diesel 4WD for their ability to pass solids, liquids, and air with equal ease, making them useful as must pumps in crushers (as open throats) and for transferring ferments to barrel (handling CO_2 comfortably). I've always been happy with using monos, particularly if there is no time pressure and jobs are not too large, while being incredibly aware of their sensitivities. Never dead head a mono (close a valve while it is operating) and never let it run dry (or at least not for more than a few seconds). A positive displacement pump, the mono will continue to move fluids regardless of the head pressure, and eventually will fail in a catastrophic and fundamentally explosive manner. Loss of wine can be a low price paid compared with the loss of credibility in the eyes of your cellar peers. Rubber stators heat quickly in the absence of liquids and a burnt rubber character in the wines is the worst-case outcome of a mono run dry for more than a few seconds. Wear and tear on the stator is increased and when in the off position a worn stator may not hold its position against the head pressure in a tank and end up running backwards—a cellar hand's worst nightmare when racking juices.

"2. Centrifugals (the fast but fickle racehorse). These really come into their own in large wineries when high transfer rates are required, with a potential to run up to two–three times faster than the fastest monos. Unfortunately, there is a price for this performance and centrifugals thrash the wine in the worst possible way by really upsetting the colloidal structure of wines with respect to the fragile equilibrium between wine's largest molecular groups: the polysaccharides, tannins, and mannoproteins, all of which contribute to structure and mouthfeel. Furthermore, they are almost pointless with ferments, requiring to be primed in the absence of gas to become operational. Performance really drops off when the head pressure becomes high but at least they can be deadheaded with no real detrimental outcome. Use only as necessary or where the generation of high in-line pressures is not desired, i.e., when delivering wine to a filtration system.

"3. Peristaltic (draught horses). These are slow, large, and heavy but oh so gentle. They can make very good must pumps as long as they don't need to pump against too much head pressure as they can be difficult to sanitise being prone to deadspots. Mimicking the same action as the human digestive tract they are a gentle but slow positive displacement pumping system that should be used more often in wineries but from what I've seen are limited by their relatively high cost and slow throughput, as well as their size and difficulty to service and maintain.

"4. Lobe (the new breed). The modern barrel pump and all round utility pump in the winery. When partnered to a VSD (variable speed drive) they have ultimate speed and flow control, are incredibly gentle and have few moving parts, meaning they are incredibly efficient, quiet and therefore expensive. The lobe pump is another positive displacement pump great for filling barrels in a controlled, gentle manner and for moving finished wine to bottling. It is not ideal for moving solids but reasonably robust on ferments. Nice pumps if you can afford them.

BOTTLING

The most natural form of bottling—and one that is still practised by some wineries—is hand bottling directly from barrels. But this is time consuming and results in a lot of variation in the wines. In particlar, there is no dissolved oxygen management, and oxygen pick-up at bottling is a major issue for wine quality. Many wineries do not audit their bottling lines to see what the level of oxygen pick-up at bottling is, and even expensive, automated bottling lines can be a source of inconsistency if they are used improperly or not maintained. We believe that automated bottling systems, involving inert gas flushing of the bottle prior to filling, and then drawing a vacuum before the closure is applied, are the best for quality in terms of consistency but this assumes that the bottling line is well set up and maintained.

The temperature of the wine is also important at bottling. Cold wines will take up more oxygen because gas is more soluble in cold liquids. Bottle rinsing is also important: do hand bottlers actually rinse bottles? We have seen lizards, flies and spiders in the bottom of bottles of wine.

8

THE NATURAL WINE MOVEMENT

Avant d'être bon, un vin doit être vrai. [Before a wine is good, it must be true.]

NICOLAS JOLY

In the classic European wine regions, most particularly in France and Italy, there exists a loose coalition of producers who have gathered under the banner of "natural wine." It is not an official organization, and there are no rules on membership. "Members" gel by virtue of working towards a common goal—that of making wines that are as natural as possible—and are linked by means of sharing the same importers for export markets, being stocked by shops specializing in natural wines, or participating in the same tastings.

The interest in "natural" or "real" wines is growing, and this movement has a strong element of counterculture to it. In some ways, natural wine producers define themselves as much by what they are opposed to as by what they stand for. It's interesting that the rise in natural wines has paralleled the growth of what could (somewhat unfairly) be called industrial branded wines and their increasing dominance of the marketplace. Could it be that the rise in natural wine is in part a production-led reaction against "industrial" wine?

One of the best ways to get a feel for natural wine is to visit Paris and tour the significant number of wine bars and *cavistes* (specialist wine shops) dedicated to natural wine. These bars are the heart of the "real wine" counterculture and have a wealth of quirky, interesting bottles from producers across the country's wine regions, all of whom have made a commitment to producing wines as naturally as possible. In France, *vin naturel* is a distinct, separate category of wine with a strong following. Despite the difficulty of pinning down the exact meaning of *natural*, the category genuinely exists.

What is a natural wine in this context? There is no strict definition, but there are common approaches that most growers who align themselves with this movement take. The chief desire shared by all is to make wines with the fewest possible manipulations or additions. Interestingly, the main emphasis among natural wine producers is on what happens in the winery; while many practice organic or biodynamic viticulture, some do work conventionally. Most commonly, though, a natural approach in the winery is coupled with vineyard management that seeks to preserve the life and fertility of the soil, eschewing herbicides and widespread use of agrochemicals. Natural wine production relies almost exclusively on yeasts present on the grape skins and in the winery environment to carry out fermentations. Sulfur dioxide (SO_2) additions are kept to a bare minimum or are done away with entirely. Typically, no SO_2 is added during the winemaking process, and just a little is added at bottling to ensure a degree of stability. Indeed, within the natural wine movement there is a group that specializes in *vins sans souffre* (wines without any added SO_2; some is produced during the fermentation process, so a little is present in all wines).

This chapter aims to take a deeper look at this natural wine movement and its goal. We'll also examine in depth the issue of SO_2 and attempts to do away with it.

JULES CHAUVET, THE FATHER OF NATURAL WINE

In France, which lies at the centre of the natural wine movement, one name is frequently cited. Jules Chauvet (1907–1989) is widely regarded as the father of the modern natural wine movement, but relatively little has been written in English about him and his methods. He was a very interesting character, though, and not easily compartmentalized into a "natural wine" box, because he was first and foremost a renowned wine scientist, as well as a winemaker. Among other things, he devised the ISO standard wine-tasting glass in the 1950s.

Chauvet had a reputation as a gifted taster and a influential tutor who based his approach to natural winemaking firmly on scientific experimentation and observation. One person who knew him well was Hans Ulrich Kesselring of the Swiss domaine Bachtobel. Sadly, Kesselring—a thoughtful, intelligent man—died somewhat prematurely in 2008, but we discussed Chauvet together after meeting in Switzerland in 2006. Kesselring had worked for a while with Chauvet and produced a book based on their discussions (*Le vin en question/Wine in Question* [Paris: Editions Jean-Paul Rocher, 1998]). Here's what he had to say:

> Chauvet was the heir to a family wine merchant business in La Chapelle de Guinchay, near Julienas in the Beaujolais. The traditional winemaking practices in this area are different from neighbouring Burgundy. In the Beaujolais the entire hand harvested clusters are transported in unique 50-litre *bennes* [buckets]. The still-intact grapes are dumped in 4,000- to 5,000-litre wooden cuvées, or cement or steel tanks. Some of the berries on

the bottom are crushed through the weight of the upper layers. This juice starts fermenting, and as a result the tank then fills with natural carbon dioxide. In this carbon dioxide–saturated atmosphere an interesting phenomenon takes place. Inside the still-intact berries, enzymes degrade the malic acid and produce ethanol. The anthocyanins are taken out of the skin; thus the colour of the grapes gives an indication of how far the maceration has gone. When the skins lose their colour to the must, they also become brittle and release their juice to the tank. Of course, this juice still has significant levels of sugar that keeps the fermentation alive. Also, this juice is lower in acidity than conventional fermentations (the malic acid degraded in the intracellular fermentation inside the berry, as described above). So the pH in the bottom juice rises and allows the bacteria to do the rest of the malolactic fermentation. When you press the grapes (often before primary fermentation is complete), often there is no malic acid left. Of course, you need more fermentation space and a bigger press due to the larger mass of the uncrushed berries. But you can skip the crusher and the must pump, and this has a positive effect on quality in itself.

Kesselring also talked about the difference between this process and carbonic maceration. "A small but important difference between *maceration Beaujolaise* (called *maceration traditionelle*) and *maceration carbonique* is that in the latter the tank is filled with carbon dioxide before the grapes arrive and the carbon dioxide hose is left in the tank, so the tank can be refilled several times when the grapes are already in there. The maceration starts immediately, not just after a few days, when the yeasts on the bottom start to do their work and produce CO_2."

He added that carbonic maceration or *maceration traditionelle* is used only for Gamays in the area, not for Pinot Noir.

When I went to wine school, in the 1970s, one of my colleagues did his diploma paper about this subject. He set up four trials: two of Pinot, two of Gamay, one of each crushed-destemmed and the other *maceration carbonique*. The tasting panel decided that for each variety the common way of the region was better, i.e., Pinot should be crushed-destemmed and Gamay should employ *maceration carbonique*.

Vin naturel is a big issue on the Continent. I went to a meeting in Parma where about fifty winegrowers showed their various natural wines. Some were quite good; others oxidized. But the definition of what is natural is not clear yet. The problems/challenges in the Mosel are not the same as in Sicily. Is chaptalization more natural than taking rainwater out under vacuum? One of the leading natural wine growers is Marcel Lapierre in Morgon. When we last visited he showed us his three different Morgons: filtered with SO_2, unfiltered with SO_2, and unfiltered without SO_2. They were all good, but slightly different. He told us that he was selling the unfiltered and unsulfured only to restaurants with a big turnover so they would get no older than three months. But most red wines improve within three to four years! When I was working with Chauvet, we did chaptalization and added 30 ppm SO_2 before bottling. For years here at Bachtobel we didn't add SO_2 to the grapes and had no problem. The malolactic fermentation started a lot more easily, without problem. But now we do a ten-day cold maceration before fermentation, and as I am scared of apiculatus yeast, we add 50 ppm SO_2 to the grapes. But next year I will try to do it without, checking the juice under the microscope.

In a 1981 interview published in the aforementioned *Le vin en question*, Kesselring questioned Chauvet about his views on the soil. "It's easy," was Chauvet's response. "Soil dominates plant." He gave the example of Beaujolais. "It is the same variety—the Gamay—from Morgon to St. Amour; every time the geological nature of the soil changes, you notice the appearance of different flavours." But, like others, Chauvet was unable to link flavours in the wine to soil characteristics. "We know that the same plant produces different flavours on different soils, but that is all we know."

Chauvet was highly critical of the way in which the character of Beaujolais wines was suffering from the greed of growers who demanded high-producing clones and chemical-based viticulture. "In Beaujolais, what interested people most was to get a crop. Whereas formerly a selection was made of seedlings which produced a small number of grapes with small berries, which produced good wines; then people became conscious that this was insufficient as regards to yields so that, later on, they would choose the biggest wine stock with the largest grapes. They got a good yield; when they got the yield they stuck with this fallacy and stuffed the vine with fertilizers." Chauvet advocated moving back to the old way of doing things. "I think that one must precisely come back to things of the past, that is, tilling the vineyards first, to stop sprinkling chemicals on the soil." He was quite opposed to the changes introduced by mechanization in the vineyards, leading to the abandonment of cultivation. "Vines are tilled no more. I regard that as very dangerous. Why? In former times when you cultivated the vine you knew that a vine cultivated correctly did produce well; it perhaps did not produce much, but it produced fine, so that the vine was healthy. Why? Because one introduced some air into the soil—and you know that soil is crammed with micro-organisms which are greedy for oxygen—those organisms could convert fertilizer into matter easily assimilated by the roots of the vine . . . and perhaps impart to it a certain resistance to diseases. But since the tractor appeared, cultivation was over." Chauvet continued, "One no longer introduces air into the soil, there are no more transformations, there is a wide use of chemicals." His view was that vines in cultivated soils were in better health and thus had more innate resistance to disease.

In the winery, Chauvet's experiments led him to favour indigenous yeasts. "We had tried every yeast selected from Burgundy, Beaujolais, Bordeaux, Côtes du Rhône, and so on, with the same must. We sterilized the must and seeded with these yeasts, and finally we had come up with a seeding of the indigenous yeasts from here. Then we had a score of tasters try all the wines; every one of them tasted and wrote down his impressions. And what happened? We saw that every yeast produced a different flavour, but it was unanimously found that the most appreciated flavour was produced by indigenous yeasts."

Most famously, Chauvet was opposed to the use of SO_2 in the winery. "I think one can do without SO_2 in a certain measure, if one has hygiene," he stated. "SO_2 is a poison. It poisons both the yeast (the yeast resists, but it gives better products when it is not poisoned by SO_2) and bacteria." Chauvet pointed out that winemakers were really caught between two stools: if they used levels of SO_2 that were too high, then malolactic fermentation didn't occur easily, but lower doses were no good against oxidasic breakdown (enzymatic oxidation from enzymes present in any rotten grapes), in which case it would be better not to treat at all, but to allow the carbon dioxide present in the fermenting wine to provide a measure of protection. Where a harvest was sound, Chauvet advocated not using any SO_2 during the fermentation process. When Kesselring questioned Chauvet about his future directions in research, he responded, "I think one must go towards an ever higher purity . . . You must come to the wine as a 'reflection of its soil,' with a minimum of chemicals both in the soil as well as in the wine . . . The older I grow, the more one wants to find truly natural wines, well made wines."

Burgundian winemaker Philippe Pacalet, who spent three years working with Chauvet before he died, and who is the nephew of another leading figure in the natural wine movement, the recently deceased Marcel Lapierre, says the following in the foreword to one of Chauvet's books:

> The processes of fermentation are energetic phenomena which change the physical/ chemical state of the materials that undergo them and, for wine, those who drink it. This energy, which is information in movement accumulated during fermentation, provokes in us, as we drink a "real wine," both sensory emotions and well-being, which go far beyond pleasure, and touch us and balance us, in the deepest manner, in our cells. In our modern epoch, when we consume more and more dead and artificial products which separate us from our true nature and affect our minds and our health, "real wine" is a source of life bringing us equilibrium and resonance with ourselves, others and our environment.

Pacalet is a well-known figure in the natural wine scene, but, like many in this unofficial club, he's not easy to compartmentalize. He believes in natural fermentation without the addition of SO_2 or yeasts, but he doesn't care for biodynamics or organics. "It's very easy to pay and become organic, not really taking any risks," he says. "But to make natural wine, you do have to take risks." Pacalet thinks that the current vine material is weak because of continued asexual reproduction. "The vines are in a degenerate state," he maintains. "Maybe we can use OGM [genetic modification] in the right way, in the hands of good people, to help here."

Pacalet uses whole bunches in his Pinot Noir fermentations, and he maintains that the stems help capture some of the heat from fermentation. He hasn't had to regulate temperature for ten years and says that different terroirs ferment at different temperatures. This view accords with the terroir concept at the heart of natural wine. Pacalet is

LITTORAI WINES' "NATURAL" WINEMAKING PHILOSOPHY

TED LEMON, Littorai Wines, Western Sonoma and Mendocino Counties, California, USA

The term *natural winemaking* is an oxymoron. Consumable wine does not occur in nature. At Littorai we prefer the older description *minimal-intervention winemaking*. The goal, however, is the same: to intervene in the fermentation and aging processes as little as possible and always to favor simple physical inputs (temperature and humidity control, moving wine by gravity flow whenever possible) rather than chemical ones. Today there exists an array of physical machinery such as spinning cone and reverse osmosis machines, some of which involve both complex physical processes and arguably some chemical intervention. It is difficult to see how any of these could fall under the category of acceptable under a natural winemaking regime. While the terms *natural winemaking* and *natural winegrowing* are not interchangeable, it would be equally difficult to defend a natural winemaking regime which is not based on "natural" vineyards. A definition of the latter lies outside the scope of this outline.

Natural winemaking can be divided into two component parts. The first is *input reduction*, and the other is *input sourcing*. *Sourcing* refers, of course, to the nature of the input applied. Such inputs include structures (buildings), equipment, and winemaking supplies. If the input is chemical, then the path of natural winemaking suggests using only organic materials, both in the winery and the vineyard. If the input is buildings, then natural winemaking would suggest that these be as "natural" or "green" as possible. "Naturalization" of equipment and supplies would address such winery staples as inert gases, refrigeration systems, lab chemicals, tanks, and all the toys of the winemaking trade. In terms of wine additives, we are quite far down the path of understanding and applying natural input sourcing. In terms of structures and equipment "naturalization," the general wine community has much work to do.

The first component of *input reduction* is reduction or elimination of wine additives. The second component involves reduction of structural inputs (buildings no larger than necessary), equipment, and supplies. This definition pretty well torpedoes the potential claim to natural winemaking for any of the monuments to ego constructed around the great winegrowing regions of the world.

At Littorai Wines our natural winemaking decisions flow from our dedication to producing wines of place, wines which reflect as accurately as possible the terroir of a given site in a given vintage. This has been my personal quest since

I began making wine as a young man in Meursault nearly thirty years ago and has continued during many years of consulting throughout California, Oregon, and New Zealand, long before we founded Littorai. If one is to claim to make wines which are reflective of a site, then logically the less input in the winery, the better. Over the years I have become willing to take greater and greater risks in pursuing this passion. Every wine producer has a different level of risk tolerance and a different philosophical bent. There is no right or wrong. Think of interventional moments as filters on a camera. With each filter the view of the vineyard changes. At first the change is subtle, but when the filters are stacked one upon the other, the vineyard withdraws, becomes unfocused, and finally is completely unrecognizable. Only the winemaking process remains.

The interplay of winery philosophy and natural winemaking considerations can be illustrated by looking at the specific example of Littorai's approach to the use of sulfur dioxide. At Littorai Wines we do not believe that *Brettanomyces* infections are reflective of the terroir of a site. We believe that high levels of *Brettanomyces* make all wines taste the same, regardless of where they come from. In other words, we see *Brettanomyces* as an inhibitor of site expression, just as many view the use of a high percentage of new oak as an inhibitor. On one side of the scale one can place the risk of brett infection and on the other the various techniques required to prevent brett development. Most of these are, in our view, as damaging to site expression as *Brettanomyces*. We reject them.

When faced with the decision between using the traditional additive SO_2 or risking that *Brettanomyces* becomes the dominant yeast strain in our cellar, we hew to a traditional terroir view of this matter. We want the production from our Hirsch vineyard to reflect the interaction of the vintage and the site. We do not want the production from Hirsch to reflect the degree of *Brettanomyces* development in a given year once the wine is in the barrel. We do not consider this to be "natural" winemaking, although more extreme proponents might see it that way. In our view, to make the argument that *Brettanomyces* development is part of natural winemaking is to make the argument that site does not matter in winemaking, that the goal of natural winemaking is to allow the wine to undergo whatever chemical and physical changes occur "naturally" during its aging process. This view decouples "natural winemaking" from "natural winegrowing." Ironically, this step brings wine production back in line with the view held by the science of wine: enology. Enology is the study of understanding and describing the potential changes grape juice and then wine can undergo during the fermenting and aging process. This decoupling from the vineyard is not consistent with our philosophy. We use good sanitation in the cellar, and we use moderate SO_2 and temperature control to inhibit brett growth. We do not sterile filter, nor, for

(continued)

that matter, do we monitor *Brettanomyces* presence via lab analysis. If, upon olfactory analysis, we believe that a given barrel has *Brettanomyces*, we sell the contents in bulk and destroy the barrel.

We do not use the words "never" or "always" at Littorai. However, we do not believe that cultured yeasts, cultured bacteria, yeast additives, fermentation aids, yeast or malolactic nutrients, enzymes, and acidification and deacidification are appropriate to the greatest expression of terroir. We harvest at optimal balance when all of the above can be avoided. As outlined above, we accept that, at this juncture in time, the moderate use of SO_2 is the most natural way to ensure that unwanted organisms do not take over the fermentation processes. The organisms *Oenococcus oeni* and *Saccharomyces cerevisiae* are the building blocks of fine wines as humans understand them both historically and in the current cultural paradigm. We would like our wines to be commercially acceptable within that paradigm. Site-inspired grapes should go into a fermentation vessel, ferment without chemical additives other than SO_2, and come out the other side as a finished wine which educated palates will find pleasing. Period. We always seek to reduce SO_2 input further but have not found the path that will permit complete elimination while remaining within both the current cultural paradigm of acceptability and our own terroir-inspired quality standards. We would welcome that day.

If a fermentation is going awry, we will intervene. We are delighted that it has become exceedingly rare for us to do so. Oxidation, aldehydes, reductive qualities, and high levels of volatile acidity are not, in our view, reflective of the terroir-based paradigm outlined above. Our "threshold" for when these are excessive is much higher than it would be at an industrial winery. And we will tolerate much higher levels of some of these components than many wineries will in the pursuit of "natural" winemaking.

There are, however, lines in the sand which we will not cross, as is the case with all winemakers. Sands shift, of course, and the lines are constantly being redrawn both at Littorai and at all wineries. This alone demonstrates that winemaking is a human process and not a "natural" one. What a delicious commentary on human nature that man would adopt a substance, learn to make it express itself in myriad forms, seek to understand everything about it, and then attempt to reduce his input to the minimum possible.

Natural wine and natural winemaking do not exist. They are an endless path of discovery, the endless quest to minimize human intervention in the production of wine. The decisions on this path are unique to a given vineyard, winery, and moment in time in human cultural experience. This is just as it should be.

FIGURE 8.1
Fermenting red wines at Fonseca's Quinta do Panascal, which are made in much the same way as they would have been hundreds of years ago.

slightly unusual among natural wine producers in that he is working in a prestigious region; many work in less fashionable regions, such as the various appellations in the Loire or in Beaujolais.

Philippe Pacalet's uncle Marcel Lapierre is one of the key figures in the influential Beaujolais natural wine movement. Mentored by Chauvet, Lapierre worked from 1980 to 1994 with Jacques Néauport, a winemaking consultant known widely by the nickname "Bidasse" who, to a degree, has taken Chauvet's mantle (he first met Chauvet in 1978). According to Pacalet, this period was very creative, with the likes of Lapierre, Guy Breton, and Jean Foillard in Beaujolais, plus Philippe Laurent in the Rhône, working closely together. After 1994 Néauport and Lapierre did not work together (Pacalet describes this as a "divorce").

Inspired by Chauvet, the Beaujolais has been the somewhat unlikely trailblazing region for natural wines, and the leaders of the movement there have been the "gang of five" from Villié-Morgon. As well as Marcel Lapierre, this group consisted of Jean Foillard, Guy Breton, Jean-Paul Thévenet, and Joseph Chamonard. Chamonard died in 1990, but his daughter stayed true to his natural winemaking approach. While all five used a similar winemaking approach, their wines show distinct differences. But all are full of interest—something that cannot be said for most modern Beaujolais. These five have now been joined by a number of other growers who are making top-quality natural expressions of Beaujolais. These include Yvon Métras, Jean-Claude Lapalu, and Jean-Paul Brun.

It is worth reiterating that Chauvet was a wine scientist who keenly observed and attempted to understand the various phenomena occurring during natural fermentations.

Successful natural winemaking isn't simply a laissez-faire process. Instead, knowledge and attention to detail in the winery are required for those who wish to improve the odds of success.

SULFUR DIOXIDE IN WINEMAKING

This is the appropriate place for us to discuss SO_2 in depth. It is the winemaking additive that is hardest to do away with, and only a relatively small band of brave souls have eliminated it entirely. SO_2 is almost universally added to wine and has been for perhaps two thousand years. This remarkable chemical acts as the molecular guardian of wine quality, and as long as too much isn't added—there are strict wine laws to ensure that this is the case—it has no negative health effects. So why would a growing band of winemakers want to do away with this useful (even vital) addition? This is one of the most extreme and interesting aspects of natural wine. Is it really possible to make high-quality wines without any SO_2 additions?

Key to understanding the effects of SO_2 is the ratio between the free and bound forms. When SO_2 is added to a wine, it dissolves, and some of it reacts with other chemical components in the wine to become bound. This bound fraction is effectively lost to the winemaker, at least temporarily, because it has insignificant antioxidant and antimicrobial properties. Various compounds present in the wine, such as acetaldehyde, ketonic acids, sugars, and dicarbonyl group molecules, are responsible for this. Winemakers routinely measure total SO_2 and free SO_2, and the difference between the two is the amount in the bound form. Importantly, an equilibrium exists between the free and bound forms such that as free SO_2 is used up, more may be released from the bound fraction. The situation is slightly more complicated than this, though—some of the bound SO_2 is bound irreversibly, while the remainder is releasable, and most of the free portion exists as the relatively inactive bisulfite anion (HSO_3^-), with just a small amount left as active molecular SO_2.

One of the key factors affecting the function of SO_2 is pH, which is a measure of how acidic or alkaline a solution is (technically it relates to the concentration of hydrogen ions in solution). A pH of 7 is neutral, and below and above this level the solution is progressively more acidic or alkaline, respectively. Thus a wine with a lower pH is more acidic. All wines are acidic (with a pH less than 7), but some are more acidic than others. Typically wines (red or white) have a pH between 3 and 4. White wines generally have lower pH than reds because of level of ripeness at harvest, because of the increased potassium levels in reds due to maceration on skins, and finally because all red wines should go through malolactic fermentation to make them microbiologically stable in the bottle. The pH level is important here in two respects. First, at higher pH levels more total SO_2 is needed to get the same level of free SO_2. Second, SO_2 is more effective at lower pH, so not only is there more of the useful free form for a given amount of addition, but also it works better.

FIGURE 8.2
A Nomblot concrete egg. These are
becoming increasingly fashionable in the
natural wine scene as alternatives to
barrels or stainless steel tanks.

SO_2 also inhibits enzymes known as oxidases, which massively speed up oxidation reactions. The most important action of SO_2 is to neutralize hydrogen peroxide, which is formed when oxygen reacts with phenolic compounds; at wine pH, peroxide is a strong oxidizing agent. The levels of these enzymes are much increased in damaged or rotten grapes, so where these are likely to be present, it is especially important to use sufficient SO_2. It follows that sweet wines made from botrytised grapes need substantially higher levels of SO_2 to protect them against oxidation. Significantly, botrytised wines are also very high in compounds that bind free SO_2, with the result that winemakers can add enormous levels and still not have significant free SO_2.

But SO_2 isn't a straight antioxidant. "There is a general misconception that sulfur dioxide will protect against oxidation," says wine scientist Roger Boulton of the University of California at Davis. "Its rate of reaction with oxygen is so slow that it cannot compete for the oxygen and stop the phenol oxidation. While it does compete for the peroxide formed, its main role is binding up the aldehyde formed, so that we do not smell the oxidation product." This all sounds a little complicated and probably needs some explanation for nonscientists. Although oxygen is often assumed to be highly reactive, it doesn't react directly with wine that is exposed to it, but requires an oxidizing agent to become truly reactive. This could be a metal catalyst, a phenolic compound, or a photosensitizer, explains wine chemist Dr. George Skouroumounis of the Australian

Wine Research Institute (AWRI), who specializes in the interaction of wine and oxygen. Boulton continues this theme: "As a wine is exposed to oxygen, the key initial reaction is the oxidation of monomeric phenols [chemicals present in red and white wines] with a special reactive group to form hydrogen peroxide." Hydrogen peroxide is very reactive and goes on to interact with other wine components. "The peroxide can be consumed by a number of other reactions, either being quenched by tannins and other phenols (dominant in red wines, much less in whites) or forming acetaldehyde by reaction with ethanol," says Boulton. Acetaldehyde is an important molecule in the oxidation of wine. Also known as ethanal, it is the oxidation product of alcohol and has an aroma described as like that of fresh-cut apples. Sherry and Madeira, made in a deliberately oxidized style, have high levels of acetaldehyde, which gives wine a flat, smooth texture in the mouth. Indeed, one description of oxidized whites is "sherried."

Red wines have a higher capacity to absorb oxygen without showing signs of oxidation because the extended skin contact that red winemaking typically employs means that more of the group of compounds known as phenolics (tannins, anthocyanins, and combinations of both) are present, and these are able to act as buffers, reacting with oxidation products such as acetaldehyde. White wines tend to lack this sort of buffering capacity and so need to be protected from air to a greater extent. As a consequence, white-wines generally need higher levels of SO_2 than reds to protect them. White wines that have been handled reductively (that is, protected against oxygen exposure through the use of stainless steel, SO_2, ascorbic acid, and inert gases—nitrogen and argon—in the winemaking process) are especially vulnerable to oxidation and need very careful protection. It is common to handle some white wines oxidatively, allowing the pressed juice to react with oxygen in the air. This causes the juice to turn brown as the phenolic compounds react with oxygen, but during fermentation these phenolic compounds are removed. Paradoxically, this juice hyperoxidation actually makes the wine more stable and long lived because the phenols that would otherwise be oxidized after fermentation are no longer present. Some grape varieties react to juice hyperoxidation better than others. Chardonnay grapes are frequently handled in this way; it doesn't work for aromatic varieties such as Sauvignon Blanc because many of the aromas are destroyed by oxygen.

Interesting data have come from the AWRI's ongoing wine bottle closure trial, which has tracked the performance of a number of different closure types over time, using a Semillon wine as the test subject. This trial has shown that the critical level of free SO_2 is 10 mg/L at the particular pH of this wine (3.1, a low level that enhances the efficacy of SO_2). When SO_2 levels have dropped below this, test bottles are rated high in the attribute "oxidized" by the sensory analysis panel, but this trait is much less common in bottles that exceed this level. The AWRI's Peter Godden has also calculated this critical point for some of the problem wines he has seen. "It is very pH dependent," he reports, "and we saw one wine in which it was 15 mg/L: that is, bottles below this level were rated exponentially higher for oxidation during sensory analysis, which correlated strongly with brown colour."

Wine scientist Richard Gibson of Scorpex Consultancy in South Australia has done some calculations of the likely impact of oxygen pickup at bottling and also transmission through the closure on wine longevity. He begins with the observation that 1 mL of oxygen reacts with 4 mg of SO_2. A headspace of 5.95 mL consisting of air will contain 1.24 mL of oxygen, equivalent to 1.78 mg, which in turn equates to 2.37 mg/L of oxygen once it is dissolved in the wine. This can react with 9.5 mg/L of SO_2. The amount of oxygen entering the bottle through closure can be calculated from the closure oxygen transfer rate (OTR). A rate of 0.01 cc/day equates to 0.019 mg/L of oxygen entering the bottle each day, which can react with 27.7 mg/L of SO_2 over a year. From these figures, the expected shelf life of a wine can be calculated. For example, a wine with 35 mg/mL free SO_2 at filling, 2 mg/L of dissolved oxygen, 0.5 mL of oxygen in the headspace, and a closure OTR of 0.008 cc/day will have a shelf life of 217 days. In real wine situations, things are a little more complex—for example, the exact amount of SO_2 consumed by 1 mg of oxygen seems to be wine dependent—but these figures are a useful theoretical framework to begin working from.

These calculations make it clear that both the total pack oxygen (TPO) at bottling and the closure oxygen transmission levels are vital factors in determining how the wine will develop over time. In reality, though, shelf life will be somewhat longer because many wines contain components that can react with oxygen, such as the polyphenolic compounds found in red wines. Still, Gibson's calculations show the importance of SO_2. He thinks that most wines will change only a little during the first phase of aging, as SO_2 fulfills its protective role. Then the wine will start to show some signs of evolution. Finally, the actual oxidation process seems to occur very quickly. Gibson thinks that this might be because when SO_2 levels drop below a certain threshold, changes in the equilibrium between free and bound SO_2 take place, releasing products of oxidation previously bound by SO_2, which make the wine rapidly taste oxidized. It should be emphasized that Gibson's calculations are just examples. As we have already mentioned, the pH of the wine will affect the efficacy of the SO_2, and also in different wines, the same amount of oxygen will cause the loss of varying amounts of SO_2. It is also possible that the rate of oxygen ingress will affect the amount of SO_2 with which it reacts.

But SO_2 is also microbicidal. It prevents the growth—and at high enough concentrations kills—fungi (yeasts) and bacteria. Usefully, SO_2 is more active against bacteria than yeasts, and so by getting the concentration right, winemakers can inhibit growth of bad bugs while allowing good yeasts to do their work. SO_2 is usually still added to the crushed grapes in wild yeast fermentations; while it kills some of the natural yeasts present on grape skins, the stronger strains survive and thus become the dominant strains for a less competitive and potentially healthier fermentation. Wines with residual sugar, wines with high pH, wines that have not completed malolactic fermentation, wines that have spent extended periods of time in oak, and unfiltered red wines are at higher risk of rogue microbial growth, so correct SO_2 addition is especially important for these wines.

But while these considerations might encourage some winemakers to add more SO_2 just to be on the safe side, Godden suggests that the best way to ensure wine quality is not to use more SO_2 but to use it more intelligently. His idea is that the key measurement for winemakers is not the free SO_2 level but the ratio of free to bound SO_2. That is, the key to effective SO_2 usage is getting the ratio of free to bound SO_2 as high as possible to maximize the benefits of the amount added. He sent us data gathered by the AWRI Analytical Service on a typical cross-section of Australian wines that show that in a range of reds, free SO_2 has been steadily increasing in recent years, while total SO_2 has been decreasing. Thus the ratio of free to total SO_2 has improved. "I consider the use of the ratio of free to total SO_2 as one of the most useful quality control measures during winemaking," says Godden. He has similar data on Australian white wines, although he feels that there is probably more room for improvement with these wines.

How is a good ratio achieved? Starting with healthy grapes is important. Grapes suffering from rot have significantly higher levels of compounds that will bind SO_2 and also of enzymes that encourage oxidation. Judicious filtration, where necessary, will also help make SO_2 additions more effective by reducing microbial populations to a level where the SO_2 is more effective against them. General cleanliness in the winery is also helpful.

Perhaps most important, though, are two critical winemaking interventions: first, controlling turbidity by careful racking, fining, and filtration (if necessary), and second, the timing and size of additions. There are three stages where wine is likely to be subject to considerable oxygen stress or risk of bug growth: at crushing, at the end of malolactic fermentation (or alcoholic fermentation where malolactic is discouraged), and at bottling. At each of these stages a healthy dollop of SO_2 is highly recommended. Crucially, for the same total addition, it is much more effective to add SO_2 in a few relatively large doses rather than many small additions, because the latter practice runs the risk of never getting free SO_2 levels high enough for it to do its job properly.

Other factors winemakers might want to consider in keeping the ratio as high as possible include the quality of the fruit and how it is harvested. Of course, higher-quality, disease-free fruit will need less SO_2. Hand-harvested fruit will need significantly lower SO_2 additions than machine-harvested fruit, which generally sees its first SO_2 addition immediately after harvesting, when the must is still macerating on skins in the vineyard.

The choice of yeast strain is an important consideration in keeping SO_2 levels down, as there are both wild and commercial yeast strains that can produce high levels of sulfur during fermentation. Leaving the wine on its lees after fermentation (free from SO_2 addition) for as long as possible can also help achieve lower total SO_2. The lees will scavenge oxygen and do the same job as SO_2 in this regard. There are associated risks, however, and winemakers who use this technique for extended periods need to keep a watchful eye on unwanted microbiological activity and/or formation of certain complex sulfides that can detract from quality. Inactive yeasts might prove to be the way forward for those producers who want to favor yeast contact without compromising wine stability during

FIGURE 8.3
Stellar Organics' No Added Sulphur Cabernet Sauvignon, which has been a
success in the U.K. supermarket Sainsbury's.

élevage. Like natural fermentation lees, certain inactive yeasts, widely available on the market, can have the desirable effect of moving the wine into a more reductive spectrum, largely through their glutathione content. Glutathione is a tripeptide that acts as an antioxidant; currently it is not legal to add it to wine except indirectly through using dead yeast cells (inactivated yeast). With these inactive yeasts you can use small levels of SO_2 with greater confidence that undesirable mercaptans will not be produced during *élevage*. For those producers working with less than ideal fruit and must, inactive yeast can be a savior in this regard. Getting the natural turbidity units (NTUs) down to low levels before fermentation through fining and prolonged settling to take out impurities and enzymes imposed by botrytis where it is present in the fruit is a standard approach to dealing with disease-affected fruit. Winemakers working with poor-quality fruit like to rack and sulfur their wines after fermentation without delay to get off the poor-quality natural lees. Inactive yeast can be added after racking to help protect the wine from oxidation.

Trying to delay the period between primary fermentation and malolactic fermentation is a technique employed in Burgundy for many years to keep SO_2 levels down. It is now widely used by many Pinot Noir producers around the world. This technique also helps keep the ratio of free-to-bound high and the total SO_2 levels lower at bottling. In other words, the earlier you finish malolactic fermentation, the sooner you have to add SO_2, and hence the greater the total SO_2 will be at bottling. Winemakers who use this approach need to consider microbiological spoilage a real threat and to keep the temperature of the

STRATEGIES FOR NATURAL WINEMAKING

ALAISTAIR MALING, Villa Maria, New Zealand

- We use less SO$_2$ in nonaromatic and/or phenolic white grapes at juice stage. This is positive as it encourages oxidation and natural phenolic dropout. Lower levels of SO$_2$ also help encourage natural fermentation and allow for easier and more successful onset and completion of malolactic fermentation (MLF) (if desired) later.
- We are looking to use more natural fermentations during white winemaking (Chardonnay: Taylors Pass Single Vineyard Chardonnay, Keltern Vineyard Single Vineyard Chardonnay; Viognier: Omahu Gravels Single Vineyard Viognier), generally seen as a positive from the increased complexity (oak integration, texture, aromatic profile). But this can also go the other way; for example, increased lag time prior to fermentation initiation can increase volatile acidity, and increased finishing time can increase acetaldehyde production and allow spoilage bacteria to become involved. When these characteristics can be kept in check somewhat, these characteristics can be seen to add complexity and interest, but it can be a fine line. We are incorporating natural fermentations more and more across our top range(s).
- We are not adding enzymes to some juices at settling (Viognier, Chardonnay), leaving more natural solids behind for the fermentations to enhance the functioning of the yeast and improve texture and complexity in the wines.
- We are fermenting at more ambient, natural temperatures rather than refrigerated whenever possible (within reason) with the above varieties in barrel, again to enhance texture, complexity, and so on.
- I'm not sure there is much advantage to be had in natural MLF versus inoculating for MLF for Bordeaux reds or Chardonnay, but we are seeing some interesting results in Pinot Noir and Syrah where we leave the wines on lees over the winter and allow the barrels to naturally warm and go through MLF in the spring. The wines that have gone through spring MLF do tend to have more richness and complexity.
- We use the seasons to naturally help make our wines, for example, to finish natural fermentations in spring and to allow for natural MLF.
- We stopped adding acid to reds this year to rely more on the grapes' natural acidity, in a positive sense looking to enhance palate texture,

perceived concentration, and drinkability. A potential downside of this is that elevated pH makes a more hospitable home for spoilage organisms, so we need to manage wines accordingly in the cellar. Added acid can leave the wines with a hardness on the palate and undermines a wine's texture, which I want to enhance.

- Using natural grape juice concentrate as opposed to bagged sugar to balance wines could be seen as being more "natural" in some ways. We are working hard on stopping fermentations to leave natural residual sugar rather than having to add natural grape juice concentrate. There is an obvious saving of dollars, and also it is better for the environment. There is little impact on wine quality.

- We naturally cold stabilise when possible, particularly for reserve wines, as it's seen as beneficial to the wine. We add cream of tartar only when we need to.

- We try to use natural gravity whenever possible rather than pumping juice/wine to move it around the winery. This is seen to be beneficial to the wine's quality.

- Filtering a wine (particularly a red) too tightly can certainly have a negative impact. Thus we manage the wines' turbidity prior to filtration (by settling and fining, etc.) to ensure this is minimized. We have never bottled unfiltered but don't believe there is a significant quality loss if the wine is not subjected to excessive pressure during the filtration. Our top-end Bordeaux reds receive a minimal coarse filtration where possible. Our 2004 Single Vineyard Omahu Merlot was bright enough in tank that the only filtration it received was the nominal Rockstopper filters on the bottling line. Our rack/return procedure (three to four times) certainly lessens the amount of filtration required prebottling.

- Natural corks can have a major negative influence on wine quality, so we don't use them.

Natural winemaking does come from knowing your vineyards. When to pick is the most important decision. If you know what wine you can realistically make at harvest, you can let the wine make itself. The notes above cover some of the things we are doing on a natural basis with the sole aim of adding more texture, complexity, and longevity to a wine. We're finding that these wines at blending time can be subdued on the nose or much tighter in structure than those made with nonnatural methods but that the wines do tend to have more mouth feel, complexity, and overall balance that is worth the effort.

(*continued*)

Natural winemaking also occurs in the vineyard, where we have embraced a number of viticultural natural organic principles over the past three to four years such as composting and promoting soil health/biology, and the use of seaweed, which hopefully reduces the need for other less naturally occurring additives. We're also finding that the canopy and fruit are often in better condition, the fruit holds on longer, and the resulting wines have more intensity and richness.

Overall, I am convinced that there is a benefit to following a more natural viticultural and winemaking practice that benefits the environment but also rewards the consumer by delivering wines with more texture, balance, complexity, and longevity.

wine as low as possible. They also need to keep a close eye on the wine to ensure that it doesn't start to develop unwanted flavour compounds such as volatile phenols and volatile acidity, to name just two, from rogue yeast and bacterial activity in the unsulfured wine.

Winemakers who want to lower SO_2 without compromising quality need to consider the type of vessel for both fermentation and *élevage*. The temperature of wine during storage is also critical because oxidation rate will be greater at higher temperatures, and more SO_2 will be needed to protect the wine if sufficient cooling facilities are not available. The more you rack the wine, the more SO_2 you generally need to add.

Given all this, why would winemakers consider not using SO_2 at all? Nonuse sounds like a recipe for quickly oxidized wine, and in theory it should be. However, many wines made without any added SO_2 taste fantastic and aren't oxidized. It's quite hard to explain this from the standpoint of wine science. Generally speaking, producers making more expensive wines can work with less SO_2 with more confidence than producers making larger volumes for supermarkets. There are two reasons. First, they are dealing with better-quality fruit, lower yields, and better natural balance. They also usually are harvesting by hand, are handling more gently (for example, gravity handling), and have better-quality lees (with more time on lees after fermentation), a longer period of *élevage* and therefore a more stable product at bottling, a better-quality closure, and shipping in refrigerated containers. Second, complexity is a key factor in the value of these wines, and some level of oxidation or *Brettanomyces* activity produces complexity. This sort of complexity that can sometimes be used to put a positive slant on a wine fault is more widely understood and accepted by consumers of expensive wine.

What seems clear, though, is that there probably is more to wine longevity than simply free SO_2 levels. Many wines without SO_2 taste fresh, have well-defined fruit characters, and are definitely not oxidized. Something is happening beyond the rather simple story recounted here. Could it be that as well as reacting with SO_2, oxygen present in the wine or entering through the closure is reacting with other wine components at the same time in ways as yet poorly understood? A long, slow *élevage* certainly seems to help protect white Burgundies, and more hurried modern *élevages* have been cited as one of the contributing factors to the premature oxidation problems encountered in many white Burgundies since the 1995 vintage.

COMMERCIAL WINEMAKING WITHOUT ADDED SO$_2$

It would be convenient for mainstream winemakers to be able to dismiss these sorts of "natural" wines as a fringe activity, irrelevant to the wine trade at large. But in March 2008 the major U.K. supermarket Sainsbury's listed one of the first commercially significant NAS (No Added Sulphur) wines, part of its "So Organic" range and retailing at £4.99.

The wine in question is a 2006 Cabernet Sauvignon from the Stellar winery in South Africa and comes with a neck tag explaining the concept behind the wine. "Sulphites (sulphur dioxide) are generally added to wine as a preservative and an antioxidant," it reads. "The warm, dry South African climate allows the production of perfect quality ripe grapes. Careful grape selection and handling, coupled with the best of modern winemaking and bottling techniques has enabled this wine to be made without the addition of sulphites. Once opened, do not store this wine." This is a rather complex message for consumers, and there is a concern that if Sainsbury's promotes this wine as being more healthful or more natural than wines with sulfites added, then shoppers will begin to question the soundness and healthfulness of the rest of its range.

What does the wine taste like? It isn't at all funky or faulty, and the dominant feature is pure, focused black currant and blackberry fruit. It has purity and freshness, and there's no sign of any oxidation. It overdelivers for the price level. When the same wine was tasted a year later, it was holding up remarkably well, with plenty of fruit left and no sign of deterioration. The follow-up vintage was ripe, fruit driven, and delicious, with real intensity.

Michelle Smith, Sainsbury's South African wine buyer at the time, said,

> When we launched Sainsbury's South African Fairtrade SO Organic Cabernet Sauvignon with "no added sulphites" back in 2008, it was a bold decision, as no one to date had really been able to successfully sell a wine of this style due to the poor perception and reality of the wines offered by producers. This was in addition to the fact that these wines could confuse customers as all other wines on shelf have "Contains Sulphites" on their back label as required by food labelling regulations. However, the wine Stellar Organics offered us ticked all the boxes on taste, quality, and value and had the massive added benefits for our customers of being both organic and Fairtrade. Three vintages later I am pleased to say it's still our best-selling organic wine and our best-selling Fairtrade wine. Marketing and selling the "no added sulphites" wine on shelf alongside those with added sulphites was always going to be a challenge, so we initially highlighted the fact via a

neck collar which explained how the wine could actually be made without the use of sulphur. The fact that our SO Organic wine has been so successful has also meant the Fairtrade funding generated from our sales has been able to provide funding for a primary school teacher for this remote farming community, which is something we are all very proud of—especially myself being a native South African who really understands the basic needs Fairtrade funding meets. After two years and only positive feedback from journalists our sales continued to grow with no negative impact on the other wines in the range. Therefore we have now added the sulphur message on the front label to make a much bolder statement about this fact.

How has Stellar achieved this? "Modern production techniques and equipment make the use of SO_2 less critical than in the past," explains Stellar's winemaker Dudley Wilson. "Standards of hygiene in cellars are much improved, and the widespread use of stainless steel makes cleaning much easier. With the selection of healthy good-quality fruit at optimum ripeness in the vineyard, there is little need to use large amounts of SO_2 at the start of the winemaking process." Wilson has also made a concerted effort to protect the wine from oxidation during the winemaking process. "Most winemakers rely on the presence of SO_2 to protect the wine when a lot more could be done by looking at dissolved oxygen in wine and understanding where it came from."

Wilson prepares the wine for bottling by protecting it with inert gases and also by measuring oxygen pickup to make sure that this protection is working. He adds that, "working with a dissolved oxygen meter has also exposed the way most common methods to inert tanks or protect wine with inert gas are more ritualistic than effective." The bottling machine he uses creates a vacuum in the empty bottle, fills it with nitrogen, and then fills it with wine. The wine is also sterile filtered just before entering the bottling machine. "The aim is to have almost no dissolved oxygen in the wine before bottling, to have no oxygen pickup during the filling process, and to have the wine sterile at bottling," says Wilson.

"On the question of shelf life," he continues, "it is my opinion that if the wine has not oxidised within the first three weeks postbottling, then it will age according to the style in which it was made. This is often dictated by the tannin profile, pH, volatile acid content, and wood influence. Thus it will be subject to much the same aging factors as a normal wine. This is assuming that there is no ingress of oxygen or microbes through or from the closure. One sometimes errs on the side of reductiveness when bottling some of these wines and they may, just after opening, exhibit some atypical bouquets. A bit of airing will invariably remedy this. Another feature to look for is the colour intensity. Even though these wines are chosen with a dense structure, the lack of bleaching SO_2 results in wines with exceptional richness of colour."

What were the motivating factors behind Stellar's decision to make NAS wines? Wilson cites two. The first was the recent legal requirement to put "Contains sulfites" on the label of any wines to which sulfur dioxide has been added. "Many people mistakenly think that organic wines are SO_2 free," says Wilson, "so we anticipated a bit of confusion when this happened." The second was the fact that in the United States the label "organic" has been restricted to wines where no SO_2 has been added. "We saw that there was a large niche to be exploited in America," explains Wilson. "I can assure you I do not refrain from using SO_2 to sleep better at night." He adds, though, that "I have learnt more about SO_2 by not using it than I have over all the previous years."

Not all wines are suitable candidates for being made without SO_2. "Generally wines that have a special tannin and colour profile are the best candidates," says Wilson. "Generally they are wines with deep colour and rich tannins. We have tried it with white wine and have had some success but the process is far more unforgiving than reds. It often requires a lot of attention and work to stabilise and bottle when we are still busy taking in red grapes. One doesn't have the safety net of tannins to mop up oxygen. Hyperoxidation and fermentation with bentonite are all options that can be explored, but the resulting style will not be as fresh and will not really work on Sauvignon Blanc."

Wilson reports that the response to his NAS wines has been very good so far, especially among consumers who have concerns about the effects of sulfites on their health. "There are probably as many people who write in claiming they can now drink wine again who have probably been affected psychosomatically as those who have found relief from a genuine intolerance towards SO_2," he adds. But there has been some hostility towards the Stellar initiative within the trade. Critics of NAS wines assert that claiming wines without added SO_2 are more natural is nonsense, because all wines contain some sulfites as a by-product of fermentation.

Stellar is not the only winery that has attempted to make a commercial SO_2-free wine. Australian giant Hardys has been marketing a range of three wines, a Cabernert Sauvignon, a Shiraz, and a Chardonnay, in its NPA (no preservatives added) range, which retails for around A$15. These wines are available only in Australia because there are concerns about how they will ship. The Chardonnay is made by using juice hyperoxidation to precipitate out all the phenolic compounds, and then it is handled reductively once fermentation is complete. Former Hardys winemaker Tony Milanowski was involved with this product line. "NPA wines were never a big seller for Hardys," Milanowski reveals. "I think we made 5,000 cases of each a year, which is minor compared to the amount of Banrock Station and Crest that was made. At my time with Hardys I think they were definitely marketing to people with specific health concerns, and not people interested in natural wine."

Wilson thinks that NAS wines are not going to become commonplace. "We will certainly be increasing the proportion of our production that is SO_2 free, but I doubt it will catch on elsewhere," he comments. "I can't claim to understand everything about not using SO_2 and still rely a lot on gut feel and intuition, not something you can write down on paper and pass on as a recipe."

CLARK SMITH AND HIS ROMAN SYRAH

Clark Smith, who founded California reverse osmosis and microoxygenation service provider Vinovation, is a bit of a paradox. You'd expect someone who has been in the business of applying high-technology solutions to improving or correcting wine to be someone easy to categorize as a modernist techie with no understanding of the heart of wine. But Smith isn't just a science guy who treats wine like milk or soft drinks, as a commodity to be tamed by technology. While he may dispute that there is such a thing as the "soul" of wine, he is primarily interested in the concept of deliciousness in wine, rejects sterile correct wines with no real personality, and has even made his own "natural" wine without the use of added SO_2.

Smith spent two years at MIT, beginning as a math major, but he says that he couldn't handle it. He then switched to chemistry, but it looked pretty well worked out. He says that he was looking for a place where inquiry into science merged with inquiry into what it is to be a living thing. He left and got a job in a liquor store, where he realized that wine was a fun playground and a place to make an impact. Two years later he started getting patents. "There are only 150 patents in the history of the wine industry," says Smith. "No one in the industry was trying to do anything new. I got interested in that." He adds that "we are trying to do something old, but we need new tools to do it." He is somewhat dismissive of reliance on wine science. "Around wine, organized inquiry is not our goal," says Smith. "Wine is liquid music!"

"Why is a major chord happy and a minor chord melancholy?" he asks. Smith talks of the illusory nature of harmony. When an orchestra tunes up, there's lots of noise but not much harmony among the instruments. "But then there's music," he says, "which is perceived as sad or joyful. It carries emotion." This sounds more like a biodynamic winegrower talking than it does a peddler of high-tech wine solutions.

Smith refers to the work of concert pianist Dr. Manfred Clynes, who has written a book on the subject of alpha rhythms. Clynes studied emotions and showed their shapes in paintings. "The idea that emotions have shapes is shared strongly among many people," says Smith. "The emotionality that wine carries is strongly shared." He starts with the idea of harmony and dissonance. "You don't need to be a musician to tell that something is out of tune." His idea in working with wines is to get them into a state where they are in tune and show harmony. To do this, two of the tools he uses are microoxygenation, to build structure, and reverse osmosis, to dial the alcohol down to find a point of harmony, called a "sweet spot." A portion of a particular wine is treated by reverse osmosis to produce a reduced-alcohol component, which is then blended back into the original wine to create a series of wines at closely spaced intervals of alcoholic strength. When groups of tasters go through these wines, some of them tend to stick out as working better than others: these are the sweet spots. "We do sweet spot tastings with 2,500 wines a year," says Smith, "and we never get a bell-curve distribution of preference. It's Gaussian, like tuning into radio stations." He reckons that just one in five of these alcohol-adjusted wines seems to work.

Perhaps Smith's most interesting wine project is his Roman Syrah. He makes it without any added SO_2 and claims that wines made with no added SO_2 show much greater aroma expression. Interestingly, this seems to be a common feature of wines made with low or no SO_2: they are very attractive aromatically. To make his wine, he needs to use a reductive variety, Syrah, grown in an organic vineyard that produces wines with very high phenolic content, which protects them from the big scourge of natural wines, oxidation. Here's how he describes the winemaking on his Grapecrafter blog:

To be safe, I began with a wine that could serve as its own preservative, one that would consume oxygen and oppose a microbial takeover on its own, and also a varietal type for which microbial complexity might be regarded as a plus. I decided to work with a high-altitude Syrah which had a lot of reductive strength from two sources: tannin and minerality. Raw unpolymerized tannin has the ability to gobble tremendous quantities of oxygen when wine is young. A beneficial side effect of micro-oxygenation is the creation of a rich, light structure which integrates aromas. Oxygen is the wire whisk in creating a tannin soufflé. This is going to keep the wine from smelling spoiled later on when the microbes have their party. Paradoxically, working properly with oxygen doesn't oxidize the wine—rather it increases its ability to take up more oxygen. The chemistry of phenolic polymerization is well understood, and in this case, Vern Singleton's 1986 paper on the vicinyl diphenol cascade explains why polymerizing tannins become more reactive than their precursors.

He's now made four successful vintages of this wine without SO_2. How does he control *Brettanomyces*, which is the other key threat to natural wines? "Brett is a hospital disease," maintains Smith, "caused by sanitation and German winemaking practices." He likens his work to doing integrated pest management (IPM) in the winery: "Beneficial organisms fight brett."

Smith sees winemaking as the work of a chef rather than that of a scientist. When a chef makes a sauce, she or he will know when she or he has gotten it right by feel. Smith builds structure in his reds by appropriate use of oxygen, which, when delivered at the right stage and in the right levels, assists the development of the tannins in appropriate ways. How much and when will differ from wine to wine; this is where the winemaker behaves like a chef. He notes that wines can usefully take much more oxygen before SO_2 additions than they can afterward.

FRANK CORNELISSEN AND HIS AMPHORAE

Frank Cornelissen is one of the most radical members of the natural winemaking brigade in that not only does he avoid using additives in the winery, but also he tries his best not to use any treatments at all in the vineyard. Cornelissen is a Belgian who began a new winery in 2001 on the slopes of Mount Etna in Sicily that is one of the most unusual projects in the world of wine. He began collecting wines with his father, and the first wine he bought was a mixed case of 1972 Domaine de la Romanée Conti. Despite the cost, he was hooked. Since then, "Wine has never left me," he says. Later he became a wine agent, and talking regularly with winemakers, he became interested in the rather philosophical question of what wine actually is. Over twenty years of tasting, he found that he liked wines that were an expression of culture, that were more evolved, and that expressed the soil more than the fruit. He decided that he wanted wines with a more natural approach and that he'd like to make wines without any treatments in the vineyard, winemaking, or bottling.

One day at a restaurant in Sicily someone brought out a sample of a wine from Etna. Impressed, he got in his car and drove to the winery. Liking what he saw, he rented some vineyards on Etna and made a wine in some abandoned sheds. This experience led him to buy an old ungrafted vineyard in 2001, which initiated the creation of his current venture.

Cornelissen's estate consists of 12 hectares on the north slopes of Mount Etna, of which 8.5 hectares are planted with ungrafted vines grown in the classic freestanding *alberello* (*gobelet* or bush vine) system. The rest is given over to olive trees, fruit trees, and bush. "I strive to abandon monoculture in order to avoid the classic diseases and have already intermixed the existing vineyards with various trees and plants," says Cornelissen. "The newly replanted *alberello* vineyard was planted directly, with original branches of the pre-phylloxera vines, thus without the grafted genetically engineered rootstock. I decided for a low density for the area's standard (approximately four thousand plants/hectare) to give a better ventilation and the ability to cultivate other plants and vegetables in between the vines."

The top wine is Magma, made from old Nerello Mascalese vines (fifty to eighty years) in the highest parts of the vineyard. Cornelissen describes the vinification as follows:

> The wine is produced in a noninterventionist way, fermented and aged according to ancient traditions in terracotta vases of approximately 400 litres each, buried in the ground in the cellar and fixed with ground volcanic rock. My aim is to avoid all treatments whatsoever in vineyard, orchard, and surroundings, in which I succeeded in 2001. Unfortunately I had to treat with Bordelaise mix in 2002 one time on June 20th which was, given the wet conditions an unbelievable achievement. [In 2003 another treatment was necessary, but he is proud that he didn't have to treat in the difficult years of 2004 and 2005.] I harvest relatively late between end of October and early November to obtain beautifully healthy and ripe grapes, but avoiding overripe grapes. The yields are about 300 grams per vine, realised early in the growing season by pruning very short. Every grape bunch is tailored and tails are cut away as well as unripe berries that are delicately picked out of the bunches . . . a monk's job!

The winemaking is crazy, but it works. Depending on the wine, fermentation takes place either in plastic tanks outside or in terra-cotta amphorae (known as *giarre*) buried

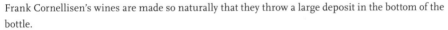

FIGURE 8.4
Frank Cornellisen's wines are made so naturally that they throw a large deposit in the bottom of the bottle.

up to their necks in crushed volcanic rock. Either way, both reds and whites have a long maceration on skins. "The skins, seeds, and nascent wine remain unseparated during the entire transformation, maintaining a cosmic link, and enabling extraction of all possible aromas of soil and territory," says Cornelissen. After fermentation, the wines are basket pressed and are then returned to amphorae for a long maturation. No additions at all are made during the winemaking process. Because no SO_2 is added, Cornelissen advises keeping the wine below 16°C during transport and storage and not decanting it.

The use of amphorae is fascinating. Cornelissen says that he traveled half the world to find the right density of clay. Amphorae allow the wine to breathe a little but don't give the tannins that wood does, nor do they alter the wine's colour. Cornelissen likes this because he doesn't want to add anything to the wine. The evaporation rate from a 400-litre amphora is about the same as from a 2,000- or 3,000-litre vat; a 250-litre amphora resembles a 1,500-litre vat, and a 100-litre amphora is close to a barrique (a standard 225-litre oak barrel). Interestingly, Cornelissen has now lined his amphorae with epoxy resin for hygeine reasons: he was experiencing elevated volatile acidity in some of the wines aged in these vessels.

Here's how Cornelissen explains the underlying motivation for his hands-off approach: "Our farming philosophy is based on our acceptance of the fact that man will never be able to understand nature's full complexity and interactions. We therefore

FIGURE 8.5
Amphorae in Portugal's Alentejo region. While those in the figure are being
used decoratively, many natural winegrowers are experimenting with
amphorae as fermentation and maturation vessels.

choose to concentrate on observing and learning the movements of Mother Earth in her
various energetic and cosmic passages and prefer to follow her indications as to what to
do, instead of deciding ourselves. Consequently, this has taken us to avoiding all possible
interventions on the land we cultivate, including any treatments, whether chemical, organic, or biodynamic, as these are all a mere reflection of the inability of man to accept
nature as she is and will be."

Most important, though, the wines are utterly compelling. They're somewhat unusual by conventional standards, but when they are judged on the basis of complexity,
interest, and length, they succeed.

Cornelissen is not the only natural winemaker to use amphorae. Also in Sicily, in Vit-
toria, COS is a biodynamic producer that uses 250- and 400-litre amphorae, buried in
the ground, for fermenting and maturing its red wines. The wines are brilliant. Perhaps
the most famous proponent of amphorae is Josko Gravner in Friuli, on the border with
Slovenia. He has been using amphorae exclusively for all his wines since 2001. Gravner
trucks his amphorae in from Georgia, the only place that can still make clay amphorae
of the required dimensions. After lengthy maceration of these white wines in amphorae,
the wines are pressed into large oak casks to finish their maturation. This region is the
birthplace of the "orange wine" movement, which is a group of producers who make
white wines using extended maceration, just as they might for reds. These wines have
tannins, which isn't usual in whites. And while they are made in an oxidative style, most

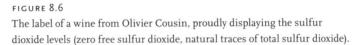

FIGURE 8.6

The label of a wine from Olivier Cousin, proudly displaying the sulfur
dioxide levels (zero free sulfur dioxide, natural traces of total sulfur dioxide).

are far from oxidized, even though the colour might seem to indicate otherwise. Orange
wines are now made in many regions, although this remains very much a small, niche
movement.

There's an inherent danger in discussing natural wine. If naturalness itself, however
it is defined, is seen as the goal, wine quality can be excluded. Is a poorly made but
thoroughly natural wine of any merit? Hard-core natural winemakers would likely suggest that no matter how good or enjoyable a wine is, if it is not honest (in the sense of being naturally made), then it is not valid—there is no real quality to it. But we feel that if
natural wine is ever to become more than a tiny niche product, it has to stand on its own
feet in terms of quality. The good news seems to be that as winemakers begin to question their methods and work more naturally, wine quality seems to improve—at least,
in interest and complexity. There need not be any trade-off of quality for naturalness.

Winemakers and salesmen of natural wines looking to broaden their reach and improve sales and profitability for their own enterprises also need to consider the difficult
question of just how important naturalness is to consumers at large. There is no question that this counterculture that is fighting to keep naturalness alive in winegrowing
has extremely good intentions, but producers who don't exhibit sensitivity to different
consumers' needs and interests (outside their own biased agenda) risk isolating a portion of the market if they choose to use extreme language in their marketing efforts.
It's a fact that not all consumers are interested in the naturalness of wine, and many of
these consumers do not appreciate having a passionate natural wine producer's beliefs
forced on them. The only way to get the message across to resistant consumers is by
talking a language that relates directly to how the wine stacks up in the glass. "Natural

wine is better-quality, more interesting wine" is a much stronger message to the majority of today's consumers than "Natural wine is better for the planet." We believe that there are plenty of natural wines on the market that confirm that with the right level of attention to detail and intervention when needed, natural wine can always be better-quality, more interesting wine. It is necessary to keep the ego in check, consider what the consumer actually wants, and do everything possible to achieve that, even if it means moving slightly closer to the centre of the continuum.

But making wine in ways that are considered natural does bring risks. If you reduce or eliminate your usage of SO_2, then you are increasing the risks of unwanted microbial action and oxidation. This raises the questions: Can winemaking problems, normally considered to be wine faults, ever be acceptable or even beneficial? And do we have too restrictive a view of wine, where we see even the slightest hint of *Brettanomyces* or volatile acidity as a fault? We examine these questions in Chapter 11.

While we are keen observers of the natural wine scene and enjoy many of the wines, we dislike the division between such "natural" wines and other wines, which by implication are therefore not natural. A dogma is springing up that natural wines must be made without any SO_2 until bottling, with indigenous yeasts carrying out fermentation, and without any other additions or manipulations save for a traditional *élevage* in the barrel. But there are degrees of naturalness in winemaking, and to limit the term *natural* to wines made in this strict manner would be unfortunate. It can be argued that wine is, in essence, a pretty natural product. Even "industrial" wines are natural in that they are simply grapes that have been crushed and fermented, with a tightly controlled set of permitted additions (none of which are flavourants). This eschewing of flavourants sets wine apart from other alcoholic beverages. To make a very strict category and then restrict the use of the term *natural* to wines in that category would hinder efforts to encourage other winemakers—including the larger companies—to work more naturally.

9

YEASTS, WILD AND CULTURED

Have you ever tasted freshly crushed grape juice? It doesn't taste much like wine. Even grape juice from the world's most famous vineyards still tastes like grape juice: it bears little relationship to the complex, thought-provoking, and sometimes very expensive liquid that it will become by the time it is bottled.

Yeasts are the primary agent of this transformation from sweet fruity juice to final wine. These unicellular microscopic fungi are responsible for alcoholic fermentation. As well as transforming the sugar in the grape must into alcohol and carbon dioxide, the complex chemistry that occurs during fermentation also involves the formation of myriad flavour molecules from precursors present in the must. Figures widely quoted suggest that of the estimated eight hundred or so volatile flavour compounds found in wine, at least four hundred are produced by yeasts. Whether or not these figures are based on actual measurements or are just an educated guess, the big picture is clear: without yeasts we wouldn't have wine.

From the earliest days of winemaking, some nine thousand years ago, until the middle of the nineteenth century (fairly recently in the winemaking timescale), the fermentation process was deeply mysterious. It was only 150 years ago that Louis Pasteur finally proved that yeasts were the agent of this change, and it wasn't until the 1970s that cultured strains of yeasts, selected from nature, were routinely used in winemaking.

Despite the importance of yeasts in moulding the flavour of wine, the literature on wine devotes remarkably little attention to them. While consumer wine magazines regularly focus on the grapevine, vineyard characteristics, and different grape varieties, they

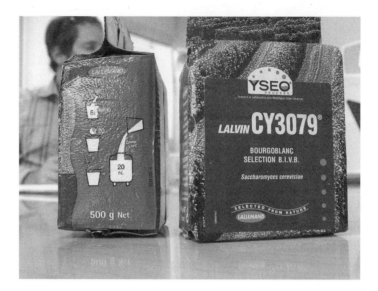

FIGURE 9.1
Packets of cultured yeasts, used by many winemakers.

virtually never touch on the microbiology of fermentation and the different species and strains of yeasts, even though these microbes are responsible for a large part of the way wine tastes and smells. That's partly because vines and grapes are easy for us to understand because we can see them. If yeasts were large enough that we could discern their characteristics with the naked eye, we'd read a lot more about them. Yeasts, along with other microbes, are hard for us visually dominated humans to get a handle on because of their microscopic size, but if we want to have a proper perspective on winemaking, we need to give them more attention. Perhaps we should imagine that fermentation vats are the size of a modest lake, and yeast cells are the size of a regular potato, but capable of growing rapidly and dividing every half hour or so. Suddenly they don't seem so abstract.

"NATURAL" FERMENTATION

Let's stretch our potato analogy to try to illustrate the "natural" fermentation process. Imagine that the composition of the lake can vary, and that rather than one type of potato, we have literally dozens, each type with subtly different growing abilities (and conveniently colour coded). Initially, the lake has just a few of each type of potato bobbing around, and an occasional potato plops in from the sky. Its surface is largely calm. Then, within twenty-four hours, these potatoes begin to grow and divide quickly. Within a short time the lake is bubbling with rapidly multiplying potatoes, feeding off the contents of the lake and in turn releasing their waste products (the word *fermentation* derives from the Latin verb meaning "to boil"). There may be as many as 5 million yeast cells in each drop of fermenting grape juice.

At first, the red, green, and yellow potatoes thrive in this seething fermentation, but within a few days blue potatoes start appearing. The nonblues die and fall to the bottom, and the blues take over, continuing their individual cycles of growth, multiplication, and death. After a couple of weeks things start to calm down, and most of the potatoes have sunk to the bottom of the lake and have formed a thick carpet of dead and dying spuds that continue to exude their contents into the water. However, a number of potatoes of different colours are still floating around in a semidormant state. It's as if they are waiting for things to change, hanging around in case there's some action.

Like the potatoes of this analogy, yeasts and bacteria are always present in the winery environment. Even in what appears to be a spotlessly clean cellar there will always be some receptive surface, such as a soldered joint in a stainless steel tank or a small crack, where microbes can hide. Barrels are a particularly good habitat for fugitive microbes because the structure of wood means that, in practice, it is almost impossible to sterilize them. Because a potential source of inoculation is nearly ubiquitous, yeasts and bacteria need only the right conditions to begin to grow. Grape must is a sugar- and nutrient-rich medium that is ideal for the growth of certain microbes, although because of its initially high sugar content, it does present them with the challenge of osmotic stress. As it ferments, it changes, and its suitability for one species or strain wanes as its suitability for another develops. This is an important concept: create the right conditions, and you can select for the population of organisms that you want to be growing at that particular time. Winemakers tend to concentrate on eradicating rogue organisms from the winery. This is a good idea, but at the same they have to make sure that the musts they are working with give a competitive advantage to the sorts of organisms they'd like to see growing.

Still, cleanliness is an important issue. There is a numbers game: the size of the inoculum (how many yeasts and bacteria are present initially) is an important factor in determining whether an infection will be a problem. It matters who gets in first—the microbes you want to be growing there or those you don't. A related issue is ensuring healthy fermentation. Yeasts require a nitrogen source and adequate oxygen, as well as a range of micronutrients. If these aren't present, then the result is a struggling or stuck fermentation. Struggling yeasts frequently produce sulfur compounds that can later cause reduction problems in the wine. Also, some yeasts affect the way in which other yeasts grow. For example, some yeast strains secrete what are known as killer factors that inhibit the growth of other strains.

Yeasts are also widespread in vineyards. They spend the winter in the upper layers of the soil or in the bark of trees and spread to the vines during the growing season via aerial transmission and insect transfer. They colonize grape skins during the maturation phase, although they never reach very high levels on intact grapes. Contrary to popular opinion, the bloom on the surface of grape skins isn't made up of yeast populations, but rather a waxlike scaly material that doesn't harbour many fungi.

Only a limited number of yeast species are present in significant quantities on grapes, the so-called native yeast populations. These include *Rhodotorula*, the apiculate yeasts *Kloeckera apiculata* and its soporiferous form *Hanseniaspora uvarum* (the most common by far), and lesser amounts of *Metschnikowia pulcherrima*, *Candida famata*, *Candida stellata*, *Pichia membranefaciens*, *Pichia fermentans*, and *Hansenula anomala*. Potential spoilage organisms such as *Brettanomyces* may also be present. It needs to be added that yeast nomenclature is rather confusing, with various names used for the same species. This isn't surprising, because until the recent development of molecular methods for typing yeast strains and species, it was rather hard to tell them apart. Unlike the potatoes in the analogy, yeasts aren't neatly colour coded.

One interesting observation is that the main wine yeast, the alcohol-tolerant *Saccharomyces cerevisiae*, is relatively rare in nature. This is something that is not widely appreciated by winemakers adverse to inoculation. Attempts to culture *S. cerevisiae* from the skins of grapes have proved unsuccessful. The only way its presence can be demonstrated is by placing grape samples in sterile bags, crushing them under aseptic conditions, and seeing what happens, an experiment that has been done in Bordeaux. At midfermentation, *S. cerevisiae*, which is undetectable on grape skins, represents almost all the yeasts isolated. In a few cases no *S. cerevisiae* is present, and apiculate yeasts do the entire fermentation.

WILD YEAST POPULATIONS

The early stages of "wild" (uninoculated) fermentations are typically dominated by around ten yeast species, the most important of which are *Kloeckera*, *Hanseniaspora*, and *Candida*. As the alcohol levels rise a little, these players bow out, and others, such as *Cryptococcus*, *Kluyveromyces*, *Metschnikowia*, and *Pichia*, step in to take their turn. It has been estimated that in an uninoculated fermentation as many as twenty to thirty strains can participate. But when alcohol levels reach 4 to 6 percent, the native species can't cope with the hostile conditions, and *S. cerevisiae* takes things from here. So the key difference between natural fermentations and those carried out by cultured yeast inoculations is in the early stages of fermentation.

There are complications, however. Most winemakers add some sulfur dioxide (SO_2) on crushing to reduce the risk of oxidation and also to kill off rogue microbes. This gives *S. cerevisiae* and the more robust native species an advantage and eliminates some of the less desirable wild yeasts and spoilage bacteria, which tend to be more sensitive to the microbicidal actions of SO_2. Temperature also affects the balance of yeast species in the fermentation. Cooler temperatures (below 14°C) favour wild yeasts such as *Kloeckera*, whereas higher temperatures aid *S. cerevisiae*.

Aside from the actual properties of the wild yeasts, spontaneous fermentations delay the onset of vigorous fermentation. In red wines this delay allows oxygen to react with anthocyanins and other phenolics present in the must, enhancing colour stability and accelerating phenolic polymerization. This enhanced exposure to oxygen before vigorous fermentation is under way could have important flavour and textural effects on the wine thus produced, quite separately from the characteristics contributed by the diverse set of wild yeasts carrying out the fermentation.

New Zealand–based yeast researcher Matthew Goddard has shown that in a natural ferment, *S. cerevisiae* engineers its environment to give itself a competitive advantage through the production of alcohol and heat. Fermentation of sugars is actually less energetically favourable than respiration of these sugars (which requires oxygen), but even in the presence of oxygen *S. cerevisiae* will still ferment these sugars and produce alcohol in the process. Goddard speculates that because *S. cerevisiae* is a specialist at consuming ripe fruits, it chooses to make ethanol to protect this valuable food resource. The ethanol acts as an antimicrobial, reducing competition, and also deters most vertebrates. Thus *S. cerevisiae* is choosing a less efficient pathway that you'd have expected evolution to eliminate unless there was some collateral benefit. This production of ethanol is therefore an example of niche construction (that is, an organism's behavior fashioning for itself an ecological niche). In his experiments, which involved natural fermentations of Kumeu River Chardonnay fruit that had been treated with a small dose of SO_2 at crushing, he found nine species of yeast taking part in the fermentation. At day one, *S. cerevisiae* wasn't present, but by day eleven it was the dominant species.

WILD VERSUS CULTURED YEASTS

An ideological divide exists between those winemakers who advocate natural fermentations and those who choose to use cultured yeasts, although many winemakers sit somewhere in the middle. At one pole, we have the likes of biodynamics guru Nicolas Joly, who maintains that "re-yeasting is absurd." At the other, there are many who share the views of yeast researcher Sakkie Pretorius (currently director of the Australian Wine Research Institute), who describes the risks involved with wild yeast ferments as "staggering." Estimates (which can only be approximate) are that worldwide, around 80 percent of fermentations are natural, and 20 percent use cultured yeasts, with the latter gaining ground. This pattern loosely follows an Old World–New World divide, with the former largely preferring to use indigenous yeasts and the latter relying on cultured strains, although this split is far from absolute.

Let's examine Pretorius's position first. There are three arguments against allowing natural fermentations. The first is risk. Because the initial inoculum of yeasts from the winery environment and grape skins is quite low, fermentation can take a while to get going. This introduces an element of risk: if bugs such as *Acetobacter* (the acetic acid bacterium that turns wine to vinegar) establish themselves before the fermentative yeast species, then the wine will be at risk of spoilage. Also, there's no guarantee that the native yeasts that establish themselves will do a good job. Like *S. cerevisiae*, all the various native yeasts exist in many different strains, some desirable, others not. In a spontaneous fermentation you take what you are given.

The second objection some winemakers make is that very few "wild" fermentations are actually wild. As harvest gets under way, the winery equipment is a ready source of inoculum, and fermentations get going a lot faster, with *S. cerevisiae* establishing itself sooner. Some studies have shown that after a few days of harvest operations, half of the yeast species isolated from the first pumping over of a spontaneously fermented red grape tank is *S. cerevisiae*. If commercial yeast strains have ever been used in a winery, there is the strong possibility that the strain of *S. cerevisiae* involved is actually a commercial strain.

The third objection is that winemakers who choose spontaneous fermentations lose an important element of control over wine style and quality. Cultured yeast strains allow winemakers to control the fermentation process and to avoid the risks of high volatile acidity or funky flavours that wild ferments can produce. If you are in charge of large quantities of someone else's wine, it's understandable that you'd want to play it safe. This is becoming a greater concern with increasing sugar levels in harvested fruit, which then result in higher levels of alcohol in the latter stages of fermentation. This raises the risk of stuck fermentations, higher levels of volatile acidity, and residual sugar in the wine at the end of fermentation. Cultured yeast strains with specific properties can also be chosen to complement the wine style being made. For example, specific cultured yeast strains are an important contributor to the highly successful New Zealand style of Sauvignon Blanc because they are able to convert the thiol precursors in the must in an efficient way. These polyfunctional thiols have recently been shown to be key to the attractive passionfruit, grapefruit, and boxtree aromas of the Marlborough Sauvignon Blanc style.

Now let us examine Joly's position. Why do winegrowers take the risk of a spontaneous wine fermentation? In many cases the motivation is ideological. Many winegrowers see natural yeasts as part of the terroir. "Natural yeast is marked by all the subtleties of the year. If you have been dumb enough to kill your yeast, you have lost something from that year," says Nicolas Joly. The use of wild yeasts is a fundamental principle of those who see naturalness as an important property of wine that separates it from "manufactured" drinks such as beer and spirits.

Others do it for quality reasons: they think that native yeasts produce wines with a fuller, rounder palate structure, higher in glycerol and other polyols, and that the fermentations tend to be slower and cooler, burning off fewer aromatics. Wines made with wild ferments are often richer textured and have more complexity. There is also a cost saving: cultured yeast has to be paid for.

Some of the risk associated with the slow start of natural fermentations can be offset by getting a starter culture (known in France as a *pied de cuve*) a few days before the start of harvest. This can then be used to kick-start fermentation. However, if the starter culture has been going for too long, then the dominant yeast will be *S. cerevisiae*, and some of the benefit of the diverse wild yeasts that thrive only at low alcohol levels found early

FIGURE 9.2
Spaghetti-like strands of yeast undergoing the drying process.

in fermentation will be lost. In addition, once a winery is well into vintage, there will be so many yeasts in the winery environment that they will likely work as the chief inoculum, and a true wild fermentation may not be possible.

ARE ALL WINEMAKING YEASTS ARTIFICIAL?

South African researcher Florian Bauer suggested a provocative thought at "Yeast's Contribution to the Sensory Profile of Wine," a symposium held in La Rioja, Spain (27–28 April 2005). Could all fermentations be artificial in the sense that the alcohol-tolerant *S. cerevisiae* doesn't occur naturally, but has evolved to fit an artificial niche created by the practice of winemaking? From archaeological records we know that winemaking is an ancient biotechnology dating back nine thousand years, and that wine yeast was the first domesticated microorganism. The activities of these early winemakers provided an artificial, rather hostile ecological niche by creating an environment high in sugar and acid that then changed to one of lower sugar levels, low oxygen, and relatively high alcohol levels. This winemaking environment would have provided significant selective pressure that could have led to evolutionary adaptations that resulted in today's wine yeast.

As we've already noted, very few commercially used *S. cerevisiae* strains can be found isolated in vineyards, even where these vineyards are close to wineries that are full of yeasts. This suggests that yeast strains are not well adapted to other "natural" environments. The implications? *S. cerevisiae* could be a domesticated, nonnatural yeast that evolved in conjunction with human activity. This conclusion is supported by the work of Alsace-based researcher Jean-Luc Legras and colleagues. He analysed twelve sections of DNA known as microsatellite loci from four hundred strains of *S. cerevisiae* isolated from around the globe and found evidence of a common origin for these strains. The conclusion? *S. cerevisiae* has likely spread around the world along with the grapevine *Vitis vinifera*.

Attractive as this theory sounds, others strongly disagree. As we've already mentioned, researcher Mat Goddard has proposed the theory that alcohol production by fermentation is an example of niche protection by yeasts—even though it is less energy efficient than respiration (the other way of breaking sugars down to get energy), the yeasts "choose" to do it to protect their food resource of rotting fruit. "*S. cerevisiae* as a species has been around some 80 million years, which is long before humans ever appeared on the planet," says Goddard. "Its ability to preferentially invade high sugar niches such as fruits has been around since fruits evolved. In fact, we think that *S. cerevisiae* evolved to inhabit the fruit niche once it appeared. This ability to ferment even in the presence of oxygen is an evolutionary adaptation to kill off other microbial competitors. It kicks out ethanol, carbon dioxide, and heat in the fruit to toxify the environment and create a selective advantage for itself." Goddard emphasiszes, "The statement that *S. cerevisiae* is a domesticated species created by humans is blatantly wrong. Within the species there are many different strains, and certainly select strains thirty or forty years ago were plucked from vineyards and other places and have been developed in labs for commercial products. They are arguably domesticated because the select variants have been enhanced in some way, but the species as a whole certainly isn't domesticated. Only recently have we had the genetic tools to be able to differentiate between these different strains. We use exactly the same technique that is used in forensic criminology situations—genetic fingerprinting—to distinguish different strains of *S. cerevisiae*. This affords us a powerful insight into the variation and relatedness of different strains that we have isolated from different areas."

Goddard has done some interesting work in West Auckland, New Zealand, in which he found different strains that were unique to that place. Significantly, they weren't related to commercial isolates. It wasn't that fermentation had taken place and that the yeasts had then been distributed back into the vineyard; these were yeasts that were present in that locale. "As you know, for a long time there has been the impression that this is not the case," he explains. "The impression in the industry has been that *S. cerevisiae* doesn't live in the natural environment; it only inhabits wineries, and that these are escaped domestic/commercial strains." His work points to yeast strains present in the vineyard as being a legitimate part of terroir.

A THIRD WAY

Is it possible to argue for a middle ground between those who see cultured yeasts as a vital winemaking tool and those who see wild yeasts as part of the terroir? In this context the term *terroir* might be unhelpful because to some it carries a supplementary meaning that it's the hand of nature and not the hand of the winemaker that is responsible for wine quality. There is an issue of agency. Many advocates of terroir deliberately downplay the role of the winemaker, even to the point of denying that humans have anything useful to contribute to wine quality. However, we feel that definitions of terroir should not exclude the human element, which preserves the all-important concept of "sense of place" while acknowledging that the winemaker is an important partner in the process of realizing the potential of the grapes that are brought into the cellar. It can be argued that proponents of this expanded definition of terroir can in fact do more as guardians of the wonderful diversity of wine styles seen around the world that have as their origin local characteristics. They can do so because they are not constrained by an ideology that refuses to acknowledge that their decisions in the cellar can do anything useful to bring out the sense of place in a wine. Subscribing to this inclusive terroir definition allows winemakers to use cultured yeasts (many of which were initially isolated from particular vineyards within the region in which these winemakers are operating) with the aim of enhancing or, perhaps less controversially, bringing out the typicity—for example, making a Puligny Montrachet that tastes more like a Puligny.

Indeed, yeast companies like to call their products "selected natural yeasts" to emphasize that they are not dreamed up in a laboratory but rather are isolated from nature, much as a farmer might store up seed from one season to use in the next. Admittedly, the same yeast companies don't help themselves by the way they frequently advertise these yeasts for sale, with lists of specific aromas and qualities that each strain will give to a wine in a very recipe-like fashion. But surely here the issue is one of intent. Is the winemaker aiming to make an honest wine expressive of its place or origin, or a spoofy wine with flavours engineered to appeal to consumer palates?

An interesting development is that yeast companies and researchers have been looking for a way to increase the complexity of inoculated fermentations by working on coinoculations and also cultured "wild" non-*Saccharomyces* yeasts. The difficulty with non-*Saccharomyces* yeasts is that they are very hard to culture, whereas different strains of *S. cerevisiae* are relatively easy to culture. However, progress is being made, and these products are already on the market. This would be of great interest to winemakers who would like to have a degree of control over the outcome of their ferments, but who would love to work with the added complexity and/or intensity that natural ferments bring.

So far, the number of available cultured non-*Saccharomyces* yeasts is limited. The yeast company Lallemand has a strong research program on the aromatic potential of non-*Saccharomyces* yeasts, combined with optimization of the production of these yeasts in dry form. This allows winemakers to take advantage of fermenting with non-*Saccharomyces* wine yeasts while maintaining control over the fermentation process. The yeast *Torulaspora delbrueckii* strain 291 is now available to winemakers in combination with specific *Saccharomyces* yeasts in sequential inoculation, which results in wines with a distinct sensory profile and mouth feel. Other yeasts are also being investigated, such as *Hanseniospora orientalis, Schizosaccharomyces pombe, Metschnikowia pulcherrima, Hansenula anomala, Candida stellata, Pichia anomala,* and *Kluyveromyces wickerhamii* to control the development of *Brettanomyces* yeast through their production of specific compounds. All those non-*Saccharomyces* yeasts are found in the natural flora of vineyards and wineries, like cultured *S. cerevisiae* used for alcoholic fermentation. CHR Hansen, another yeast company, has a reasonably broad portfolio of non-*Saccharomyces* products. Prelude is a single-species culture of *Torulaspora delbrueckii*, and the company also offers blends. Melody and Harmony are both blends of *Kluyveromyces thermotolerans, Torulaspora delbrueckii,* and a strain of *S. cerevisiae*. Rhythm and Symphony are both blends of *Kluyveromyces thermotolerans* and *S. cerevisiae*.

Work is also ongoing on carrying out malolactic fermentation at the same time as alcoholic fermentation by coinoculating with both *Oenococcus oeni* and *S. cerevisiae*. If this could be done successfully it could be of interest, because not only would it shorten the whole fermentation process for wines where malolactic fermentation is desirable, but also it would remove the key *Brettanomyces* risk period for red wines between the completion of alcoholic fermentation and the onset of malolactic fermentation. This is risky because SO$_2$ levels must be kept low so as not to inhibit malolactic fermentation.

While this may not seem to be relevant to extreme natural winemaking, it is important for more commercial winemaking where reducing risk of problems in this way can reduce the need for inputs or manipulations later in the winemaking process. For those interested in working more naturally but constrained by commercial considerations or risk-adverse management structures, this is an important discussion.

A BREWING STORM: GENETICALLY MODIFIED YEAST STRAINS

Finally, we'd like to touch on possibly the most controversial issue surrounding wine yeasts—the use of genetically modified (GM) yeasts in winemaking. Plenty of these yeasts already exist, but they haven't previously been commercialized because of the negative reactions of consumers to GM food products, which don't seem to be budging much.

Now, however, a GM yeast strain called ML01 has been commercialized and is authorized for use in the United States. This yeast, made by Springer Oenologie, has two extra genes (a malate transporter gene from *Schizosaccharomyces pombe* [another yeast] and the malolactic enzyme gene from *Oenococcus oeni* [a bacterium]) that allow it to carry out malolactic fermentation (normally done by bacteria after alcoholic fermentation has been completed) at the same time as alcoholic fermentation. Concurrent malolactic and alcoholic fermentations have several advantages, one of which is that the resulting wine is less likely to contain biogenic amines that are produced by bacterial malolactic fermentation. In the United States, yeasts are classified as processing agents, and thus wines made with this yeast would need no declaration that they contained GM ingredients. In many other countries, such as New Zealand and Australia, the regulations are more stringent. There are also other commercially available yeast strains made through genetic engineering technology, but which are not officially classified as GM yeasts. These are a series of strains produced by a company called Phyterra and are engineered to reduce production of ethyl carbamate and hydrogen sulfide. Phyterra is able to claim their yeasts are not genetically modified because their technology involves a reshuffling of genetic material within the yeast, rather than introducing genes from outside.

Is anyone making wine using GM yeast? Yes, but those who are doing so aren't telling anyone, for understandable reasons. In response, the Australian Wine Research Institute has issued a statement declaring that no GM yeasts will be used in Australian wine for the foreseeable future. But because GM technology can much more easily produce yeasts with desirable properties than conventional breeding (and there are some traits that conventional breeding cannot select for), research continues apace globally on GM yeast technology. This technology seems at odds with wine's image as a natural product, but its supporters argue that what they are doing is not creating fake wines, but unlocking the latent flavour and aroma potential of grape must by using yeasts with special properties. One yeast researcher has even gone on record as stating that the best wines are yet to come. However, many scientists favour a cautious approach. If GM yeasts become widespread, the danger is that wine will be seen as just another manufactured beverage. If we kill the "naturalness" of wine, we run the risk of destroying the whole venture.

CAN NATURAL WINE BE MADE WITH CULTURED YEASTS?

One of the tenets of the natural wine movement is that fermentation should be carried out by means of the natural yeasts present in the vineyard and winery, and that cultured yeasts should not be used. Is this a fair and logical stipulation? As we have discussed here, it could be argued that the use of selected natural yeasts that are then cultured and sold, just as seeds are kept for the next harvest by farmers and agricultural companies, is not necessarily at odds with a natural winemaking approach. If we can accept that winemaking is a partnership between humans and nature in which winemakers have a very important role to play, then giving skilled winemakers an extra level of control by allowing them to choose which yeasts to use to conduct fermentation could lead to wines that are better expressions of their site than those whose fermentation is left to chance.

The assertion that cultured yeasts are an artificial creation seems somewhat alarmist. Calling them "industrial yeasts" and implying that all winemakers who use them are choosing them with a view to faking their wines with yeasts designed to produce specific flavour compounds is unfair. The reality is more complex than this.

A more pragmatic and less dogmatic approach to the question whether the use of cultured yeasts is acceptable for natural wines is indicated by the realization that the yeasts participating in a natural ferment are not necessarily those present on the grapes in the vineyard. While some believe that the natural yeast population is part of the terroir, others equally committed to the notion of terroir disagree with this assertion.

As a consequence, we argue for a broader view of natural wine that allows the use of cultured yeasts selected from nature where winemakers make this choice with a view to making wines that are more representative of their origin than might otherwise have resulted if fermentation was left to chance. This should become an especially attractive proposition when cultured non-*Saccharomyces* yeasts become available. At the same time, we also applaud winemakers who are able to achieve excellent results without any inoculation. We support the slightly heretical view that in some cases fermentations involving yeast technology can enhance the diversity of wine, and in some cases make wines that more faithfully reflect their terroirs, noting that in some cases wild ferments contain elevated levels of aromatic chemicals such as volatile sulfur compounds that can obscure terroir. The proof is in the wine.

MALOLACTIC FERMENTATION

We recognize that this chapter is all about yeasts, but we also feel that it's worth discussing briefly the process of malolactic fermentation (MLF) because this is a vital process in the production of the majority of wines made today. It is a secondary fermentation carried out by bacteria, as opposed to yeasts, and it is called malolactic because one of the things these bacteria do is convert malic to lactic acid. Almost all red wines need to go through MLF, chiefly for microbiological stability (i.e. to avoid an uncontrolled fermentation at a later stage in bottle that can destroy the wine). In addition, many white wines and sparkling wines go through MLF—in fact, more than many wine professionals might appreciate. It's not just your reds and your big rich chardonnay styles that rely on what is commonly known as "the secondary fermentation." Producers in cooler regions such as Germany, the Loire Valley, Alsace, Champagne, and Austria, among others, embrace partial or even full MLF to gain a "natural" reduction in total acidity, which results in textural balance and improved complexity.

During MLF many other compounds known as secondary metabolites are produced. The two most well known of these are ethyl lactate and diacetyl. These secondary metabolites can undoubtedly improve the complexity and the quality of the wine, but they can also impair wine quality if there is a lack of balance/harmony with other aromas in the wine. Common descriptors used by winemakers to describe the impact MLF can have are as follows: "smoky," "spicy," "reminiscent of dried fruits," "more body," "enhanced tannins," and "better length." It's no secret that winemakers tend to think of yeast as being far more important than bacteria in their respective fermentations. With this in mind, we feel that winemakers around the world (irrespective of how natural they are) need to take MLF a lot more seriously. Another perceived benefit from spontaneous MLFs as compared to inoculated MLFs is that the final wine is likely to have a lower total SO_2. Half a year without SO_2 can be great for wine, but it can also be its downfall, leading to oxidation, rogue microbial activity, and an array of faults. If however, the impact of these negative factors is limited during this extended MLF (and it is possible), the resulting wine can show better color, more ample texture, and a more vibrant aromatic profile. There's a lot to gain, but even more to lose if a winemaker doesn't look closely at MLF and the various management techniques at his or her disposal. As stated above, we believe that spontaneous MLF can sometimes improve complexity, but we also feel that there are a lot of risks (both sensory and economic) that need to be considered before confirming an MLF strategy.

During spontaneous MLF carried out by indigenous *Lactobacillus* and *Pediococcus*, wine quality can be damaged. In particular, excessive volatile acidity or diacetyl can be formed. These compounds will not only mask the primary flavors in the wine and interfere with site expression/terroir, but also at certain levels they are considered a fault. Most winemakers try to avoid acetic acid production as it can provide a prickly quality on the bouquet while also adding to sourness. Diacetyl is less clear-cut and many believe that at low levels (in the right wine style) a small amount of its buttery expression can be quite appealing. At higher concentrations diacetyl becomes less attractive because it comes across as nutty and caramelized.

As is the case with spontaneous "primary" fermentations, one of the big problems associated with spontaneous MLFs is that they can take a long time to complete. During this extended period without high free SO_2, other microorganisms (in particular *Brettanomyces*, addressed in detail in Chapter 11), can flourish producing volatile phenols, among other compounds, that at excessive levels can significantly impair wine quality. It's clear from our research in writing this book that many winemakers have experienced difficulties in the form of slow or stuck ferments trying to get their wine through MLF (even when they inoculate with a commercial strain), so these problems are certainly not restricted to winemakers taking the spontaneous path. One thing is clear however, slow/stuck MLFs seem to be more of an issue with spontaneous fermentations. The problem rests with inadequate MLF management. A key factor aiding an efficient and healthy MLF is selecting the right inoculum for the wine: one that is comfortable with the pH and one that is compatible with the yeast strain chosen for primary fermentation. It's certainly not impossible to get good results with spontaneous MLF, but it's a lot more difficult than using an inoculum. For those who are using inoculum with mixed results, our suggestion is they talk to their bacteria producers to see where they're going wrong. Quite aside from the cost, if you are using inoculum then you should make sure you are giving yourself the best chance of success.

Aside from quality, there's another issue to consider: health. The scientific literature confirms that uncontrolled growth of microorganisms can generate harmful secondary compounds, such as biogenic amines (histamine, putrescine, cadaverine), that are not only allergens, but can also have a negative impact on the sensory profile. Research also shows that potentially carcinogenic compounds such as ethyl carbamate and ochratoxin A can also be produced at higher levels in spontaneous MLFs. This may be a factor to consider in choosing whether or not to allow a natural MLF.

10

RIPENESS AND ALCOHOL LEVELS

International fine wine consumers are tiring of the high alcohol, sweet flavoured "terroirless" red wines made from superripe grapes and especially made from Shiraz and from Australia. Consumers are rapidly becoming more sophisticated and discriminating and are seeking out savoury wines of finesse and complexity where the flavours are related to the terroir or place of origin and faithful to the story of the wine.

BRIAN CROSER, FEBRUARY 2010

One of the themes of this book is that wines made as naturally as possible tend to be more expressive of their origins. When winemakers work with a light hand, wines have the potential to show a sense of place. Conversely, too much intervention in the winery can obscure the varietal and regional origin of a wine. Examples of this are the use of too much new oak and overextraction. But one of the chief ways in which varietal/regional character—terroir, if you will—can be lost is poor work in the vineyard.

If grapes are in poor hygienic condition or are picked in an unripe state, or yields are too high (leading to dilute wines with less concentrated flavours), wine quality suffers. Perhaps a more pervasive problem for high-end wines, however, is the current trend to pick ever later, leaving the grapes on the vine until they are superripe. Leaving the grapes on the vine for extended periods is often referred to as extra "hang time," and the consequence of this practice is that the resulting wines display a very sweet, fruity, lush profile tending towards jamminess, as well as very high alcohol levels. Such wines require substantial tartaric acid additions early in the winemaking process and in some cases undergo later manipulations to reduce alcohol levels.

The general trend of rising alcohol levels worldwide has been well documented in both New World and Old World wine regions. This trend is likely to be due to several factors, including the demonstrable climate change (specifically, a warming trend) that has occurred in wine regions across the globe over the past fifty years. But a key factor has undoubtedly been changing attitudes towards what constitutes ripeness, allied with conscious decisions to pick grapes later. Of course, picking too early is equally detrimental to quality, and in this context, delaying harvest a little—sometimes a decision allied to a fair degree of risk—can be a vital step in getting an extra bit of quality. But the chief problem with ambitious wines these days seems to be that they are made from grapes picked too late.

In this chapter we'll be looking at these topical issues: What are the consequences of high levels of ripeness? Do growers really need to pick so late that they then have to practice highly interventionist winemaking to compensate? What is the chief problem with high alcohol levels, and what can be done in the vineyard and the winery to counter this problem?

THE GRAPE-RIPENING PROCESS

The vine produces grapes in order to reproduce itself sexually. The grape itself is designed to be appealing to birds, and the vine sacrifices some of its resources in order to make it worthwhile for the birds to eat the grapes and thus disperse the seeds over a wide area, with a dollop of fertilizer. After successful flowering and completion of the vine's sex act, berry development begins. The berries are initially hard and green, camouflaged and rendered unpalatable by bitter-tasting tannins and green-tasting methoxypyrazines, as well as high acid levels. As ripening progresses, sugars begin to accumulate, acid and methoxypyrazine levels fall, and the tannins begin to rearrange themselves chemically such that they taste less astringent. The eventual result is a deliciously sweet, colourful berry that birds find hard to resist. (Recent research shows that initially all grapes would have been "red" grapes, that is, blue black in colour; white grapes are the consequence of a mutation that probably occurred after grapevine domestication.)

In the natural environment of the grapevine these changes are timed such that the grapes become palatable to birds when the seeds are ready for dispersal, and a visual indicator is provided by the change in colour from green to reddish black. (Another aside is needed here. We're talking here of red varieties, but our discussion applies in some degree also to whites. However, certain characteristics of grapes that are less than fully ripe, such as greenness or herbaceousness, work quite well in some white styles. Bear in mind that most white wines are made with very little skin contact, and thus the tannins in the grape skins aren't going to influence flavour very much.)

But if you were to make a red wine from grapes when they reached the stage at which birds like to eat them, it wouldn't taste very nice. The acidity would be too high; the grapes, while tasting sweet, wouldn't have enough sugar to achieve desired levels of alcohol; and the tannins would taste distinctly "green" and astringent. We would certainly choose to let the grapes ripen longer on the vine so that quality wine production would be possible. We're fussier than the birds. The key issue is how much longer.

It is common to divide the grape-ripening process into sugar ripeness and physiological ripeness (also referred to as phenolic or flavour ripeness). The highest goal of

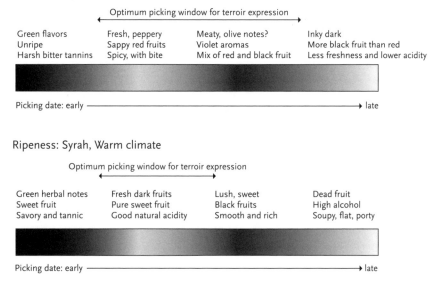

Ripeness: Syrah, Cool climate

Optimum picking window for terroir expression

Green flavors	Fresh, peppery	Meaty, olive notes?	Inky dark
Unripe	Sappy red fruits	Violet aromas	More black fruit than red
Harsh bitter tannins	Spicy, with bite	Mix of red and black fruit	Less freshness and lower acidity

Picking date: early ⟶ late

Ripeness: Syrah, Warm climate

Optimum picking window for terroir expression

Green herbal notes	Fresh dark fruits	Lush, sweet	Dead fruit
Sweet fruit	Pure sweet fruit	Black fruits	High alcohol
Savory and tannic	Good natural acidity	Smooth and rich	Soupy, flat, porty

Picking date: early ⟶ late

FIGURE 10.1

Windows of ripeness in Syrah: a theoretical depiction.

viticulture is to achieve this transition in harmony, such that all the processes—sugar accumulation, acid lowering, methoxypyrazine degradation, and tannin softening—all coincide at a suitable harvest date. Of course, in many regions and in many vintages it's rare for physiological ripeness to occur exactly at the desired sugar ripeness. Given a choice, most winemakers will opt to pick at physiological or flavour ripeness rather than aim for ideal sugar levels in their grapes. This is where winemakers are faced with either living with the consequence of picking at physiological ripeness—elevated alcohol levels—or doing something about it in the winery. If they can, most will opt to achieve this balance in the vineyard by using the viticulturalist's tool kit. We will say more about this later.

Photosynthesis is the driving force behind ripening. It is the process by which plants harness light energy to produce sugars, which are then transported around the plant via specialized vascular conducting tissue called phloem. The green tissues of a plant are photosynthetic, and these are called source tissues. Tissues at which the sugars are targeted are called sinks. Source-sink relationships are important in the ripening process. In a grapevine in midseason, the two strongest sinks are the growing tips of the shoots and the developing fruit. In a vineyard that has good natural balance, the vigour of the vine will be controlled such that at veraison—the stage in ripening where the grapes change colour, expand, and begin to accumulate sugars—the shoots will have ceased growing, and the fruit will become the predominant sink for the sugars produced during photosynthesis. If the supply of nitrogen and water in a vineyard is too

WINDOWS FOR PICKING AND THE INTERNATIONAL STYLE OF RED WINE

JAMIE GOODE and SAM HARROP

For most vineyards and varieties, there is a window for picking when the grapes fall within acceptable parameters for ripeness, ranging from the cusp of greenness to the first signs of overripeness. Where the grower chooses to pick between these points is a stylistic issue. The current vogue is to go to the overripeness end of the spectrum, and in some cases beyond. This often results in boring wines without any sense of place.

It is increasingly common to encounter expensive, ambitious red wines in what is dubbed the "international" style. They share the same sweet, dark, fruit-flavoured profile, with deep colour, soft tannins, and lots of concentration. In an attempt to give them some bite and interest, there's usually a whack of spice from new oak. They are seductive and have an immediate appeal—they're the sorts of wines that usually appeal to nongeeks—but they quickly become boring.

These wines also have too much alcohol. In the context of a table wine, high alcohol has a profound effect on how other wine components express themselves. The high alcohol is usually obvious to the nose, and it also has an effect on the palate, usually by adding a little sweetness together with a bit of bitterness on the finish. Perhaps most important, the tannic composition of these wines compromises their aging capacity. Of course, it's not the destiny of all wine—not even all fine wine—to be cellared. But when people buy expensive red wines with a high Parker score, they usually do so with a view to future drinking and put them in their cellars.

Tannins are a complicated subject. They are polymers made up of phenolic compounds and have a marked astringent flavour. In both ripening grapes and wine, tannins undergo a range of modifications, including complexing with pigments and increasing and decreasing in chain length. These chemical modifications change the sensory properties of the tannins in ways that scientists are still busy working out. The simplistic view is that as they increase in length, they become less astringent, but reality is more complex. As we discuss in the text, grapes become more palatable to birds as they change colour from green to red, and one of these changes is that the tannins are modified on the vine to become less astringent. Part of red winemaking involves managing the extraction of tannins from the grape skins and then helping those tannins rearrange (for example, by the use of the limited oxygen pickup that oak barrels allow) such that the resulting wine has an appropriate structure. It follows that it is also important to pick the grapes when the tannins are at the right stage. Pick too late, and the tannins will have already undergone lots of modification on the vine. The wine may taste soft and sweet, but there will be very little further room for the tannins to develop. If a winemaker intends to produce a *vin de garde*, then she or he will need to consider the state of the tannins, a decision that will affect picking time and winemaking choices.

Can you have your cake and eat it too? Can you have a wine that is ripe and lush in its youth and has the requisite tannic structure? Only if there is some fairly serious tannin present that is masked by the sweetness of the fruit, as occurs with very good vintage Port, or perhaps if the wine is very ripe but very heavily oaked, containing spicy oak tannins. Usually, though, one wouldn't predict a good future for red wines that have been picked late and whose tannins have resolved on the vine.

high, it can lead to excessive vigour, which creates several problems. The first is that the large canopies continue growing throughout the ripening process and compete for resources with the fruit. Second, this vigour can also lead to fruit shading, which is usually bad news because the acid balance in the grapes is altered by such shading, and the accumulation of tannins and anthocyanins in the skins is reduced. Third, vigorous growth also creates dense canopies where fungal diseases flourish in the increased humidity that comes from restricted airflow.

The actual factors that govern ripening of grapes are not completely understood at a molecular level, although recent genomic studies have been able to pinpoint the many different genes that are up- or down-regulated (that is switched on to produce specific proteins, or turned off to stop producing proteins) during the ripening process. We know that light has a role, particularly in affecting methoxypyrazine levels in the grapes. High levels of ultraviolet light, such as those experienced in vineyards at higher altitudes, can increase skin thickness and alter the nature of the tannins in the skins, as well as their quantity. Large diurnal temperature shifts, with cool nights, seems to help preserve acidity in grapes by slowing the process of nighttime respiration in the berries. Latitude has an effect, too: vines grown at higher latitudes experience longer summer day length and therefore photosynthesize longer. In cooler areas, growing seasons are longer because the grapes take longer to mature, and harvest usually occurs in autumn conditions rather than in late summer. Also, in more northerly (northern hemisphere) or southerly (southern hemisphere) regions, daylength fluctuates significantly from the peak of summer to harvest time. Both of these factors could make a difference in the final stages of ripening. Could it be that when ripening finishes in autumnal conditions, those grapes can more easily achieve a state at harvest where they show better balance of flavor and sugar? Yields will also affect the ripening process, and while lower yields are generally thought to be good, it could be that ultralow yields encourage too-high ripeness levels.

Temperature is a key factor in ripening. While high temperatures generally accelerate plant growth, once temperatures reach a certain point, the risk of evaporative loss is so high that the vine closes its stomata. Stomata are small gas-exchange pores on the surface of plant tissues that allow carbon dioxide, necessary for photosynthesis, to enter. However, some evaporative water loss (known as transpiration) occurs when they are open, and in hot conditions this loss is high enough to cause the pores to shut and photosynthesis to stop. When applied properly, the techniques of regulated deficit irrigation and partial root drying have been shown to aid grape ripening by altering the vines' stress-signaling responses in ways that help the fruit. This signaling is done by the plant hormone abscisic acid, and at the right time in the ripening cycle these irrigation techniques, where they are available, can be used to improve grape quality, as well as to save water, because they stimulate abscisic acid production by the roots which then signals to the rest of the plant. It is likely that the best terroirs do this sort of timed water restriction naturally.

There's an important difference here between cooler and warmer winegrowing regions, which loosely translates to a difference between the Old World and the New World. In classic European wine regions, sugar level has been the usual guide to harvest date, and the higher the sugar levels, the better. Growers are often paid a premium for higher sugar levels because they mean riper grapes and better wine. Once potential alcohol levels reach 12 percent or so, it's time to pick because physiological ripeness will usually have been achieved. Also, because harvest time coincides with the onset of autumn rains, there is often pressure to get the grapes in as soon as possible. In some cases harvesting occurs at sugar levels that need to be supplemented by chaptalization. The luxury of leaving grapes on the vine until ideal ripening levels are achieved is not always an option in these relatively cool wine regions.

In New World regions, vintage time frequently occurs during settled, warm conditions, and growers can leave the grapes on the vine pretty much as long as they like. Also, because harvest occurs in warmer conditions, sugar levels aren't a good indicator of physiological ripeness. This can be a problem because sugar is easy to measure in the field, but there are no simple assays of physiological ripeness other than taste. The result is that in these warmer regions, harvesting can occur at very high sugar levels. Acidity is frequently corrected in the winery, so the fall in grape acid levels that occurs with increasing ripeness is not seen as a huge problem.

But with global warming, even the classic European wine regions are finding it difficult to synchronize sugar and physiological ripeness. While warm regions have always had to worry about too-high sugar levels, cooler regions are finding sugars a less reliable indicator of ripening than they used to be and are having to wait for physiological ripeness, which occurs only at sugar levels higher than might be desirable. The consequence is that across the world, alcohol levels have risen. However, the problem is still more acute in the warmer New World regions.

Some of this rise has occurred because growers, quite rightly, have not wanted to have unripe, green characters in their red wines, and they have preferred to have full flavour development in their whites rather than tart, green, rather lean wines. But some of this rise can be attributed to deliberate stylistic choices by winegrowers. They are choosing to wait before picking because they are aiming at wines with a sweeter, lusher fruit profile and softer tannins. Consumer preferences, they argue, have changed. Even at the high end of the market, people want concentrated, dark, sweetly fruited red wines with a new-oak sheen—wines of impact and immediate appeal. After all, this is the style that has appealed so well to influential critics, particularly in the United States. It is widely known as the "international" style of red wine because wines made in this way—with this set of viticultural and winemaking choices—tend to taste rather similar, no matter where they come from. *Surmaturité* (over-maturity) denies wine typicity.

There are other problems in dealing with very ripe grapes. One is that increased sugar ripeness occurs in tandem with decreased yeast-assimilable nitrogen (YAN) levels. Lower YAN levels mean that winemakers have to supplement more, typically by adding the nitrogen source diammonium phosphate (DAP), which can lead to problems because if it is added all at once, it acts like a yeast version of fast food, causing the yeasts to grow rapidly and then struggle. Low YAN is problematic because it leads to reduced protein synthesis and decreased sugar transport into the yeast cell, which can then cause sluggish or incomplete fermentations. It can also lead to problems with the production of hydrogen sulfide, which leads to the wine fault known as reduction. Another problem is that in highly alcoholic wines, potassium is less soluble, which can lead to a problem with tartaric acid falling out of solution during winemaking when it combines with potassium. This compounds the problem that low acidity is already an issue in warm-climate wine made from late-picked grapes, but the high alcohol these wines frequently show causes the acid levels to drop even further. The result of the obsession with tannin ripeness is that the late picking it encourages causes the stability of must and aromatics to become more fragile and runs the risk of losing any sense of typicity. It is as if the wine has become a drug addict, needing more and more supplements and additions to keep it happy.

Acidity problems can also arise through overuse of fruit-zone leaf plucking. While removing the leaves in the fruiting zone has the dual benefit of encouraging air circulation (to reduce the risk of fungal disease) and exposing the bunches to sunlight (this may help reduce levels of methoxypyrazines and allow the fruit to ripen better), it risks causing movement of potassium ions into the fruit. Higher levels of potassium, as we have just mentioned, lead to problems with lower acidity levels in wine. In some warm regions, therefore, some fruit shading may be beneficial. A single wire trellis resulting in umbrella sprawl, commonly found in some Australian regions, may have some wisdom to it. It can also be argued that this is a more "natural" way of trellising a vine than a vertical shoot positioning (VSP) system with leaf-zone plucking. Another viticultural issue of interest here is yield, and related to this vine age (often very old vines have extremely low yields). Sometimes yields can be too low. In warmer years or regions, sometimes larger yields can be better. In the Loire, for example, in 2003, a very warm year, some of the best red wines were from the cooperatives, which used grapes from vineyards with higher yields—these were more balanced and longer lived, showing more typicity.

In the past, the way of dealing with firm tannic structure in high-end red wines was careful *élevage* and then time in the bottle. Producers are now worried that consumers and critics won't have patience with these sorts of wines, and so they join the international-style bandwagon, picking late and then adding acid and a new-oak sheen in the winery. These wines invariably have relatively high alcohol levels because of the decision to aim for higher ripeness.

"Alcohol levels are a vexed question," agrees Australian wine guru Brian Croser. "The biggest factor is the decision by most winemakers to pick later regardless of the physiological condition of the grapes. There are a lot of wines made from grapes past the use-by date, shrivelled and physiologically dying or dead." Croser calls this phenomenon "dead grape syndrome" and suggests that it "pertains to the best regions of the table wine world."

"I heard something recently which absolutely shocked me," reveals Californian winemaker Randall Grahm: "'Twenty-eight is the new twenty-four.' (He was referring to the level of Brix at which grapes are typically harvested.) Wineries are now going for extreme levels of maturity—very popular with certain critics who shall remain nameless—and going back to fix the other elements of the wine, potential alcohol, acidity, and perhaps tannin as well. Certainly, we are now in the realm of the confectioner, rather than the vigneron."

The recipe for making an international-style blockbuster red wine is the antithesis of natural winemaking. First, the grapes are picked late, when they are phenolically ripe, and then are extracted to hell and back in the winery, with three to five *délestages* (a red winemaking process in which the fermenting wine is removed from the skins to another vat, and then returned to the first vat by pumping it on top of the skins) and then microoxygenation to polymerize the tannins. Microoxygenated wines tend to be less stable because they are further along their evolution, and in general, riper-styled wines don't age as well, so these wines tend not to age gracefully. Late-picked grapes are lower in acidity and require additions of acid. Sulfur dioxide works less well in higher-pH wines, so more needs to be added. Riper grapes have lower YAN levels, which call for supplementation or risk sluggish or stuck fermentations, and potassium is less soluble in higher-alcohol wines, risking the loss of acidity, which is already an issue. In addition, these wines often rely on new oak for structure, and wood tannins are a problem because they never soften. It seems that in recent years, oak quality has worsened considerably, perhaps because of less seasoning. Demand has gone up, certainly, and this could lead to a lowering of quality. Tannins from new wood seem to be more overt and sharper these days.

Some winegrowers pick late because they have to; picking any earlier would result in unripe characters, chiefly greenness, in their wines. They would also argue that picking earlier wouldn't give them the flavour profile that they seek. But there's a feeling that some growers are picking almost perversely late and could very well pick earlier if they chose to, thus solving some of the problems of high alcohol very simply. Also, there's the question whether all greenness is to be feared in red wines. Classic Bordeaux wines in the past often had a marked green component in their youth and then evolved gracefully; they also commonly had alcohol levels of 12 percent. Classic Rioja and Chianti wines have also shown noticeable green characters in their youth. There is good greenness, some argue, and bad greenness.

"Viticultural practice has been revolutionized in the New World and sharpened up in the Old World," says Brian Croser. "We now have very efficient solar panels in our vineyards (vertical canopies with good bud spacing, improved clones and rootstocks, good soil nutrition and water management), all leading to the highly desirable result of more rapid and complete ripening with more anabolic spillover into flavour and colour and better-retained acids." Croser's point is that improved viticulture should lead to earlier picking dates, but these are rarely practiced. "A bit like the cork/Stelvin issue [the conflict between supporters of natural cork and screwcaps], there is an element of peer pressure, herd instinct, and browbeating that bullies winemakers to avoid early picking despite the fact that our best vineyards are now set up to facilitate this by achieving early ripeness," he laments.

"There is some feeling that, in general, New World wines appear to attain the holy grail of physiological maturity at higher levels of potential alcohol relative to Old World wines," says Randall Grahm.

The reasons for that I would suggest might be the following (with appropriate remediation proposed):

1. There is first the question of the length of daylight hours during the growing season, which is dependent on the latitude, i.e., the higher the latitude, the larger the swing in duration of sunlight from the midseason to the late season. Maybe this triggers some sort of hormonal process in the plant relative to its ripening pattern, and gives the Old World grapes a little goose to get on with it. Alas, nothing to be done in the New World short of a Dr. Evil–like correction to the earth's rotational axis.

2. In the New World, grapes are generally grown in areas that are strictly speaking warmer than they need to be to fully ripen the fruit (especially if they are cropped at much higher yield levels than one would typically find in Europe, as is generally the case). They are grown this way because they can be—our

FIGURE 10.2
Overripe grapes that have started to shrivel.

extraordinarily long growing season allows growers to imagine at least that they can hang these absurdly high crop levels. Growing grapes in cooler climates with restricted yields would certainly help bring the vines into better balance.

3. Style of farming, especially the utilization of drip irrigation, tends to disfavour deeper rooted vines, and this generally leads to problems of dehydration in warm years. This is especially problematic in varieties such as Syrah and Zinfandel. Dry farmed vines, especially older ones, seem to be in just better balance: they throw more appropriate crops and ripen them surely and evenly.

4. Size of vines. It is generally our wont to create larger vines, more widely spaced than our European counterparts. These bigger vines have more carbohydrate reserves stored in them during the winter and generally grow like crazy in the spring. Perhaps it takes longer for the vine to get the hormonal message that it is time to stop growing and get on with the business of ripening its fruit. (Though it could be argued that this phenomenon may well be counterbalanced by the European phenomenon of summer rain, which can also disrupt the ripening program.) There is the feeling among some people that the larger vines, whether owing to the greater distance between the roots and the trunks and/or the proportionately larger amount of fruit on an individual vine, tend to dilute the mineral concentration of new world wines (which in itself doesn't bear on the ripening curve, though it may make the wines seem to taste more alcoholic). But my belief is that smaller vines are more efficient machines,

especially with devigorating rootstock, which tend to have a shorter vegetative cycle, i.e., give the plants the signal that it's time to start the ripening.

Brian Croser highlights some of the viticultural steps that he feels can be taken to counter excessive sugar levels at full ripeness:

1. It is necessary to ensure the leaf to fruit ratio is adequate but not excessive ($0.7\,m^2$/kg of fruit). Many of the modern vertical canopy vineyards have much too much solar power for the crop load exacerbated by crop thinning (2–$3\,m^2$/kg fruit). Nor does just raising the crop level to achieve the lower ratio achieve the right result. Small vines with small crop loads is the answer. I have chosen canopy heights of 500 to 700 mm, not 1 metre plus, with the fruiting wire close to the ground at 0.5 m, not 1 metre plus.

2. Ensure the daylight photosynthetic and net sugar accumulation time is matched by a nighttime anabolic phase ensuring optimum conversion of sugar to colour and flavour. Low day/night differentials, low vines receiving ground warmth all night is one way to go (Fleurieu Peninsula); another is to allow daytime high temperature to limit the photosynthetic duration and efficiency and to use the cooler but still physiologically appropriate temperatures at night to allow optimum anabolism. Again small low vines are the answer (Piccadilly Valley). Piccadilly and Fleurieu have the same heat summation about 1170 degree days C and in each case the need is to optimise anabolic phase at night. Sugar accumulation is slower at Piccadilly because of daytime temperatures and picking is later than Fleurieu.

3. The ripening signals (abscisic acid) are really important to make the anabolic conversion phase go and that relates to the unmanageable average air and soil temperature but the manipulable irrigation regime (partial root zone drying). In the Piccadilly and Fleurieu nature has to take charge of that process but I ensure irrigation is minimized and timed not to interfere with the autumn phase. This is harder on the Fleurieu than Piccadilly. Site slope and soil porosity have to do the work on the Fleurieu to create the right drought stress levels to get the juices running.

REDUCING ALCOHOL IN THE WINERY

Thus there are a number of steps that can be taken in the vineyard to help synchronize sugar and phenolic ripeness. Should all these fail, technologies now exist to correct high alcohol levels in the winery.

First, we should mention the old trick of adding water to must. It is very common in warm climate regions, but it is illegal (although the regulations in California do allow a fairly generous amount of water when winemaking processing additives are added).

THE VITICULTURAL TOOL KIT

DAVID BOOTH, Viticulturalist Working in Portugal's Alentejo Region

Green, astringent, thin, unripe fruit character in wine is at the top of my personal hates for red wine, very closely followed by clumsy additions of tartaric acid. This very closely relates to the question of achieving excellent physiological ripeness at sensible sugar levels. The short answer is yes, it is possible, but only if you are in the world's most perfect viticultural region when all the different lines of the graph come together at the perfect moment for harvest. I do not know where this mythical 100-point vineyard is, but I can tell you it is not in the Alentejo. So let's look at the six items that we have in the grape quality tool kit and see what might be possible to do to get less than perfect vineyard sites to produce their very best.

1. Crop thinning. Getting the ratio down to one good shoot per bunch is vital if you are attempting to be serious. Do the first pass some time between fruit set and veraison (the lower the vigour of the site, the earlier you should do it). Pulling off all bunches from short shoots is vital. Then at the end of veraison do another pass to remove any bunches on good long shoots that are slow to colour. One of the main objectives of crop thinning is creating homogeneity in fruit. Will low crop levels accelerate phenolic development before sugar development races out of control? Possibly.

2. Canopy management. Good canopy management rules apply, but I cannot see how they directly affect the ripening issue. A big solar panel is important if you want superripe fruit, but with lots of sugar too.

3. Soil water management. This is the main control. I see well-managed deficit irrigation in the month preceding harvest like the joystick of a light aircraft, with the viticulturalist trying to put down the plane on a very short landing strip. A lot of high sugar levels in hot climates are not real sugar maturity but berry dehydration that produces an apparent rise in sugar level. Many growers do not irrigate close to harvest, believing that it will dilute the fruit. The result is that they often harvest horrible, astringent, unripe grapes as soon as they record 13.5 percent potential alcohol in the vineyard. We sample berry weight from a 500-berry sample every two days. This test is very good at detecting dehydration before you can actually see it appearing as golf-ball dimples on the skin of the berry. We then do a very short,

frequent, shallow irrigation—down to say 40 cm, just to keep the berries hydrated but without diluting them and keeping the vines in a state of moderate/severe water deficit so that they will have stomatal closure and no photosynthesis for most of the day. If we see the berry weight go up, I ease off on the irrigation. All the time we are tasting and looking at seed, skin, and pulp maturity and accurately measuring phenolic content so we have some numbers and can track the development of the curves on the graph. I suspect that deep stony soils have a natural ability to place deep-rooted old vines under water-deficit conditions and then slowly meter in water. A skillfully managed irrigation system is trying to imitate this effect, just as modern canopy management is trying to imitate the canopy environment of the old low-vigour vineyard.

4. Harvest date. Explained in tool 3.

5. Zoning. Also vital. Identify, manage, monitor, and harvest well-defined areas of homogeneous fruit on the same date. Then at least if you have some fruit with good potential alcohol and good phenolics, you don't end up mixing it in with some horrible unripe or dehydrated stuff.

6. Biological and biodynamic viticulture. This one is a bit of a struggle, but I am increasingly coming to the conclusion that these methods can be legitimately included in the quality tool kit, with the caveat that they will not work if they are used in isolation; they stand a chance of producing really vibrant, high-quality fruit only if they are used in the context of excellent viticultural practice. I get the impression that many farmers using these methods are not especially good farmers and make their wine in dirty cellars using ancient pumps and presses and as a result produce appalling wines.

Adding water is problematic. While there's little risk of being caught, there are techniques (such as isotope analysis) that can show whether water has been added. In addition, adding tap water can cause problems in the wine, first through the presence of chlorine in tap water (as opposed to groundwater), which can cause fermentation problems, and also because of the risk of geosmin contamination (this earthy-smelling compound is often found in water, especially in warm summer conditions where algal blooms are common).

Three legal technologies are used to reduce alcohol. The first is reverse osmosis, which relies on a technology called cross-flow filtration. A portion of the wine is put through a cross-flow filter, which acts a bit like kidney tubules in that the liquid being filtered isn't

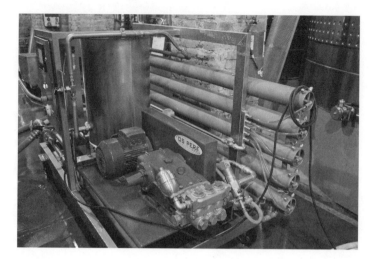

FIGURE 10.3
A reverse osmosis machine in the cellar of an Argentine winery.

forced through a membrane but instead runs through a tube under pressure, the walls of which are made of the filtration membrane. The advantage of this technique is that the flow of liquid keeps the membrane pores from clogging. However, the surface area of membrane required is enormous. This surface area is achieved by using a column consisting of numerous small tubes. As the wine passes through, a mixture chiefly composed of water, acetic acid, and alcohol is separated from it. The alcohol is then removed by distillation. The water can then be recombined with the wine to produce a lower-alcohol wine that can be blended back into the original larger batch to produce wine with the desired alcoholic strength. The second technique, called Memstar, is similar but relies solely on membranes, with a second membrane step for separating the water and alcohol fraction rather than a distilling column. The cost of a reverse osmosis set-up starts at around $50,000, whereas a Memstar starts at around $100,000. Both these techniques require the wine to be passed through at pressure, and there is a little loss of flavor. But they are the only option for estate wines that are legally not allowed to leave the winery premises.

The third technique, the spinning cone, achieves the same ends by rather different means. Originally invented for making heavy water for the nuclear industry, but commercialized for wine by the U.S. company Conetech, the spinning cone column contains around forty upside-down cones, of which half are fixed and half spin. In a vacuum environment, the cones spin the wine into thin liquid films, and a cool vapour rises off the wine, carrying the volatiles from the liquid. In the first pass, the ultralight component consisting of the delicate flavours and aromas is carried off and condensed. This is known as the *essence*, and it is saved to be recombined with the wine later. The second pass takes off as much alcohol as you want to remove. Theoretically, you could then recombine the remaining low-alcohol wine with the essence and the alcohol and end up with the same wine you started with.

Currently, Conetech treats wines from around six hundred clients worldwide, and in 2010 it treated 6 million gallons. However, because it treats only a small proportion of each wine—around 10 percent—that is then blended back, around 50 million gallons of wine have the alcohol level reduced in this way. As well as a plant in California, Conetech also has plants in Chile, South Africa, and Spain. The cost of the spinning cone machine is around US$1 million.

The rules are potentially a problem for this sort of technology. In the United States, spinning cones have been authorized for alcohol reduction, but in Europe this technique used to be allowed only on an experimental basis. This meant that you were allowed to treat 50,000 hectolitres, but the wine couldn't leave the country of origin. But in November 2008 the EU regulations changed to make it legal to remove up to two percent of alcohol where specific local appellation laws permitted this (in many AOCs in France, for example, this is still not permitted).

Tasting a series of samples of the same wine with the alcohol reduced, both by the spinning cone and by reverse osmosis, reveals how much of an impact the presence of alcohol has on the perception of other wine components. "Alcohol is a masking agent," says Conetech's head winemaker Scott Burr, "so taking it away reveals what's there. It also adds sweetness to the palate."

How does a winemaker decide how much alcohol should be reduced? "A big client who we've been working with a long time might specify they want their wine at 13.85 percent," says Burr. "A smaller client might say they have a Zinfandel at 16.8 percent alcohol, so we do a run, take the 4 percent component and blend wines at a bunch of different alcohol levels," he says. "I don't tell the client what the alcohol level should be." In regard to which wines are more successful, Burr says that there is not a curve; instead, there are sweet spots. "There are all kinds of different ones. The more oak, the bigger the variance."

Clark Smith, a California winemaker whose previous company Vinovation was the leading practitioner of reverse osmosis in the United States, reckons that 45 percent of premium California wines are alcohol adjusted, either by reverse osmosis or by the spinning cone. Alcohol reduction is becoming a widely adopted tool throughout the wine-growing world, but it is not without controversy, simply because it's seen as a rather artificial technique that subjects a portion of the wine to fairly dramatic physical forces.

Clearly, such interventionist strategies don't fit well with the concept of natural wine. But there is an interesting, almost philosophical question here. If a grower is stuck in a position where he or she is forced to choose between flavour development and sensible alcohol levels, whatever he or she does in the vineyard, might this justify the use of alcohol-reduction technologies as a last resort? They do sound horridly manipulative, and most fine wine producers prefer to do as little winemaking intervention as possible. But the tantalizing possibility remains that wines that speak more eloquently of their

FIGURE 10.4

The same wine with different alcohol levels, which have been adjusted using the spinning cone method.

origins—the vineyard site or terroir they came from—could be realized by the use of these tools. We know it sounds like heresy, but could alcohol-reduction techniques in the wine cellar assist in the expression of terroir that traditionally minded winegrowers seek? Could reverse osmosis or the spinning cone have an important role to play in fine wine production, compensating for the effects of global warming?

The argument would be that technologies such as this are just tools, and tools are morally neutral—it is how they are used that matters. A winegrower who genuinely wants to make a wine that expresses the vineyard site optimally, but finds the wine's ability to do this hindered by the masking, sweetening effect of high alcohol, could use such a tool to produce a better wine that has more of a sense of place to it (in theory, at least).

"In the past, I confess to having used some technological methods (spinning cone and reverse osmosis) to remove alcohol from our wines," admits Randall Grahm, "but I am now quite opposed to the practice (and of adding water as well—known as 'Jesus Units' in the trade). If you are doing the right work in the vineyard, you should not be compelled to resort to these extreme solutions."

He continues: "In the winery, the most practical solution that we have found to keeping alcoholic degree in check has been the use of open-top fermenters, warm fermentation temperatures, and especially the use of indigenous yeasts. The 'wild' yeasts have at least for us been absolutely brilliant; they tend to give us a much longer, more even fermentation (and also don't stick). But what is particularly cool is that the fermentation process is far less efficient, owing to the successive populations and obscure yeast wars going on between species. They're essentially converting the sugar in the grapes into biomass rather than alcohol and one ends up with very low sugar to alcohol conversion levels, in some cases approximately 0.51–0.52 (Brix to percentage alcohol)."

This last point is quite controversial. The conversion level Grahm quotes is contested by some yeast researchers we contacted; they don't think that the yeasts would convert sugar to biomass, and they add that even in an indigenous fermentation, most of the fermentation will be by means of *Saccharomyces cerevisiae* species, which will have a higher conversion factor, about the same as that of selected yeast species.

One of the current objectives of yeast research is to produce wine yeast strains that are less efficient at converting sugar to alcohol. Such strains already exist, but the two key problems have been finding non-GM yeasts that have these properties, and finding strains that use the sugar to produce alternative fermentation products that have desirable sensory properties. GM strains of *S. cerevisiae* can produce wines that have 2 percent lower alcohol, but they couldn't be used in wine because of the hostile consumer climate toward GM organisms. The greatest variation in alcohol levels that has been demonstrated with natural fermentations with non-GM *S. cerevisiae* is 0.2 percent, which is much less than the variation achieved by modifying the fermenter design. Still, GM yeast seems a bit like a sticking-plaster solution to a more fundamental problem, and the major focus of those looking to produce wines with more sensible alcohol levels should be on viticultural practice.

11

WINE FAULTS

A common criticism of natural wines is that they're prone to develop faults. In particular, most scientifically trained winemakers consider that practices such as working with low sulfur dioxide (SO_2) levels (or, indeed, no SO_2 at all), using indigenous yeasts, not adjusting must acidity or adding nutrients, and avoiding filtration are recipes for all manner of wine problems. So it is important to discuss the topic of wine faults in the context of making wine more naturally. Indeed, one of the motivations for intervening—both by adding things to wine and by using technical innovations in the winery—is to reduce the risk of delivering faulty wine to the consumer.

However, it is important to clarify exactly what constitutes a wine fault. While some traits—most notably, cork taint—are always faults, context and level (to a degree) determine whether others are viewed as faults. Winemakers, who are trained to spot faults in wines at a very early stage in their development, tend to be less tolerant of the presence of any fault in a wine than consumers generally are. Also, New World winemakers tend to be better at detecting faults and are also less tolerant of them than Old World winemakers, who have often grown up in a culture where low levels of certain faults are considered part of the wine style. Not all "natural" wines are faulty, but in some cases natural wines display traces of "faults" that seem to work in the context of these wines. Are wines like these, with "faults" as part of their personality, acceptable and legitimate expressions of their terroirs? This is an interesting and somewhat divisive question that we will try to address in this chapter.

CORK TAINT

Cork taint isn't terribly relevant to the topic of natural wine, because it is independent of the winemaking, but instead is a fault shared equally among all wines that are sealed with natural cork. Suffice it to say that a small proportion of wines sealed with cork are tainted by the haloanisole 2,4,6-trichloroanisole (more commonly referred to as TCA), which gives them a musty taint. The level of cork taint is hard to pin down, but large surveys of its incidence (for example, data from the faults clinic of the International Wine Challenge) indicate a rate of around 3.5 percent. Efforts have been under way to reduce levels of cork taint, so in the next few years this level may drop. In the past, taint levels above 5 percent have been cited by some, so perhaps they are already dropping. Of course, not all musty taints are the fault of the cork: contamination from haloanisoles in wood structures and pallets has affected the wines of a number of wineries. But the vast majority of musty taints seem to be from the cork, because large surveys find almost no musty-tainted wines sealed with screwcaps or synthetic cork. Both of these alternative closures are manufactured from synthetic materials. In the case of synthetic corks, low density polyethylene (LDPE), and in the case of screwcaps, the closure material in contact with wine is polyvinylidene chloride (PVDC), although the cap itself is made from aluminium. While it is possible for these materials to pick up environmental taints during the manufacturing process or while they are stored, this seems to be very rare.

Many natural winemakers claim that cork is the only natural closure option. Indeed, cork is a natural product with a low carbon footprint, and cork forests are a wonderful sustainable ecosystem that supports rural communities in countries such as Portugal and Spain where the majority of the cork oak forests are located. But issues with taint and variable oxygen transmission mean that some winemakers are not prepared to risk their wine quality, no matter how strong cork's green credentials are. For now, those who wish to use a cork-based closure but insist on freedom from taint and on consistent oxygen transmission have an alternative in Oeneo's Diam, which is technically a cork made from small granules of natural cork that have been cleaned from any taint and then recombined with a small amount of synthetic component and moulded into a cylinder, from which the corks are made.

BRETTANOMYCES

The topic of *Brettanomyces* is highly relevant not just to natural wine but to almost all red wines. The problem can also occur in some white wines.

Brettanomyces, commonly called brett, is a genus of yeast, also known as *Dekkera* (the yeast can exist in two states, and the latter name is used for the sexual, spore-producing form). While several species names are commonly used, the current classification has just two species of wine-relevant brett, *B. bruxellensis* and *B. anomala*, of which the former is much more important.

Brett is a problem in winemaking because it is resilient and can persist when conditions are unfavourable, only to grow again later when things change. In practical terms, this means that it does its real damage after alcoholic fermentation is complete. Brett is slow growing and tough and doesn't need much to feed on. It is a major problem because it produces some distinctive flavours that, at higher levels, can ruin wines.

Brett causes many sensory effects (see Table 11.1). The first sign is reduced varietal character, followed by the degradation of certain fruity aromas by esterases. These are enzymes that cause the breakdown of esters, a chemical group important in conferring fruitiness. Brett hits lighter wine styles particularly badly. Pinot Noir, for example, loses its delicate bright cherry and violet characters. This loss of fruit can be an early cue of the presence of brett while the wine is in the barrel. But brett doesn't just produce esterases that rob the wine of flavour: it also produces certain flavour compounds that can dominate the wine and mask the varietal and site characteristics. Hints of smoke and spice begin to appear; the chief culprit here is a compound called 4-ethylguaiacol. As the infection progresses, the wine starts to smell and taste medicinal (largely because of 4-ethylphenol) and to lose its fruity flesh, exposing the structural bones. Typically, the acid and tannins stick out a bit. Finally, the wine smells of barnyards and bandages.

It is quite difficult to teach people how to spot brett because the characteristics of bretty wines vary depending on the substrates that were initially available to the brett cells as they multiplied, the precise strain of brett involved, and the context of the other flavours present in the wine. Different combinations and relative concentrations of spoilage compounds produce different overall effects. Some bretty wines are more earthy and spicy; others are more at the fecal and animal-sheds end of the spectrum.

Although it is difficult to determine the prevalence of brett, we can say that it is far from rare in red wines. Wine scientist Pascal Chatonnet, who was responsible for much of the groundbreaking research on this subject, surveyed the incidence of brett in a variety of red wines in 1993 and found that just under a third had levels of 4-ethylphenol above 600 mg/L (4-ethylphenol is found only in wines that have a brett infection and hence is used as a diagnostic indicator for the presence of brett; most people can spot it at around 420 mg/L, but this varies with the style of wine). He says that he thinks that the incidence now is higher. A further clue about the extent of this problem is given by data from the International Wine Challenge, where brett consistently makes up around a third of all wine faults (typically 15,000 bottles of wine are tasted each year, and some 5 to 7 percent of these are deemed faulty). Indeed, over the years 2006–2009, brett has shown signs of increasing, as Chatonnet has suggested, although in 2010 the levels fell a little.

There's a widespread misconception that brett contamination is a hallmark of wineries with poor hygiene. "Brett can occur in the cleanest cellars," says New Zealand winemaker Matt Thomson, who is an expert on the subject. Brett has been identified in every wine region where people have looked for it. Thomson thinks that oak is largely

TABLE 11.1.   Some Compounds Produced by *Brettanomyces*
and Their Aromatic Impact

Compound	Sensory impact
4-ethylphenol	Bandage, medicinal, phenolic, horsey
4-ethylguaiacol	Spicy, smoky, phenolic, cloves
Isovaleric acid	Sweaty, rancid, cheesey
4-ethylcatechol	Medicinal, stables
2-phenylethanol	Honey, spice, lilac
Guaiacol	Smoky
Ethyldecanoate	
Trans-2-nonenal	
Isoamyl alcohol	
Ethyl-2-methylbutyrate	

to blame for many infections, because brett can live in oak and is almost impossible to get out by cleaning (it is so resilient that it will survive most cleaning attempts). "If you use new oak, you will get brett: it is not something you can associate just with a dirty cellar."

Brett likes oak. It particularly likes toasted new barrels and has been found 8 mm deep in staves. This makes it very hard to remove by steam or ozone cleaning. It can feed off a compound, cellobiose, that is formed when barrels are toasted. Thomson goes further, suggesting that brett is not only associated with new oak, but also may be associated with specific coopers who Thomson has identified as having a problem with bretty barrels, although he won't name them. Brett is also associated with old barrels.

Thomson also thinks that brett is a growing problem. "I am convinced that in large numbers of wineries in both the New and Old Worlds, brett is a new thing." He theorizes that there has been a relatively recent change in the way oak barrels are produced. "Something happened with the huge demand for new oak in the 1980s. Coopers had a boom period and started doing something different, and there was a change."

What can be done to avoid brett, according to Thomson? This is where things get interesting, because many of the steps that need to be taken in order to ensure clean wines run counter to the sort of winemaking approach you'd want to take to make interesting wines.

The first is to avoid barrels. Stainless steel can be cleaned properly, which vastly reduces the risk. Second, you need to avoid cross-contamination. When Thomson is taking barrel samples, he uses plastic barrel thieves (devices used to take samples from barrels for tasting) that are sterilized after each use. He also avoids doing rack and return where the wine would go from several barrels to be mixed in one tank: instead, each barrel is racked separately to the tank and returned, and the tank is cleaned before the procedure is repeated with the next barrel. Few winemakers are this careful.

The next stage is to keep pH low, either by acidifying or by harvesting earlier. This is crucial in the fight against brett. Because brett is so widespread, you want to make your wine an uninviting habitat for its growth. To put this the other way, if you make your wine a favourable place for brett to grow, it will. Low pH is important for two reasons. First, brett doesn't like more acidic media. Second, at lower pH any SO_2 additions will be much more effective, and more of the SO_2 will be in the active (free molecular) form. Harvesting earlier will ensure that your sugars (and thus potential alcohol levels) are lower, allowing for a healthier primary fermentation with less residual sugar left at the end. As sugar is a major substrate for brett, less residual sugar during *élevage* usually means less brett activity.

Another important prevention measure is to keep the time from the end of alcoholic fermentation to the end of malolactic fermentation as short as possible. SO_2 levels have to be kept low in order to facilitate malolactic fermentation, which makes this a risky time for potential brett growth. For this reason, inoculating with lactic acid bacteria for malolactic fermentation is advisable, and after it is complete, it's a good idea to add a dose of SO_2 to protect the wine for the rest of its time in the barrel or tank. Coinoculation with cultured strains of yeast and lactic acid bacteria has shown good results and may be of help here.

Other preventive steps include avoiding lees aging, keeping barrels topped up (full to the brim), keeping cellar temperatures low, avoiding temperature changes, and aggressively cleaning new and used barrels. There is also even a specific fining agent made from chitosan of fungal origin that has just been released. The producer of this product is advising use after primary ferment and before malolactic fermentation to reduce brett populations significantly during this lag phase. Incoulating with a commercial *S. cerevisiae* strain will also give you more chance of a healthier, faster ferment with lower sugars at the end of ferment and thus lower the risk of brett activity during *élevage*.

If brett has been at work on a wine, there are two ways in which a winemaker can deal with it. The first is to strip out the remaining brett cells, either by filtration or by the use of a chemical called dimethyl dicarbamate (DMDC, also known by its trade name Velcorin). This is extremely toxic to microbes but breaks down into harmless products once it has done its job. The wine will still have the impact of the compounds associated with brett, but at least it won't get any worse and will be stable in the bottle. The second approach, once the wine is stable, is to use modern cross-flow filtration technologies to remove compounds such as 4-ethylphenol in a selective manner. This approach is quite new and hasn't yet been widely adopted.

We now come to the thorny question: is brett always a problem, or are there contexts in which it is okay? If you were a winemaker, you'd probably want to avoid it altogether because it is so difficult to control. But, perhaps through luck, some wines seem to work even though they have noticeable brett. Unlike many other wine faults, which are more clear-cut, the issue becomes a matter of personal preference. Wines that seem to successfully carry brett are often those from warmer climates, where the sweetness of the fruit seems to be complemented quite well by the earthy, spicy funk of brett. However, some people will find brett objectionable no matter what the context is.

If brett occurs naturally in many red wines, should we simply accept it as part of natural winemaking? The problem with this position is that brett obscures the sense of place of a wine because bretty wines all begin to taste similar to one another. It seems silly to spend a lot of time and effort working in a more natural way in the vineyard in order to have wines that reflect their origins, and then to lose this character in the winery through allowing brett to stamp its rather extreme character on the wine. Ted Lemon of the California winery Littorai explains this viewpoint brilliantly on page 146.

In some ways dealing with brett is a balancing act. Some of the methods of brett control are rather extreme manipulations that natural winemakers would be averse to. They will have to work as hard as they can to prevent brett without the use of some of these tools, with a resulting degree of risk. In any case, a heightened understanding of brett will help avoid its worst excesses.

REDUCTION

Reduction is one of the most interesting and topical of all wine faults; one that is currently much discussed in winemaking circles. The term is used to describe sensory characteristics of wine caused by the presence of a suite of volatile sulfur compounds (VSCs, whose presence is commonly referred to as "sulfur-like odors" or SLOs; see Table 11.2). The term *reduction* is actually a bit of a misnomer: it was coined because these characteristics frequently develop in wine that has a very low redox potential (a measure of the affinity of a solution for electrons in chemical reactions, and thus for it to undergo reduction, hence the term "reduced"), such as occurs when barrels are left for a long time without racking, but these sulfur compounds can theoretically also be present in wine that is oxidized. However, it is such a well-recognized, convenient, and widely used term that we'll stick with it. Sometimes the term *sulfides* is used as a catchall to describe reduction issues, but this is technically incorrect and involves a serious risk of confusion because mercaptans (thiols) and thioesters are involved in reduction, as well as sulfides and disulfides.

These sulfur-containing compounds are the responsibility of the yeasts. The chemistry involved is rather complex and still not very well understood, but here's a simplified summary of what is currently thought to be the situation. Most of the hydrogen sulfide and other volatile sulfur compounds are thought to be produced by yeasts through the pathway yeasts themselves use to make the sulfur-containing amino acids methionine and cysteine. This is called the sulfate reductive assimilation pathway or sulfate reduction sequence (SRS). If the yeasts are short of methionine and cysteine (and grape juice is often deficient in these amino acids), they switch on a pathway that takes up

TABLE 11.2. Volatile Sulfur Compounds in Wine

Compound	Sensory impact	Notes
Hydrogen sulfide	Rotten eggs, sewage.	This is the most prevalent compound, made by yeasts when they use one of the sulfur-containing amino acids as a nitrogen source. Stress also encourages its formation.
Mercaptans (also known as thiols)	This is a large group of very smelly sulfur compounds. Terms such as cabbagey, rubbery, struck flint, or burnt rubber are used as descriptors.	If hydrogen sulfide isn't removed quickly, it can result in mercaptan production. This is a big worry for winemakers.
Ethyl mercaptan	Burnt match, sulfidy, earthy.	Often negative, but can be positive in the right wine environment at certain levels.
Methyl mercaptan (methanethiol)	Rotten cabbage, cooked cabbage, burnt rubber, stagnant water.	One of the compounds implicated in screwcap reduction.
Dimethyl sulfide	Cooked vegetables, cooked corn, canned tomato at high levels; blackcurrant drink concentrate at lower levels. Quince, truffle.	

(continued)

TABLE 11.2. (continued)

Compound	Sensory impact	Notes
Diethyl sulfide	Rubbery	
carbon disulfide	Sweet, ethereal, slightly green, sulfidy.	
Dimethyl disulfide	Vegetal, cabbage, onionlike at high levels.	
Diethyl disulfide	Garlic, burnt rubber.	
4-mercapto-4-methylpentan-2-one (4MMP), 3-mercaptohexan-1-ol (3MH), 3-mercaptohexyl acetate (3MHA)	Tropical fruit or passion fruit, boxwood, and grapefruit at low levels; cat's urine or sweatiness at higher levels.	Common in Sauvignon Blanc but also found in red wines where they can contribute to the blackcurrant fruit aroma. An example of sulfur flavours that can be positive in the right environment.
Benzenemethanethiol	Smoky/gunflint aromas.	Can be positive in the right context and at the right levels.
Methylthioesters: S-methyl thioacetate S-methyl thioproponate S-methyl thio	Cooked cauliflower, cheese and chives.	
Furfurylthiol	Roast coffee, popcorn.	Thought to form from toasted oak staves during fermentation.

sulfate, and through several chemical steps, this is reduced into sulfide. Normally, this sulfide is then taken and used to form methionine and cysteine in a further step, but if the precursors to these amino acids are not present, for example because of a deficiency of nitrogen in a form available to the yeast, the sulfide may be released as hydrogen sulfide. This is then released into the wine.

H_2S is reactive and can combine with other wine components to form the volatile sulfur compounds that we are discussing. In addition, high levels of sulfite from sulfur dioxide (SO_2) can diffuse into the yeast cell and bypass regulatory mechanisms, causing H_2S production. Elemental sulfur in the must can also cause the same problem.

It seems that putting yeasts under stress in various ways can also cause reductive problems, presumably through autolysis of dead yeast cells, although the mechanisms are not entirely understood. The ability of yeasts to produce H_2S is highly strain dependent and is therefore at least partly genetic. Some yeast cells naturally produce much less H_2S than others.

Another important reaction in yeasts also involves sulfur compounds. In a quite separate pathway, yeasts produce a range of volatile thiols from must precursors that add a fruity quality to the wine. These are particularly important in Sauvignon Blanc aroma, where they contribute passion fruit, boxwood, and grapefruit aromas (at higher levels they can make the wine taste a bit "sweaty"). Again, some yeast strains are much better at liberating thiols from precursors than others, so a genetic component is clearly at work.

One reason that reduction has become a hot topic of late is the growing use of screwcaps. Corks allow a little oxygen transmission, which means that the redox potential will be higher in bottles sealed with corks than in bottles sealed with screwcaps, which allow much less oxygen transmission. The low redox potential of wines sealed with screwcaps can mislead winemakers: they can bottle a wine that is free from noticeable SLOs, only to have the SLOs that are present be modified by the low redox environment into a smellier form, with the result being "reduction" noticeable to tasters. One such reaction is the reduction of disulfides to mercaptans (thiols). As a result, winemakers need to change the way they prepare their wines for bottling if they intend to use screwcaps. The wine needs to be free of any reductive tendencies at all. Frequently, copper fining trials will be done before bottling. Copper removes mercaptans, but not disulfides, and winemakers will look at using as little as necessary to clean the wine up. In addition, winemakers will be looking more carefully at the nutrients present in the must during fermentation: a healthy ferment is likely to give rise to fewer SLOs in the first place.

Kiwi winemaker (Stonecroft, Hawkes Bay) and PhD chemist Alan Limmer has written widely on the subject, bringing his knowledge of wine chemistry to bear. Limmer has pointed out that screwcap reduction is not a problem that can be completely eliminated simply by more careful winemaking. "In essence we are talking about thiol accumulation, post-bottling, from complex sulfides which do not respond to pre-bottling copper treatment," claims Limmer, in response to the assertion that fining with copper removes reduction defects. "This reaction occurs in all wines containing the appropriate precursors, irrespective of closure type. But the varying levels of oxygen ingress between closures lead to significantly different outcomes from a sensory point of view."

Limmer's explanation of screwcap reduction is that sulfides present in the wine at bottling need a small level of oxygen ingress through the closure; otherwise they can become reduced to thiols. So the use of a closure, such as cork, that allows a little oxygen ingress (but not too much) is a necessary concession to the vagaries of sulfur chemistry. Limmer points out, "Controlling ferments to not produce the complex sulfides is beyond our means currently. This sulfide behavior of the ferment is more controlled by the yeast genetics than the winemaker."

However, new work from the Australian Wine Research Industry shows some unexpected results. Dr. Elizabeth Waters and her colleagues have found that hydrogen sulfur is in some cases generated in the wine after bottling when closures with very low oxygen transmission are used. The mechanism for this is as yet unclear. In addition, the same set of studies has shown that copper additions can, in some cases, result in increased formation of hydrogen sulfide during wine storage: quite the opposite effect of what these additions are intended for.

How is reduction recognized? In its worst manifestations, reduction is easy to spot: hydrogen sulfide gives eggy, drainlike aromas that spoil the wine. Any such wine is clearly faulty. But the most commonly encountered forms of reduction are more subtle. The form seen most often is "struck match/flint," presumably due to mercaptans. This form of reduction can be attractive in the right sort of context, but many people find it objectionable. In its most subtle form, it enhances the minerality of white wines, and it is often encountered in white Burgundies, where it can add to complexity.

Related to this 'good' reduction is the cabbage/cooked-vegetable character that comes from either mercaptans or disulfides. Again, this is sometimes found in white Burgundies, and although it's initially off-putting, it can produce complexity. Reduction also manifests itself in a slight rubbery quality, which is most often spotted in red wines. There are also strong smoky, roast coffee aromas in some reds that suggest high-toast oak but are actually due to volatile sulfur compounds. It should be added that low-level reduction may have only a small sensory impact on the aroma of wine but can affect the palate, obscuring the fruit expression and adding hardness to it. Thus it is also an issue of mouth feel.

One of the difficulties with this discussion is that the perception of SLOs seems to depend quite highly on the context of the wine. Also, at different concentrations the various SLOs will have a different sensory impact, which makes it hard to be sure what the signature impact of a specific sulfur compound is. In turn, this makes specific diagnosis of "reduction" faults difficult for tasters.

A distinction needs to be drawn here between reduction and the sensory characteristics of sulfur dioxide. Sulfur dioxide is added to almost all wines as a preservative and to counter the effects of oxidation. Very occasionally, it is added at levels where it crosses the sensory threshold, and then the wine will have a slightly acrid, sulfury edge to it.

While the development of SLOs in wine is normally best avoided, there are some circumstances where they can contribute something positive. New Zealand winemaker James Healey points out some of these. "In Champagne the bready/brioche character from aging for a period on lees is a result of a certain type of reduction in association with autolysis and liberation of the contents of yeast cells into the wine. The reductive characters from fermentation of Chardonnay juice containing highish solid concentrations result in accentuated nuttiness and improved texture after ageing on lees for some time. And the 'cat's pee' or sweaty character that develops during fermentation of Sauvignon Blanc from cooler climates is the result of a certain reduction-related compound."

Consultant winemaker Dominique Delteil also gives examples of the different manifestations of reduction. "First, a very ripe Languedoc Syrah macerated to reach liquorice aromas, and then aged in oak. In that wine, hints of 'burnt match' could be very interesting from a sensory point of view. They will match the ripe fruit/vanilla style. Most wine drinkers will appreciate that because those aromas are in a very sweet aromatic environment, so they won't express as dominant. Second, a cool-climate unripe Cabernet Sauvignon. Let's suppose that this wine has exactly (chemically speaking) the same amount of the sulfur compounds that gave the interesting light 'burnt match' in the above Syrah. In that wine those chemicals will give a different sensation that the same taster will translate as 'leek,' 'green bean,' and eventually 'garlic.'"

This complexity makes reduction one of the most interesting and intriguing topics in the wine trade. A fascinating idea is that what is often thought of as minerality in wine could actually (in some, if not all, cases) be due to reductive characters.

Portuguese winemaker Dirk Niepoort thinks that what often ended up as minerality in some famous wines was actually caused by certain imperfections in the must due to the terroir. "For example, because of a lack of a certain nutrient in a must from a certain terroir, fermentation would create off-flavours during the fermentation which in the end would give the so typical character of that area," he hypothesizes. "Certain treatment habits in the vineyards (for example, sulfur treatments done late) can create some residues in the must that influence fermentation, producing some reduction, which are cleaned up by the time the wines are bottled but give a lot of character."

OXIDATION AND VOLATILE ACIDITY

We consider these two faults together because one causes the other.

OXIDATION

Oxidation is covered in some length in Chapter 8, where we discuss the use of SO_2. While oxygen is needed in some wines at certain stages—for example, during red wine fermentation and in very small quantities during barrel aging of wines—winemaking is mostly a reductive process in which good practice seeks to exclude it because wine contains many flavour compounds that are adversely affected by oxygen. In particular, fresh fruity aromas are highly vulnerable to the impact of oxygen, and wines exposed to too much oxygen lose their fruitiness, fade in colour (or, in the case of whites, darken, turning golden and then orange or brown), and generally become less attractive.

Wine is a complex liquid consisting of a multitude of different chemicals, many of which are created by yeasts during the fermentation process. As with any mixture of chemical entities, these chemicals will rearrange themselves into the most favorable energetic state. This is the principle of entropy. In simplistic terms, the various molecules will swap tiny charged particles called electrons, and the nature of this swapping is determined by what is known as the redox state of the wine. In any chemical reaction between two partners, one entity gains electrons (is reduced), and the other loses them (is oxidized). These processes occur in tandem, and it follows that you don't always need to have oxygen present for oxidation to occur. The redox potential of a particular wine determines what sort of state of its component molecules is most energetically favorable. That is, the reactions that take place in wine are affected by the redox potential. This potential shifts according to how much oxygen the wine is exposed to. It follows that it will be lowest in bottled wine and highest in barrels after topping up and stirring. It will also be lower in wines sealed with closures with lower oxygen transmission (such as tin-lined screwcaps) than it is in those with higher gas transmission (such as synthetic corks). Exposure to air increases the redox potential; oxygen becomes dissolved in the wine and fuels oxidation reactions.

What sorts of reactions happen when wine is exposed to oxygen? Oxygen, which is often assumed to be highly reactive, doesn't react directly with wine but requires an oxidizing agent to become truly reactive. It then forms the highly reactive compound hydrogen peroxide, which goes on to interact with other wine components. It might react with tannins and other phenols (of which there are more in red wines), it might form acetaldehyde by reacting with ethanol, or it might be bound by SO_2.

Acetaldehyde, the oxidation product of alcohol, is an important molecule in the oxidation of wine as discussed in Chapter 8. It has an appley aroma, and is perhaps best appreciated in the smell of a Fino Sherry. Red wines have a much better capacity for absorbing oxygen without showing oxidative changes because of the presence of high levels of polyphenols. This is also discussed in Chapter 8.

SO_2 protects wine from oxidation. White wines are typically bottled with at least 30 mg/L of free sulfur dioxide. Over time this level declines, and when it drops below about 10 mg/L, the wine begins to show signs of oxidation. But, as we discuss in Chapter 8, the science is a bit more complicated than this.

Exposure of the developing wine to oxygen at certain stages is crucial to successful winemaking. The problem is that there's a lot of guesswork involved. Traditional winemaking practices have serendipitously controlled oxygen exposure by using oak barrels and processes such as racking, often to good effect but sometimes not. One of the successes of modern winemaking has been the use of stainless steel tanks and practices that protect the must and evolving wine from oxygen throughout the winemaking process. This is known as reductive winemaking, and it has been central to the development of fruit-driven wine styles. Some winemakers, however, deliberately expose their white wine musts to oxygen to oxidize many of the phenolic compounds present (this is known as oxidative juice handling). These musts turn dark in color, but from then on the wine is handled reductively. The resulting white wine is actually longer lived and more resistant to oxidation.

To the nose, both reds and whites exposed to excessive oxygen lose their fresh, fruity aromas and become flat. In whites you can pick out the notes of apple and cider caused by acetaldehyde. The wine smells of sherry. Reds smell tired and fruitless and can sometimes develop a caramel-like quality. The palate of oxidized red wines also changes: they tend to become dry and slightly bitter.

It is much easier to spot oxidation in young wines than in old ones, and this fact raises the thorny question of the role of oxidation in wine aging. Conventional wisdom says that wine aging is an anaerobic process, taking place to best effect in the absence of external oxygen. This view is supported by anecdotal reports that old wines with the smallest ullages (the gas space between the bottom of the cork and the surface of the wine), where the cork has presumably sealed best, tend to taste the best. Studies in Australia comparing Chardonnay sealed in glass ampoules, in bottles sealed by screwcaps, and in bottles sealed by natural cork suggest that wines sealed hermetically, with no oxygen ingress, will still develop, but at the cost of some reduction defects. It could be that the only requirement for oxygen during wine aging is for just a trace, early on, to avoid reduction problems, and that the best aging then ensues when the seal is as tight as possible.

Heat increases the rate of chemical reactions, including oxidation events, but it also encourages chemical reactions that wouldn't take place at lower temperatures. This is one reason that wines kept at elevated temperatures age not only faster but also worse. Swings in temperature encourage the rate of oxidation of wine because as the temperature rises and falls, the pressure of the headspace above the wine changes, and there is a small exchange of air between the atmosphere and the wine bottle. There is also evidence that corks in contact with air (standing-up bottles) have a higher rate of gas exchange than those where the wine abuts the cork surface, which confirms the wisdom of laying wine down in cellars.

A current controversy in the wine world concerns the premature, random oxidation of white Burgundy from the 1995, 1996, and perhaps subsequent vintages. The phenomenon is extremely worrisome: customers are finding that in a case of high-end white Burgundies from the same producer, vineyard, and vintage, some will be pristine, while others will be lifeless, dark colored, and oxidized. No one knows exactly why, although several theories have been advanced. The random nature of the problem points to cork problems, but it's likely that some factor is making the wines excessively fragile, and the natural variation in cork oxygen transmission is then exposing this fragility by causing only some bottles to oxidize.

Some wine styles are deliberately oxidized. Many Sherries, all tawny Ports and all Madeiras are made in a way in which deliberate oxidation is part of the wine style. But for most wines, unlimited exposure to oxygen is fatal. However, a degree of oxidation is acceptable in some wines. After all, the aging process often involves development of the wine in response to very slow exposure to oxygen. How much is too much is a question of degree. Oxidation characters are common, but by no means universal, in wines made naturally with very low or no additions of SO_2. It is hard to say when these characters are faulty and when they promote complexity; to some degree it is a matter of personal taste and also of the context of the wine.

VOLATILE ACIDITY

Volatile acidity, as the name suggests, is that part of the acidity of a wine that is released from the wine as a vapour at room temperature and thus makes itself known to the nose—aromatic acidity, if you will. Winemakers normally split acidity measurements into three components, with some overlap among them. First, there is the total acidity, which is a measure of how much acid is in the wine solution. This is expressed in grams per litre, in terms of either tartaric acid equivalent or sulfuric acid equivalent (the latter measure is commonly used in France but not elsewhere). Then there is the measure called pH: the lower the pH, the more acid the solution (from school, you'll probably remember that this is shown by litmus paper turning red), and the higher the pH, the more alkaline it is (litmus paper turns blue). The pH level is a very useful measurement for wine, but for many complex reasons it doesn't correspond exactly to the total acidity, which is why both pH and total acidity are routinely measured. Finally, there is volatile acidity, which is a measure mainly of acetic acid, but also of lesser quantities of butyric, formic, and propionic acids. Another compound often mentioned in the context of volatile acidity is ethyl acetate, which is produced by chemical modification (esterification) of acetic acid and smells of nail varnish.

Just as all wines have acidity—it is a fundamental component—all wines have volatile acidity. However, volatile acidity is something winemakers try to minimize, and it is almost always bad if reaches a detectable level. In this sense, it is a rarity: a wine fault that is a clear-cut problem, to be avoided as much as is possible. "Volatile acidity is always a problem," says wine consultant Pascal Chatonnet. "It's a fundamental problem of wine stability." Indeed, it is not possible to produce wine without at least some volatile acidity, because varying levels of acetic acid are produced by all the microbes involved in fermentation, as well as by acetic acid bacteria that are present in all wines.

"Volatile acidity is produced by yeasts during fermentation," explains another leading winemaking consultant, Tony Jordan, "but most of the yeasts we use produce a level that is well below threshold." Under normal fermentation conditions the classic wine yeast *Saccharomyces cerevisiae* produces up to 100 mg/L of acetic acid. "There are some notorious VA-producing yeasts," adds Jordan, "so unless you want VA, you avoid them.

Wild yeast fermentations are more problematic. Often if they are slow to start or stick, volatile acidity becomes an issue." Under high sugar conditions, *S. cerevisiae* can produce considerably higher levels of acetic acid, and lactic acid bacteria, which carry out malolactic fermentations in almost all reds and some whites, produce small amounts of acetic acid. But if alcoholic fermentation stops and the lactic acid bacteria start work on unfermented sugars in the must, then this potential for acetic acid production is greatly increased. However, the chief microbes responsible for volatile acidity problems are the acetic acid bacteria.

There are two genera of these acetic acid bacteria, *Acetobacter* and *Gluconobacter*, and in wine the most frequently encountered species are *G. oxydans*, *A. aceti*, and *A. pasteurianus*. These bacteria are quite common and are ideally adapted for growing in sugar- and alcohol-rich environments. Studies have shown that even under conditions where they aren't able to grow or proliferate, they persist in wine, ready to get going again should the wine environment suddenly become favourable for growth. The key fact about their biology is that their metabolism is aerobic; that is, they need oxygen in order to grow. If at any stage in the wine's development the level of dissolved oxygen rises, the bacteria will begin growing and producing acetic acid.

What do they do? In the presence of oxygen, *Acetobacter* oxidizes ethanol to acetaldehyde and then to acetic acid, while *Gluconobacter* prefers glucose, which it oxidizes to ketonic compounds. As a result, *Acetobacter* is more common in wines where fermentation is under way, and it is the chief culprit underlying most volatile acidity problems, while *Gluconobacter* is more prevalent in musts and on grapes. *Acetobacter* can also turn the acetic acid it produces into ethyl acetate, which is detectable at about a quarter of the concentration of acetic acid.

The problem of volatile acidity can begin in the vineyard. All ripe grapes have populations of acetic acid bacteria on them—this is why all wines contain at least small populations of these bacteria—but rotten or damaged grapes have particularly high concentrations. In this case, where the grape skins are broken, fermentation can begin before the grapes are picked; in these conditions there is plenty of oxygen around, so the bacteria turn the alcohol into acetic acid, and as a result the must can have a relatively high level of volatile acidity even before fermentation begins.

In the winery, the keys to keeping volatile acidity levels down are good hygiene and protecting the developing wine from oxygen. Tony Jordan cites poor cellar hygiene coupled with poor barrel topping or ullaged tanks without a good inert gas cover as the chief causes of volatile acidity in wine. Oxygen exposure is bad for two reasons. First, oxygen reacts directly with components in the wine, modifying some of the important aroma components and also producing acetaldehyde, which makes the wine taste flat and oxidized. Second, there are viable populations of acetic acid bacteria in almost all wines, and given the right conditions, they will grow. Their chief requirement is for oxygen, but higher temperatures and pH (less acid conditions) also encourage their growth. Each time the wine is exposed to another bit of oxygen, for example, during racking, or if a barrel isn't topped up, they can grow a bit more and produce more acetic acid. Even when wines are protected by 25 to 30 mg/L of the almost universally used antimicrobial and antioxidant compound SO_2 in its active free form—a very respectable level that will keep a lid on microbial problems while it is maintained—the bacterial populations remain viable, waiting for their next chance to grow.

If a winemaker has done her or his job properly, most finished wines will typically have acetic acid levels of 0.3–0.5 g/L (if yeasts typically make 100 mg/L, this means that the bacteria are contributing 200–400 mg/L). This is below the level at which we can detect it, which is known as the aroma threshold. The aroma threshold for acetic acid depends on the context of the wine and the sensitivity of the person sniffing, but is between 0.6 and 0.9 g/L. Wine-producing countries have laws specifying the maximum allowable concentrations of acetic acid in wine. In the EU, they are 1.07 g/L of acetic acid for white and rosé wines and 1.2 g/L for reds. In Australia, the limit is 1.5 g/L, while the United States specifies 1.1 g/L for whites and 1.2 g/L for reds. There are usually special rules for wines barrel aged for a long time or for sweet wines, which may exceed these limits.

High levels of volatile acidity are also a problem because they can cause one of a winemaker's greatest nightmares: a stuck fermentation. Acetic acid bacteria produce yeast-inhibiting substances, and there is evidence that acetic acid itself is toxic to wine yeasts. Once a fermentation has "stuck"—in other words, the alcohol-producing yeast *S. cerevisiae* has stopped turning sugar into alcohol even though there is still sugar left in the must—the wine is at real risk: it is a sitting duck for the proliferation of even more acetic acid bacteria, and fermentation may never begin again.

What can winemakers do about volatile acidity? Their best bet is to prevent it from occurring, and the most effective protective strategy is to keep air away from wine. We asked Tony Jordan whether he took steps to avoid volatile acidity in his winemaking. "All the time," he responded. "You need to be very careful with hygiene in equipment and storage vessels. You should make sure rigorous cellar practice is followed at all times, such as topping regimes, inert gas cover, and, of course, you should make sure you are tasting all your wines regularly and the lab is monitoring routinely for VA amongst other things."

In wines that are bottled young and kept in stainless steel tanks during their development, volatile acidity can fairly easily be avoided by not using damaged or rotten grapes, using SO_2 sensibly, not letting the pH get too high, and using techniques such as blanketing the wine with inert gases. For wines that are aged for some time in barrels, this becomes a little more difficult. Similar strategies can be employed, but one of the reasons for using barrels is to allow controlled exposure to oxygen during a wine's upbringing. In this case, it's especially important to keep the barrels topped up and to monitor the levels of free SO_2 to ensure that they are protecting the wine effectively against bacterial growth.

How can volatile acidity be spotted in a wine? It's not encountered very often, perhaps because the gap between the sensory threshold (0.6–0.9 g/L) and the legal limit (just over 1g/L, depending on wine style and country) isn't very large. Most well-made commercial wine styles don't show it. We have tasted wines spiked with both excessive acetic acid and excess ethyl acetate. Acetic acid at 1.5 g/L adds a lifted, vinegary edge to the wine. Ethyl acetate, which is commonly found alongside acetic acid, adds a nail-varnish-like quality at 250 mg/L. At lower levels, volatile acidity can make itself known in more subtle ways. Australian wine judges have a descriptive term for the nose of a wine: *lifted*. A lifted nose is one where a little bit of volatile acidity is present, and it's sometimes found in red wines that have been barrel aged for a long time. It's not always negative. Indeed, one can argue that a little bit of volatile acidity can be positive. Tony Jordan agrees: "VA just above threshold can look good in many reds. Apart from stickies [an Australian term for sweet wines], I don't like it in whites." He adds, "Volatile acidity is very much part of many botrytis styles, though too much is too much." It is quite a challenge for winemakers to keep volatile acidity low in sweet wines because the high sugar content makes yeasts struggle a bit, and even more so in wines made from botrytised grapes because these come into the winery with higher levels of acetic bacteria. "These are stressed fermentations," says Jordan, "but good attention to yeast selection, nutrient status throughout the ferment, and fermentation rate helps."

Finally, what can winemakers do if they have a barrel or tank of wine with a volatile acidity problem? There are three choices. The first is to dump the wine. The second is to blend it with a sufficient volume of wine with a low acetic acid level so the final level of the wine is below the aroma threshold. The third is to use reverse osmosis, as discussed in Chapter 10. This relies on the use of a special filtration technique that strips out a colourless permeate consisting of water, alcohol, and small molecules including the offending acetic acid. This permeate is then passed through an ion exchange column, which removes the acetic acid, and the remainder, now free of acetic acid, is recombined with the wine. Reverse osmosis and ion exchange can also be used on wines that have stuck in the middle of fermentation; once the acetic acid has been removed, fermentation often starts again.

THE CARBON FOOTPRINT OF WINE

Natural wines are full of good intentions. They are full of fossil fuel, too.

ERIC TEXIER, WINEGROWER IN THE RHÔNE

The issue of global warming (or, more correctly, climate change) is a huge current concern for the wine industry. Carbon dioxide is one of a number of greenhouse gases that perform an important role in the atmosphere. These gases allow solar radiation to warm the planet, and then they act as a sort of gaseous insulating layer that stops some of this heat from escaping. Without the greenhouse effect, surface temperatures on earth would be some 30°C lower, and life as we know it wouldn't exist. But human activity has increased atmospheric carbon dioxide levels, largely as a result of the burning of fossil fuels. Consequently, the greenhouse effect has become more intense, and global average temperatures have risen.

The Intergovernmental Panel on Climate Change (IPCC) is a scientific body that provides policy makers with objective information on this complex subject. Its latest report, from 2007 (the Fourth Assessment Report; see www.ipcc.ch), makes disturbing reading. It shows clear trends of increasing average temperatures, rising sea levels, and increased melting of the polar ice caps. These changes all occur in tandem with increasing atmospheric greenhouse gas levels. Whatever we do to reduce greenhouse gas emissions, there will still be future temperature rises because of the amount that we've already put into the atmosphere, but the lower we manage to get our emissions, the lower these rises will be.

This chapter examines how the wine industry might address its own carbon footprint. Although this topic isn't directly relevant to the subject of this book, any winegrower who wants to work as naturally as possible should also want to work sustainably, in sympathy with the environment. Carbon dioxide emissions pollute the environment as much as agrochemical runoff, so we feel that this is a legitimate topic for a book on authentic and natural wine to cover.

Interestingly, the natural wine movement seems to ignore the issue of sustainability.

Eric Texier, a grower in the Rhône known for his natural approach, is one of the few members of the unofficial natural wine movement who raise this issue, and he is somewhat critical of his peers. He claims that they focus on limited aspects of naturalness in wine and ignore real sustainability. "As I started growing grapes organically (according to the Ecocert rules), I could see that my oil consumption was raised quite a bit for my Brézème vineyard," he says in a piece he wrote for the *Saignée* blog (http://saignee. wordpress.com), whose author Cory Cartwright ran a thirty-two–day series focusing on natural wine in 2010. "During 1999, I burned about 550 liters of diesel for 4.2 ha. At that time, these vineyards were chemically weeded and treated. During 2008, a tough year for mildew though, I burned 980 liters of diesel for the same 4.2 ha. These same vineyards are now ploughed under the row, cultivated between the rows and treated with so-called 'organic' molecules (copper sulphate, sulphur)."

Texier reckons that ploughing under the vine instead of using Roundup (the trade name for glyphosate, an herbicide) results in 20 mL of fossil fuel burned for each bottle. He says that back in 1995, when he started making natural wines, "they were traditional, artisanal wines made from organic grapes, and sustainability was part of the picture." He complains that now, very few in the natural wine world are interested when he voices his doubts about the use of copper as a fungicide (it is a heavy metal that lasts for a long time in the soil, killing mycorrhizae and other soil fungi) or the excessive use of fossil fuels that organic viticulture necessitates. "Sustainability is rarely a subject of discussion. SO_2, carbonic maceration, filtration, amphorae, Jules Chauvet, even Che Guevara are much more fashionable than fossil fuel consumption or carbon footprint in the present natural wine discussion."

WINE PRODUCTION IN A CHANGING CLIMATE

That our climate is changing is an indisputable fact. But how do we know that the current rise in global temperatures is due to human activity, not just part of a bigger trend or cycle? And how do we know that the predicted impact of greenhouse gas emissions is correct? We can't be totally sure, because understanding the world's climate is an incredibly complicated business. However, while a decade ago some scientists (and some rather notable American politicians) were quite sceptical about the issue of global warming, there is now more of a consensus that it is actually human activity that is responsible for this climate change. The projections about what will happen if we carry on as we are now doing vary, but mostly along the scale of bad to very bad: very few now doubt that the consequences of such action would be serious indeed.

This is largely all discouraging news for the wine industry. The world's great vineyards are carefully sited so that grape variety, soils, and climate all work in unison. Shift the climate, and the quality of the wine will likely suffer. However, in the short term, some countries whose vineyards are on the climatic margins for viticulture have undoubtedly benefited from global warming. Germany and the United Kingdom are good examples. Renowned German winemaker Helmut Dönnhoff cites figures showing that between 1988 and now, the average temperatures in his region, the Nahe, have increased by a degree, and flowering is a week or ten days earlier. "I want global warming to stop now," he says. "It's perfect: we are the winners at the moment." He says that because of climate change he hasn't had a bad vintage since 1988.

In some well-publicized research, Gregory Jones, a scientist from Southern Oregon University in the United States, has examined the implications of climate change for the wine industry. His results have probably been discussed a bit too much now, but that's simply because they are the only data of this kind. Jones and colleagues analysed fifty years of climate data from twenty-seven different wine regions and compared them with Sotheby's 100-point vintage ratings, looking for any trends. They also looked at the projected temperature changes over the next fifty years. The results show that growing-season temperatures have increased by an average of 2°C over the last fifty years. Surprisingly, in tandem with this rise in temperatures, the quality of vintages has also improved, although a confounding factor here is that winemaking and viticulture have also improved over this period, and with the increased interest in fine wine, producers have been able to justify greater efforts because of the higher prices the best wines fetch.

But winegrowers are not worried only about global warming. Along with rising temperatures, the incidence of exceptional weather events appears to have increased, and climate scientists reckon that the climate will become even more erratic in the future. Previously predictable seasonal patterns have been disturbed; hurricanes and storms are more frequent; droughts are more severe; and there has been an increase in unseasonably warm or cool spells. All of these are bad news for winegrowers, because while you can adapt to steady warming trends, you can't do anything about unpredictability. One of the biggest worries concerns the future of the Gulf Stream—the warm Atlantic current that currently ensures that the United Kingdom and Atlantic-influenced western Europe have a warmer climate than they would otherwise enjoy, given their northerly latitude. If it were to disappear, then some of Europe's greatest wine regions would be devastated, and there are signs that the flow is already weakening.

What about the next fifty years? If Jones's predictions are correct, most wine regions can expect an average increase of 2.04°C on top of the 2°C temperature rise seen over the past fifty years. While this may benefit some cooler regions and may open up some new areas for viticulture, warmer regions could suffer badly. In some cases the careful matching of grape variety to vineyard site may have to be reconsidered. The wine industry, however, is filled with passionate, resourceful, and determined people, and so the

FIGURE 12.1

Chilean winery Cono Sur is trying to communicate about carbon footprint issues with consumers who buy their wines.

hope is that growers across the globe will be able to adapt and improvise to continue making great wine even in the face of a changing climate.

It is for this reason that the wine trade, along with the rest of society, has recently taken a keen interest in its carbon footprint. While the carbon footprint of the wine trade is just a small fraction of the total amount, we still, like all of society, have an obligation to challenge ourselves to reduce this footprint. But what exactly is the carbon footprint of wine, and what can be done about it?

IDENTIFYING FOOTPRINT PROCESSES

There are two stages in the process of identifying the carbon footprint of wine. The first is to list all the processes, from grape to wine glass, where there is a net production of carbon dioxide (or other greenhouse gases) that otherwise would not have occurred. The second is to attempt to quantify these processes—a more difficult task.

In the vineyard, agricultural operations involving tractors or other vehicles are likely to be a big contributor. The fewer the passes through the vineyard by tractor, the lower the footprint. Some wineries use biodiesel to power their tractors. Alternatively, some wineries are considering the use of electric tractors that are charged by solar power, which may be an attractive option in the future.

Sprays have two levels of footprint: first, the energy required to manufacture the spray, and second, the fuel burned in delivering the spray. The calculation is complex because while a practice such as manual tillage of the soil may seem more environmentally friendly than the use of herbicides, it may require more mechanical input and thus have a higher carbon footprint. Likewise, biodynamic preparations have a carbon footprint in preparation—they aren't usually dynamized by hand—and in application to the vines and the soil.

Pumping water for irrigation uses power and therefore has a footprint, as may the wastewater treatment process that is part of being a good environmental steward.

Frost protection involving the use of propellers, burners, or helicopters is likely to be a rare event but involves some level of footprint.

Cooling the winery's buildings (or heating them in the winter in cooler regions) may require quite a lot of power. The more efficient the winery's design and the better the insulation, the less energy will be needed. Practices such as opening winery doors or windows at night to allow cooler air in may help passive cooling of the facility.

Pumps in the winery use power, as does lighting the winery where this is required. Switching to modern energy-efficient lighting will help, and in some regions subsidies may be available.

Cooling tanks require a major energy input. Many fermentations take place at low temperatures. At various stages in winemaking, significant cooling of large volumes of wine is necessary, for example, during cold stabilization. Techniques being developed to carry out stabilization of white wines without chilling to very low temperatures could result in reduction of winery footprint. But products such as metatartaric acid and carboxymethyl cellulose (CMC) have a manufacturing footprint that needs to be considered before these are introduced as solutions.

There can even be unintended and unexpected consequences of working more naturally in the vineyard. For example, compost heaps that are not managed properly can release methane, which is a much worse greenhouse gas than carbon dioxide.

Travel for marketing and selling wine is a carbon footprint that is rarely considered.

Carbon dioxide released during fermentation doesn't count towards the winery footprint because the carbon used has been sequestered from atmospheric CO_2 during photosynthesis in the vines. Some wineries are now capturing the CO_2 released during fermentation, however, and using it for inert gas cover during processing to combat oxidation.

Two inputs that wineries will find hard to avoid are those for packaging wine (dry goods) and transporting wine. If a winery is to be truly carbon neutral, it should cover the entire process from grape to wine glass and cannot ignore the transport chain to the consumer. We'll return to this important issue later in considering the packaging of wine (including the closure) and its transport.

QUANTIFYING FOOTPRINTS

In a paper published in 2009 (*Journal of Wine Research* Vol 20, pp. 15–26), Tyler Colman and Pablo Päster have attempted to calculate the carbon life cycle of wine, taking into account all elements of wine production, from vineyard to consumption. They calculate that grape production has a relatively high carbon footprint, citing figures of 50–100 kg of agrochemicals to produce 1 ton of grapes (as opposed to 40 kilograms per ton for corn), and mechanization requiring 130 litres of fuel per ton of grapes (as opposed to 22.7 litres per ton for corn). In addition, 550,000 litres of water are needed to produce a ton of grapes, and 100 g CO_2e (carbon dioxide equivalent, a measure of greenhouse gas emissions) is used in electricity or natural gas to produce a bottle of wine.

But the greatest impact of wine production is that of transportation both of the dry goods used in the winery and—more significantly—of the wine to the consumer. Cartons of bottled wine are heavy, and transporting them has a significant environmental impact. Colman and Päster use the following emission factors for different modes of cargo transportation (all in grams of CO_2e per ton of cargo for each kilometre transported; $g.t^{-1}.km^{-1}$):

Container shipping	52.1
Container shipping using reefers (refrigerated containers)	67.1
Train transport	200
Trucking	252
Air Cargo	570

In calculations that presumably weren't well received by the California wine industry, they suggested that a bottle of wine shipped from Australia to Chicago might have a lower carbon footprint than a bottle of cult California Cabernet also going to Chicago (life-cycle CO_2e 3.44 kg versus 4.5 kg) because cult Cabernets usually come in very heavy bottles and are worth enough to make air freight feasible. "To underscore the fact that not all transportation miles are alike, many New Yorkers may be surprised that holding bottle mass constant, it is more 'green' to drink wine from Bordeaux (1.8 kg) with a long sea voyage as opposed to a wine from Napa (2.6 kg) with a long truck trip," state the authors.

They also attempt to calculate the total greenhouse gas (GHG) impact of the world wine industry: "Assuming average greenhouse gas emissions of 2 kg per liter and a global production volume of 2,668,300,000 liters in 2001, the global GHG emissions from wine production and distribution are 5,336,600 tons. If the total global anthropogenic GHG emissions are 6.3 billion tons, the production and distribution of wine represents 0.08 percent of global GHG emissions. While this percentage seems small, it is equivalent to the fossil fuel combustion emissions of roughly 1,000,000 passenger vehicles over a year."

What can the wine industry do to lessen the carbon footprint of wine? The chief culprits seem to be transportation and packaging of wine. While it may not be possible to eliminate transportation, changing the way wine is packaged is the lowest-hanging fruit—the easiest way for the wine industry to reduce its carbon footprint.

BULK SHIPPING

One of the largest changes in the way wine is transported during recent decades has been the rise of bulk shipping. Many wines, especially those at the more commercial end of the spectrum, are now shipped in bulk using 25,000-litre flextanks. These are like large bladders that fit inside a shipping container and are then filled with wine. In the destination country the flextanks are then unloaded at the bottling plant and packaged appropriately for the market. The advantage of using flextanks is that they are the most economical way of shipping wine, without any packaging. Also, where relatively high-oxygen-transmission packaging such as bag-in-box, Tetrapak, or polyethylene teraphthalate (PET) is used, transit time, which can be considerable, isn't deducted from the shelf life of the wine. The disadvantage is that wine quality can suffer unless care is taken to minimize oxygen pickup during transfer operations. However, shipping wine in bulk (assuming that dissolved oxygen, sulfur dioxide, and temperature are managed properly, and that operators at both ends know what they are doing) could result in better product on store shelves, especially if the wine has to travel a long way. This is because buffering that comes from wine being in a large-volume container insulates it somewhat from temperature changes.

LIGHTWEIGHTING

For those wine producers who need, for a variety of reasons, to stick with glass bottles, there has been an industry push towards reducing the weight of glass, known as *lightweighting*. The average bottle weight is currently around 500 g, whereas the lightest 75 cL bottle weighs around 300 g, so there is plenty of scope for saving weight. As an example, the Chilean producer Errazuriz has recently started using a new, specially designed lightweight bottle that looks much classier than the existing alternatives. Journalists have also started to protest against heavy bottles. Wine writer Jancis Robinson has for a few years outed producers using extremely heavy bottles (which are usually intended to confer seriousness on "icon" wines), and fellow wine writer Tim Atkin has recently announced that he will refuse to review wine in very heavy bottles.

ALTERNATIVES TO GLASS

In recent years, moves have been made to replace glass, which, while being cheap and excellent at protecting wine from the ingress of oxygen, is heavy and has a tendency to break.

BAG-IN-BOX

Putting wine in a plastic bag with a tap suits those consumers who drink modestly or infrequently. As a glass is drawn from a wine box, the internal bag collapses, so there is no need for air to enter to fill the gap left by the vacated wine. This avoids any oxygen ingress and subsequent oxidation, with the consequence that the residual wine is kept fresh for some time. Bag-in-box is also an economical way to ship wine because a pallet of bag-in-box wine holds 80 percent more wine and is less than two-thirds the weight of the equivalent volume of glass-bottled wine, thus reducing the carbon footprint. Boxes also appeal to retailers because they are easy to merchandise (they fit on shelves better, they are easier to handle, and they are non-breakable).

The drawback of bag-in-box is the high oxygen transmission of the bag material, which can result in rapid product evolution and short shelf life. There are two main bag materials: metallized polyester and coextrusion with ethyl vinyl alcohol (EVOH). Both have drawbacks. Metallized polyester bags can suffer from flex cracking during transport, which can quadruple the oxygen transmission level; EVOH doesn't suffer from this problem but works less well at higher temperatures and humidities. Another source of oxygen transmission is the tap, which is plastic, and there is also some extra oxygen pickup during filling. All these factors result in a shelf life of just nine months or so, which has led to a move towards filling bags at their destination market. In addition, the sulfur dioxide levels of bag-in-box products are usually elevated to counter the higher oxygen transmission.

Sweden is perhaps the most interesting case study for bag-in-box wine because this format accounts for more than half of all still light wine sales (53 percent in January 2009). This is largely because of the Swedish alcohol monopoly, the Systembolaget, which creates unusual market conditions. First, there are no price promotions, which makes bag-in-box the cheapest way to buy wine. Also, because there are only four hundred monopoly shops, consumers prefer to stock up in large shopping trips, and bag-in-box is the easiest way to do this. Bag-in box is also dominant in the Norweigan wine market, and is growing in popularity in Denmark. In other countries, such as the United Kingdom, France, Australia, and the United States, bag-in-box continues to be a strong presence on the market, showing some growth but looking unlikely to expand much further at the expense of glass.

PET

The latest development in packaging is the appearance of 75 cL (standard-sized) PET bottles. PET, a plastic whose more formal name is polyethylene teraphthalate, has been used for wine before, most commonly with small 25 cL bottles, and also with 1.5-litre bottles of inexpensive wine from the south of France. But only recently has it been used for 75 cL bottles designed to be a replacement for glass. Two wines, a New Zealand Sauvignon Blanc and an Australian Shiraz Rosé, were launched by the United Kingdom supermarket Sainsbury's in PET in 2007, and Australian producer Wolf Blass has launched two of its Green Label wines in PET internationally. The Systembolaget in Sweden put out a tender for six wines in PET in 2008; the winning producers were Mitchelton (Victoria, Australia) and Paul Sapin (a *négociant* and bottler based in Beaujolais, France).

Potential advantages include weight (a typical 75 cL glass bottle weighs around 400 g; the same size in PET weighs 54 g, making transportation more efficient), robustness (PET bottles don't break, which makes them safer and easier to transport), size (they are considerably smaller), and recyclability (green glass, the colour most commonly used for wine, has limited use recycled in many countries).

The main potential disadvantage of PET, like bag-in-box, is in preserving wine quality. PET allows more oxygen ingress than glass, and thus the wine loses freshness more quickly and has a shorter shelf life. As with all plastics, PET allows diffusion of oxygen. To counter this, barrier technologies and oxygen scavengers are incorporated into PET construction. Barrier technologies lose their effectiveness at higher temperatures, which is one of the reasons that it's inadvisable to ship PET bottles over long distances. In addition, bottles begin to age after they are manufactured because the oxygen scavengers start working immediately.

Also, plastic items have an increasingly negative image in the eyes of consumers. Convincing them that plastic is an environmentally friendly option will be difficult, and it will be hard to get away from the cheap look of plastic bottles. But if PET bottles are used creatively, they could become an intrinsic component of the image of new brands rather than just lighter, smaller versions of existing brands.

TETRA PRISMA

Perhaps the most "alternative" of the alternatives to glass bottles for wine is Tetra Prisma, from Tetrapak. While Tetrapak's Tetra Brick has been used for quite a while as a way of packaging wine, it hasn't really caught on. The better-looking Tetra Prisma is a new development and has lately been making waves in the wine world. The French company Boisset has been a market leader with this packaging: its French Rabbit brand of Vin de Pays d'Oc wines was designed with Tetra Prisma as an intrinsic component. It was launched in August 2005 and exists only in Tetra Prisma. Technically speaking, Tetra Prisma has an aluminium foil layer sandwiched between polyethylene, with an outer cardboard skin. Barrier properties of this foil are good because the flex cracking that occurs in the foil layer of bags is unlikely to occur here. Unlike bag-in-box, there is no oxygen ingress through the cap because the cap pierces the foil only when the pack is opened. Boisset claims that Tetra Prisma reduces packaging by 90 percent compared with glass and is fully recyclable.

In 2008 the successful southern French producer Mont Tauch released one of its low-priced Village du Sud range, old-vines Grenache, in Tetra Prisma. It uses an environmental justification for this decision but is also championing Tetra's other benefits: ease of opening and resealing, light weight, robustness, and collapsability. A spokesperson for Mont Tauch revealed that the wine is not prepared differently for Tetra Prisma, and that the expected shelf life is six months, better than for bag-in-box, although bag-in-box producers might argue this point. Mont Tauch has found that the Swedish and Canadian markets are the most receptive to this alternative packaging. Interestingly, in both Canada and Sweden, alcoholic beverage buying is controlled by a government-backed alcohol monopoly. Perhaps the influence of the Liquor Control Board of Ontario, which first listed Tetra Prisma wine in August 2005 and now offers sixty different wines in this packaging, is one explanation for the high success of this format in Canada.

POUCHES/BLADDERS

A variation on the bag-in-box theme that has recently shown promise is the wine pouch, which is effectively the bag without the box. Two prominent brands, Arniston Bay of South Africa and Palandri of Australia, have been released in a foil/plastic pouch called the E-Pak.

CANS

Ring-pull cans are available and are widely stocked by supermarkets, but their use remains a niche involving cheap wines and shows little sign of growth.

It seems that alternatives to glass bottles for wine could have a bright future in markets where consumer attitudes are open, and that concerns over the carbon footprint of wine could be the main driver. Alternative packaging is not something that consumers necessarily want, but it seems that they will embrace it if retailers push it, using green motives as the story. But the possibility remains that glass alternatives could be used creatively as an innovative aspect of new brand design. Almost all the alternatives to glass reduce the shelf life of wine, so the supply chain and inventory management need to be good if consumers are to be presented with wines in optimal condition.

CLOSURE CARBON FOOTPRINTS

What about wine bottle closures? Cynics might suggest that when there is a bandwagon running through town, people will jump on it, and the two major closure manufacturers with the most to gain from a carbon audit of their businesses have both commissioned surveys focusing on sustainability, carbon footprints, and environmental issues. But while there's clearly a strong motive for them to do this work, it would be unfair to suggest that such surveys are solely illegitimate attempts to bash the competition.

The first study was conducted by the French company Oeneo Bouchage. This is the firm behind one of the new generation of wine closures looking to take on the three market leaders: natural cork, synthetics, and screwcaps. Its product, Diam, is what is known as a technical cork. It is made from small pieces of ground-up cork combined with synthetic microspheres and a binding agent to form what looks and feels like a natural cork but is more regular and has a grainy complexion. The significant detail is that the cork

THE RETAILER'S PERSPECTIVE

JUSTIN HOWARD SNEYD, Former Head of Waitrose Wine Department and
Currently Head of Wine at Direct Wines in the United Kingdom

Lots of people are rushing into alternative packaging at the moment, but a lot of real understanding is needed to get to the bottom of what is good and bad for the environment. The totality of the decision is important: it is simplistic to say that U.K. bottling is good if you are shipping the bottles you use from Italy, for example. And with lightweight packaging, you may be using fewer grams of material, but if that material is made from petrochemicals, it may be worse for the environment than glass. As a retailer, we really need some way of measuring all this. There's also an extra layer of complexity contributed by social effects: shipping wine to the United Kingdom in bulk and bottling in the United Kingdom may put people out of work in the source country. How do you know whether you have really done the better thing?

particles are rendered taint free by washing them—somewhat ironically, given the topic of this chapter—in carbon dioxide kept at a temperature and pressure at which it is in a state called *supercritical*. In this state it has the cleaning power of a liquid but the penetration power of a gas.

Oeneo's report, carried out by a French consultancy, Cairn Environment, used the Bilan Carbone method (developed by the French Environmental Protection Agency) for assessing greenhouse gas emissions. Three closures were examined: natural cork, screwcaps (which it manufactures as part of its closures portfolio), and Diam. Of course, in-neck closures are accompanied by capsules, so the impact of these was taken into account. The results show clearly that natural cork has the lowest carbon footprint, and screwcaps the worst, with Diam somewhere between (see Table 12.1). What about synthetic closures? No figures are yet available, but it is likely that they come in somewhere between Diam and screwcap.

Let's try to put these figures in some kind of perspective. One million glass bottles, averaging 400 g each, have a carbon footprint of 183 tons. If screwcaps have a footprint of 35.9 tons per million units, this is around a fifth of the impact of glass bottles, so in the context of a bottle of wine, the difference appears to be significant. The second survey, released in July 2007, was carried out by Amorim, the world's largest cork producer, responsible for 50 percent of the world's corks by volume and 70 percent by value. The document is an independently audited sustainability report with a broad

TABLE 12.1.　Contribution of Closures to the Carbon Footprint of Wine

	Unit mass (grams)	Tons of CO_2 equivalent per million units[a]
Natural cork with PVC capsule	4.8	11.9
Diam with PVC capsule[b]	5.8	24.7
Diam with aluminium capsule	5.95	28.9
Screwcap made from 35% recycled aluminium[c]	4.92	52.3
Screwcap made from 70% recycled aluminium	4.92	35.9
Glass bottle	400	183.3

[a]These data have significant error bars (this means that there is some uncertainty about the range of values that are obtained because of uncertainties about the levels of emissions from incoming materials).

[b]The Diam figure is larger than the figure for cork because of the energy cost of the cleaning process by which taint is removed from the cork granules by carbon dioxide at its critical point, and because this closure incorporates a synthetic component. The PVC capsule is responsible for a 16% increase in the figure for a Diam closure alone. Some wineries are now using PET for capsules rather than PVC (which is not environmentally good).

[c]The greenhouse gas emissions of aluminium depend on how much of it is recycled.

SOURCE: Oeneo-sponsored report, July 2007.

scope that addresses several issues. With regard to global warming, this report highlights the positive impact of natural cork forests in retaining CO_2 (4.8 million tons annually in Portugal, 5 percent of the country's total emissions); the role of corks as a carbon sink during the product life cycle; the fact that Amorim supplies 46 percent of its energy needs from vegetal biomass, including cork dust; and the way Amorim is using lower-polluting maritime transport for its products where possible. The report also touches on the significance of cork forests as a form of sustainable development, balancing ecosystem conservation, creation of wealth, and social development. "By providing environmentally sound jobs to countless farming communities," states the report, "cork forests not only foster biodiversity but also provide the means to sustain and retain populations on the land, preventing additional migrations to already overcrowded cities." "Without cork, some of these areas would be deserted," adds Carlos de Jesus, communications director for Amorim. But he adds that this environmental angle "is not a panacea for the cork industry: it works only if aligned with a policy of research and development and quality control." It is also worth considering the prospect of a failed cork industry: although cork has other uses than wine bottle closures, the closures market is the most profitable. Without it, the cork forests might be at risk, with significant environmental implications, if they are no longer managed properly.

These surveys sound like bad news for screwcaps. But how significant will these sorts of data prove in the real world? It is unlikely that consumers will suddenly let these closure carbon footprint considerations affect their wine-buying habits. It is also unlikely that influential retailers will specify natural cork as a closure type on the basis of environmental impact.

More significantly, quibbling over small amounts of carbon emissions may be rather a moot point. New Zealand winemaker Steve Smith MW of Craggy Range argues that with the cost savings from buying screwcaps rather than more expensive alternatives, such as Diam, he can more than offset the extra carbon footprint. "The increased carbon footprint of a screwcap works out at $0.00679 \, kg \, CO_2$ per unit. To put that into perspective, it is the equivalent to driving 18 metres in a 2,000 cc car." But while this illustration seems impressive, the macro issues still need to be considered. Besides, if more people begin using alternatives such as Diam, their cost may come down.

Smith points out that in New Zealand there are programs such as EBEX 21 (Emissions/Biodiversity Exchange in the 21st Century; www.ebex21.co.nz) that use carbon credits to establish regenerating, permanent CO_2 sinks on private property that otherwise would not be funded. "This is a professional, audited system that not only provides an opportunity to develop carbon sinks, but also will leave a wonderful legacy of new native forests for future generations. These regenerating native forests would not have happened without the funding gained from carbon trading." Smith adds, "Tradable credits are now regarded as the most realistic approach to enable a worldwide reduction in carbon loading by encouraging reduction of carbon emissions (because a cost will come with emitting carbon) but most importantly funding carbon sinks that otherwise would not have happened." By his calculation, if he uses screwcap as a closure rather than Diam plus aluminium capsule and puts the margin he saves towards buying carbon credits, he will be operating with a significantly smaller carbon footprint.

"There is an almost overwhelming trend in the world today to develop marketing strategies using 'carbon footprint' as a justification for supporting one product at the expense of others," says Smith. "The current debate in the Northern Hemisphere on food miles as a justification for buying local is a true reflection of using flawed conclusions to establish trade protection. It is very likely a case of NZ wine sent by container on a boat to London uses less carbon in transport than sending a case of wine to London from Bordeaux by truck."

DOING SOMETHING ABOUT IT: GOING CARBON NEUTRAL

How can the wine industry respond to these calculations and reduce its carbon footprint? One way is by following the lead of several pioneering wineries that have now gone "carbon neutral." The first winery to do this was Grove Mill in New Zealand. In the United States, Parducci in Mendocino County, California, led the way.

Because wine production is unlikely ever to have zero emissions, a two-pronged strategy is needed. The first is to reduce emissions as much as possible; the second is to offset any remaining emissions that can't be eliminated. This offsetting involves the

FIGURE 12.2
New Zealand winery Grove Mill was the first to go fully carbon zero.

buying of carbon credits, and providing that it is done through a reputable company or organization, it is a legitimate step. The money is usually used to plant trees that otherwise wouldn't have been planted. However, this is not a very intellectually satisfying solution. These trees will take a long time to soak up CO_2, and it's not as though we can all live as we please and plant gazillions of trees to offset our activity. There is likely to be a very real limit to the number of trees that can be planted, and if everyone decided to offset his or her activity, potential forest areas, and the capacity of such organizations to plant forests, would be rapidly exhausted.

One option for wineries is to use power that is sustainably generated, through wind or solar power, for example. This would incur extra cost, but it is possible to contract with companies that deal with only sustainably generated power. While the actual electricity you receive through the power grid may have been generated in a number of ways, these companies put into the grid as much electricity from sustainable sources as their customers use.

Another option is for wineries to generate their own electricity. Because most wineries are in sunny locations, solar power is the obvious choice. It requires a large capital outlay, but in many cases subsidies and creative sources of financing exist. As an example, Saintsbury winery in Carneros, Napa, recently (2009) installed a large solar panel array that generates as much power as it uses each year. The array cost a lot of money, but with subsidies and a leaseback arrangement on the finance, the monthly cost is not much more than the winery was paying before, and after eight years it will own the panel array. Its intention is to increase generating capacity so that it can charge electric

FIGURE 12.3
Close-up of a solar panel at the Trefethen winery in the Napa Valley.

FIGURE 12.4
This carport is also a large array of solar panels at the Saintsbury winery in
Napa's Carneros subregion.

vehicles to do work in the vineyard, thus reducing its footprint even further. Such solar
power projects are not unusual in wineries, particularly in the United States. In Oregon, both Stoller and Torii Mor have incorporated them into the designs of their new
wineries.

To achieve sustainability, it makes sense to build wineries that are as energy efficient
as possible. Of course, this is possible only where new installations are being put in place.

In the United States, there is a relatively new certification scheme for buildings, called Leadership in Energy and Environmental Design (LEED). Stoller was the first winery in the USA to achieve LEED certification for its winery, and more are following suit.

In conclusion, while there is much posturing and marketing spin concerning carbon footprints, they are increasingly being taken seriously by many wineries. As we mentioned earlier, these sorts of considerations are not directly relevant to wine quality. However, we would expect that winegrowers serious about issues of authenticity in his or her wines should also take an interest in treading lightly in an environmental sense. Perhaps the strongest push, however, will come from retailers, who are taking a keen interest in the carbon footprint of their product ranges. In many cases this interest is being driven by legislation.

13

MARKETING AUTHENTIC WINE

Stories rule. Stories make us vote, or buy an iPod or give money to a charity.
Stories trump science every time.

SETH GODIN

Wine is a wonderful gift from nature. The vine sends its roots deep into the living earth. They struggle in search of water and nutrients, in communion with the unseen but vital world of soil microbes. Above the ground, the vineyard teems with life. A large community of grasses, herbs, and wildflowers supports a complex array of insect life, and the vine, with its verdant canopy, sends out its flowers and produces a crop of grapes. The attentive grower watches over this process and almost feels the energy of life in the air, tending the vineyard sensitively and with a light hand. During the warm days of summer the grapes ripen to the point that when the seasons begin to change and autumn is arriving, it is time to begin the harvest, not too soon and not to late. There is a time for everything. Listen to the vineyard, and it will speak to you; you will know when to act. The grower knows that these grapes contain within them the full potential of the wine that is to come; it is the winegrower's job merely to bring out that potential, to let the story of this place— the vineyard—be told with clarity in the wine. But it is an important and skilled job nonetheless. In the cellar, the winegrower works sensitively, doing all that is necessary to avoid failure but being careful not to do too much lest the fragile essence of terroir be lost. Patience and restraint are required in equal measure. Leaving the wine to tell about its place is almost an act of faith; the grower allows the whisper of the vineyard to steer the direction of the wine. Finally, the wine is bottled. It tells a story, first of that place, and second of that year. It is unique. It is special. Wine, that wonderful gift of nature.

This is the story of any authentic wine. It is a story worth telling. It resonates with people's desire for truth, and it is not told often enough in this age of industrial wine production. We tend to accept that cheap wines need to be tricked up, manipulated, and added to in order to make them palatable to modern consumers, but do they really need to be? Would it be disastrous to make large quantities of inexpensive wines more naturally, avoiding faults but allowing them to taste of where they came from, even if their flavours were simpler and less concentrated than those of their more expensive terroir wine cousins?

Are those who think that throwing this rich heritage away and creating dumbed-down ersatz wine brands that will yield them vast profits good captains of the wine industry? Has the strategy been successful thus far? Not as far as we can see, in the battleground of the supermarket wine aisles, where top wine brands challenge each other solely on the basis of price. These brands have a limited life cycle and eventually die on their own swords. Retailers push brand owners on pricing and profit margin until brand owners reach the breaking point. This heavily branded segment—pushing for commoditisation, dismissing quality and authenticity, and ignoring the wonderful story of wine and why it is special—is not only sailing into a storm for its own business but also, collectively, is the storm that encroaches on the wine industry at large. This is where the dumbing down, the consumer focus groups, and the sweetened fruit have led us. Are we confident that we are on the right path? Shouldn't we instead be looking to draw people in with the story of wine as a product of nature, expressing diverse, interesting flavours that are genuine in the sense that this wine is what the agroecosystem of the vineyard, with the vine as one of the key players, has yielded us, in conjunction with the climate of that year? And if so, how do we go about doing this practically? To answer these questions, we need to look at how wine has been marketed over the past twenty years.

WINE MARKETING

We need to say at the outset that neither of us is a marketing expert. But for a number of years, in different contexts, we have been keen observers of the wine business globally, with an interest in both the technical and marketing aspects of wine, and the following discussion is based on our observations.

Marketing in the wine industry to date has been underfunded and overly simplistic when compared with other industries—almost embarrassingly so. The major reason for this is the structure of the industry, which as a whole is highly fragmented and runs on small (if any) profit margins. At the commercial end of the market, until recently, supply and retail-sector marketing efforts have been, at best, a glorified term for a sales strategy based purely on price promotion. What about the other marketing Ps? (The four Ps of marketing are product, price, place, and promotion.) In effect, the marketer in any wine organization was (and in most organizations today still is) the salesperson. The New World has performed better than the Old World in sophistication and effectiveness of marketing activity, and this goes some way towards explaining the great success many New World wine-producing regions have experienced in the export market over

FIGURE 13.1
Compost in the hands of biodynamic winegrower James Millton.

the past twenty years. But also key is the fact that many New World winery groups were, not very long ago, start-ups with more need to focus on return on capital to stay in business. The Old World had little need to repay capital because of legacy. In addition, the Old World has been slower to accept rationalization and the economies of scale that come with it. In short, over the past two decades Old World winemakers have not been as hungry as New World ones, and this has been reflected in the way the two wine-producing worlds have approached the market. Of course, we cannot deny that New World producers have an easier message to communicate, that is, the variety as opposed to the region. They have fewer restrictions on labeling and have therefore been able to capitalize on the consumer's lack of understanding of the product by breaking marketing down to the simplest messages, variety and brand.

Successful producers at the premium end of the market, irrespective of region of origin, naturally employ sophisticated marketing techniques without massive budgets. This is a lesson that many producers and wine sellers need to learn. To create a pull effect for your product, you must be smart and use all four Ps in the mix. You need to communicate a consistent and dynamic message and to exploit public relations as much as possible. Because wine is a very complicated product for consumers to grasp, third-party (journalistic) endorsement is vital in making a successful premium brand (indeed, any brand). Winning over key trade opinion—makers or gatekeepers—is also vital. Thus spending time talking to journalists, top sommeliers, and other key members of the trade in all markets in which you aspire to be represented is critical.

Along these lines, if marketing is to be defined as activity to promote sales, the single biggest marketing effort in the wine world over the past 20 years has been driven by one man—Robert M. Parker, Jr. In the absence of a consolidated marketing effort from the industry, Parker—neither a winemaker nor a retailer, but an educated consumer—saw an opportunity to provide independent advice to other consumers on which wines to buy. His idea sounds simple, but the effect on the wine industry has been unprecedented and polarizing. Targeting the affluent baby boomer generation, Parker has created a multimillion dollar business that employs several people and likely has more influence on U.S. wine sales than the *Wine Spectator*, a consumer wine magazine with an enormous circulation.

The typical boomer, characterized by a curious blend of material aspiration and need for external affirmation, is an easy target of efficacious marketing. In Robert Parker the boomer found his or her hero. A boomer himself, Parker offered wealthy consumers without much wine knowledge a VIP pass to the top. He told them, in the simplest possible terms (a numerical score), which were the best wines, and they followed his judgments.

It's hard to put people into neat boxes, but sometimes a little generalization is useful. In wine marketing, there do appear to be generational differences that can be useful for helping us see the bigger picture a little more easily. You could call this "capturing the spirit of the age." Such generalizations can be useful in thinking about how to market to broad groups of people.

Over the past twenty years, a large part of the budget for wine marketing has targeted the baby boomer generation, persons born between 1946 and 1965. This is understandable: many people come to wine as adults, and many boomers have the disposable income to indulge their wine interest.

In his role as consumer champion, Parker has developed a powerful kingmaking ability. Only the *Wine Spectator*, with its huge circulation, has anything like the influence he—a single person—has on wine sales in the United States. Elsewhere in the world of wine there are important opinion makers, but they have a fraction of the reach to consumers that Parker has.

As a market for wine, the boomers have proved a rich mine, but they are not getting any younger. The new generation of consumers is alternatively referred to as "Generation Y" or "millennials." These are people who were born between 1981 and 1992 and are currently teenagers and young adults. They are the children of the Baby Boomers. Sandwiched between these two groups is Generation X (born between 1966 and 1980).

The millennials are generalized as being largely turned off by the quest for money and status that has driven their parents. They value work/life balance, want truth, and are more receptive to stories than to facts. Going through life without witnessing real hardship, they don't have the fear and insecurity that has driven their parents to achieve. And they are the Internet generation; social media, in particular, plays an important part in their lives. As a bunch, they are independent, innovative, and creative. Critics say that they are work-shy dreamers who expect to get everything handed to them on a plate. These are the people the wine industry needs to connect with.

And what of the members of Generation X? They're a confusing bunch—on the one hand, boomeresque; on the other, Generation Y. The Internet revolution has captured many Generation Xers, and through social media, many have effectively become honorary members of Generation Y.

The question for the wine industry now is how to appeal to the upcoming generations of wine drinkers without alienating its existing customer base. We think that the message of the naturalness/authenticity of wine resonates well with the millennials and should be part of marketing to this generation, the wine consumers of tomorrow.

MARKETING WINE TO THE NEW GENERATION OF DRINKERS

Traditional marketing is changing. Now, rather than addressing advertising messages to people or speaking down to them, marketing is about joining a conversation. It is a much more distributed activity than in the past, harder to control, but open to a wider range of players. In part, this is because of the opportunities afforded by new media; in part, it is because of the changing attitudes of the millennials, who are less receptive to traditional marketing approaches. They seek truth and question more deeply the messages delivered to them.

With their reliance on social media and indifference to authority, the millennials herald the demise of the supreme wine critic. In the future, it will not be scores that sell wines, but stories. Authentic, interesting stories that resonate with listeners' experience and attitudes are powerful marketing messages. Whoever delivers these stories must be credible, transparent, and engaged in genuine conversation with his or her listeners. Winegrowers, whatever their size, need to package their own authentic stories and get them to the market. They need to make the jobs of retailers, sommeliers, and journalists easy. Retailers, sommeliers, and journalists need to take more responsibility for selecting and recommending authentic wines so that even if the consumer can't tell the difference in wine quality, she or he is getting satisfaction from other nonsensory factors associated with the product. Wine is very much more than simply a liquid in a glass, and the perception of wine is based on more than simply its chemical makeup. The context and the story play a huge part in the actual perception of wine. After all, wine is one of the few products where consumption is closely linked to packaging. The bottle sits in front of you on the table as you consume it, reminding you of its origin, its heritage, and its story. This is why label design and the information on the label are critical for wine.

SOME CONSIDERATIONS FOR KEY WINE INDUSTRY STAKEHOLDERS
FOR WINERIES

Generally speaking, small wineries are doing a much better job of marketing and selling authentic wines than larger wineries. We can't understand why the larger wineries with larger marketing budgets are not doing a better job. These larger wineries need not employ Hugo Boss–clad marketing consultants to tell them how they should do it; they should simply look at case studies of successful smaller wineries, which are having to work harder and more creatively to fight over the scraps. As always, the best solutions are not only the simplest but also are often right under the nose.

This brings natural wine into the picture because the most natural expressions of wine have the best story to tell. There are two reasons for this. First, more natural approaches in the vineyard and winery allow differences in flavour to be expressed, which have as their basis differences in terroir. The result is a diversity of wines possessing a sense of place. There is no more compelling story in wine than that of terroir—a link between the product and the locale and culture that caused its creation. Second, working naturally, respecting the environment, and showing awareness of issues of social capital and carbon footprints are also compelling stories. We shouldn't take the issue of social capital lightly. The wine industry employs many people whose lives are strongly based on the practice of winegrowing. One of the things that most enthuses filmmaker Michael Seresin about his biodynamically run New Zealand vineyard Seresin Estate is the fact that he has a diverse bunch of employees who really enjoy coming to work each day. His vineyards and winery are happy places to work, he says. It must be much more fulfilling to work with the rhythms of the biodynamic calendar and spray natural preparations than it is to nuke a vineyard with herbicides and eradicate insect life with pesticides, regardless of the efficacy of each approach.

The environmental aspect is another important story. Like every other business, the wine trade needs to take into account the change in public sentiment about the environment, but in this case the need is even more pressing because wine has benefited from its image as a natural, authentic product. The fact that most consumers simply aren't aware of just what is sprayed on vineyards and some of the additions and trickery that take place in wineries gives the wine industry no room for complacency, because as society wakes up to environmental issues, people will begin asking more penetrating questions about where their food and drink come from. For this reason, winegrowers worldwide have just a short period of grace to set their house in order, reducing the environmental impact of their practices and being able to justify any agricultural inputs they make.

On the flip side, there is also a positive message here. Consumers' heightened awareness of environmental responsibility and working in sustainable ways means that people are increasingly willing to let these issues guide their purchasing and even to pay more for products that have green credentials. Expect to see green issues influencing purchasing decisions to become more prevalent in coming years.

One of our motivations for writing this book was that we wanted to try to make the case for retaining a diversity of wine styles and to make the wine industry pause to reflect on its current trajectory. For example, in the vineyard there is no acceptable way of working that is not sustainable: it is morally wrong for us to spend the capital of the next generation.

FIGURE 13.2

U.S. winery Parducci is keen to emphasize its sustainable credentials.

Ultimately, we are pragmatists, though, and recognize that the only way for conservation efforts to be a success is to make them pay. If we can encourage the wine industry to think about using naturalness and authenticity as a marketing angle, there's a possibility that the trade will realize that rather than being a problem to be ironed out, the complexity of the current wine offering is one of its marketable strengths, and it is wines made in a natural way that possess the diversity and sense of place that make wine unique.

FOR MULTIPLE GROCERS (SUPERMARKETS)

Don't give up on wine. It's a unique product and, as such, is incremental business for you. Despite profit contributions that are lower than you might want, it has a vital role to play in the long-term success of your business. Protect its authenticity, and you protect future revenue streams for your business.

Obviously there is much more to any marketing campaign than just price, and any retailer serious about making a sustainable business out of wine needs to consider factors that define authenticity. Resources should be employed to get these stories to the consumer. Most wineries have an authentic story to tell, so tell it.

If wine falls into direct competition with the other alcoholic beverages, it will lose the battle. Wine does not compete directly with RTDs (ready-to-drink alcoholic beverages), spirits and beers. Take away the diversity, the heritage, the naturalness, and the authenticity from the product, pushing it in the direction of the commodity, and the retailer will lose the majority of this business. Consumers won't buy RTDs as a substitute; they will go to specialists (if they still exist) for a more interesting, authentic product.

Supermarkets with their simplistic marketing models focusing for the most part on price promotion, are not acting in a way that is in the long-term interests of their shareholders. Quality is often compromised to achieve deep discounting. A dissatisfied consumer who buys a poor-quality discounted brand in your store might well have a tainted image of your store as a result of her or his experience. Placing too much emphasis on pricing and not enough on quality will inevitably affect the value of your business's brand.

Distribution within the industry cares only for short-term returns. It's an expensive business. Producers spend cash (and plenty of it) months and sometimes years before they see a return. If the future competitors with wine are RTDs, then there is going to be a clear-cut winner, and it will not be wine. Unlike wine, RTDs don't rely on a seasonal crop for their main ingredient. These products can be made at any time to a specification and at much lower cost. Margins are higher, and returns are faster.

While the world of RTDs can make good business sense, the world of wine is a lot less promising as an investment opportunity. Sanity checks for new entrants into the winegrowing business should be compulsory. Despite a widespread and clear understanding of this problem, more and more individuals every year spend their retirement funds planting vines and building smart wineries. Why is this happening?

Therein lies the beauty of wine production (large and small, rich and poor) and why we need to protect it. In the capitalistic, money-hungry world we live in, the wine industry offers a glimmer of hope. Could there be other motives for setting up a business than mere profit? This is one of the wine industry's unique qualities, and it is one that we should cherish. Passion, lifestyle, tradition, emotion, heritage, legacy, and culture are just a few returns that investors in the industry look for while they pour their money down the drain. There was a time when the majority of wine retailers understood and supported this folly. Unfortunately, retailers with less compassionate shareholders than they had in the past have moved the goalposts, embracing Darwinian notions of natural selection. Like it or not, shareholders have eyes only for the size of their dividend. So the industry is confronted with a difficult situation and will not be able to escape from it without some level of long-term vision from retailers. Retailers need to practice restraint in their cost cutting and margin hunting in the wine category. They need to believe once again in the notion that retail is only as strong as its supply base. Winemakers need to be encouraged and supported to make better, more authentic, more socially responsible wines for the consumer, not just competing on price alone. With support from the market, might disheartened wine growers start making better, more authentic wines?

If retailers need to employ marketing for successful business activity, then they should build these costs into their margin. We believe that it is unethical to pass them on to the production sector in an underhanded way (as is currently done in the multiple-grocer [supermarket] sector), especially when they are already deprived of little if any profit. The winery has to cover its own marketing costs; why can't the same be expected of the retailer? Isn't that just good honest business?

We urge major retailers, producers, and other stakeholders to work together in a common initiative that supports and encourages marketing campaigns for authentic wine and in doing so provides a brighter future for wine and the communities around the world that rely on its success in the market.

FOR SPECIALIST RETAILERS

Continue what you are doing. Sell the story, the point of difference, the experience. Look to those who are doing it well, who are succeeding, and emulate them. There is no point in reinventing the wheel. Specialist retailers have a valuable role to play because they can help communicate the necessarily complex story of wine. One of the problems faced by modern retailing is the lack of any connection with consumers, and wine suffers badly from this. In some ways, specialist retailers, with well-trained, helpful staff who are able to talk to their customers, are fulfilling a vital role in wine education. They are able to learn about their customers' preferences and tastes and help them progress in their journey into wine. In fact, establishing a relationship with a good wine merchant is perhaps the most enjoyable way to learn about wine.

FOR RESTAURANTS

Like specialist retailers, sommeliers have a vital function in helping people enjoy and understand what they are drinking. Invest in educating your sommeliers and wine waiters. Help culture their passion and enthusiasm for wine, because these qualities are contagious, and sommeliers are important ambassadors for interesting wines. Challenge your producers—even your favourite one—to make more authentic wines. And challenge importers to get serious about authentic wine. If you share the stories of each wine with your customers, you will make their dining and drinking experience even better.

FOR OTHER INDUSTRY BODIES

One of the glaring problems for any marketer looking to promote authentic wine is that the majority of consumers lack understanding of what wine is, let alone what authentic wine might be. If we look at the definition of authentic wine we stated in the introduction of this book, then it becomes a rather complex set of messages to try to get across to the consumer. It's all very well for us to champion authentic wine, but how is this message to be communicated?

But look again at some of the discussion points in this book, and it becomes clear that marketing authentic wine need not be as difficult as you might have thought. There are already organized controlling and certifying bodies (although they demonstrate varying levels of professionalism) in place in most, if not all, of these areas. As noted in the relevant chapters, certifying bodies exist for sustainable wine growing (restricted nationally), organics (many hundreds of registered bodies), and even biodynamic viticulture (just two, with global reach). There is a burgeoning natural wine group in place, although it is currently an unofficial alliance without strict rules. And most wine regions have official bodies that protect the geographic origin of their wines.

We were originally going to title this book *Natural Wine,* but the term *natural* has too many problems for it to be used as an umbrella marketing term, not least that it is indefinable. But we do believe that the term *authentic wine* can be useful as a marketing term, bringing together such issues as sustainability, environmental sensitivity, noninterventionist winemaking, and the diversity that comes from terroir. When one attempts to market authentic wine, the obvious starting point is for wineries and retailers alike to market those wines that are certified by an official, accepted body to verify their position as a sustainable wine, an organic wine, a biodynamic wine, a fair-trade wine, an environmentally respectful wine, or a terroir wine. But these organizations need to look to the organic movement for inspiration and to have recourse to a central organization that controls standards globally. Of all these categories, organics is the only one that is properly understood by consumers, and this is in large part due to the harmonization of standards worldwide, even though the work of certification is spread among hundreds of different bodies.

What will certainly reduce the chances for success of authentic wine will be the existence of too many competing organizations with different standards and different marketing and communication agendas. By having competing certification organizations, such as those we see in the biodynamics movement, we are also limiting the resources available for these organizations to create effective marketing tools for their members. Professional, sensible, goal-focused organizations are needed to control standards for their members and to work closely with their membership base to come up with concise, simple marketing messages that allow consumers an understanding of why their wines are worth purchasing alongside others. There is a need for less politics and more action. With regard to geographic origin, the extensive rationalization of AOCs and DOCs is needed, rather than the proliferation of ever-smaller wine regions, often where there is little justification in the underlying geology, or climate, or even taste of the wines. A more serious natural wine organization needs to be developed if the message about natural wine is not to become hopelessly confused. Sustainable viticulture and winemaking need a marketing message that they currently lack. What good is it for New Zealand to develop a different message concerning sustainability from that of South Africa for the same end consumers? Would it be possible to pool resources and create a globally recognized standard for sustainable viticulture that is based on common standards and delivers a simple, consistent marketing message?

We believe that even more powerful would be an umbrella term, *authentic wine*, with a single logo and message that embraces the various topics discussed in this book.

14

CONCLUSION

Wine is not an industry that generates huge profit. It's an industry where
passionate people are totally absorbed in the process, culture, history and
mystique that surrounds it.

ALAN BRADY, CENTRAL OTAGO PIONEER

People have a hunger for the authentic. Consider the crowds who flock to view the work of a now long-dead painter, such as Vermeer. His thirty-four surviving paintings are distributed among a number of different galleries, and many people travel specifically to see them. With today's technology it would be possible to produce copies of all of them at a level at which only an expert with the help of technology would be able to tell them from the original. Yet if you were to set up a display of accurate copies of all thirty-four, we suspect that few would visit. People want to see the real thing. They long for the authentic.

You can imagine a similar experiment with wine. A group of tasters could be presented with three wines that tasted very similar: a bottle of Domaine de la Romanée Conti Echézeaux and two much cheaper wines that had been skillfully doctored to match the sensory profile of the Echézeaux to a degree that even experts confused them, so our group of tasters would fail to spot any difference in the three wines. We suspect that when the wines were unveiled, there would be little interest in purchasing the doctored wines at, say, one-twentieth the price of the Echézeaux, even though they delivered the same sensory experience when tasted blind. Authenticity matters.

In this book we have discussed many aspects of naturalness and authenticity in wine. It is not a simple story; indeed, it is almost impossible to come up with a definition that has broad applicability and doesn't simply box natural wine into a tiny niche. Even the natural wine movement recognizes that definitions have to be a little fluid. While there are some agreements (for example, on the use of selected yeasts and almost all chemical additions), there are differences of opinion on the use of sulfur dioxide (some use just a little at bottling, a few use none at all) and vineyard management (not all are biodynamic, and a few are not even organic). We argue that it is important to see naturalness as a continuum, and that the whole industry should take a shift in the direction of naturalness. For some, the journey will be a long one, leading all the way to naturalness, while commercial realities may cause others to stop a little short of the target. But wouldn't it be great if the whole wine industry could become certified sustainable in the vineyard, could lower its carbon footprint, and could eschew the use of unnecessary additions and physical manipulations in the winery? On the flip side, this discussion of naturalness is important and timely because of the danger that flavour additives could creep into wine, which would be a disaster.

The wine industry is at a crossroads. Wine is a wonderful natural, authentic product. Do we emphasize this naturalness, celebrate the diversity of wine, and put our house in order by steering away from unneeded additions and manipulations? Or do we allow wine to become simply another manufactured beverage whose flavours are manipulated to match perceived consumer preferences? Should all commercial wines be allowed to taste the same: simple, uncomplicated, sweet, and fruity? Do we appeal merely to the common palate—the consumer's innate sense of deliciousness that has been such a successful target for soft-drink manufacturers, fast-food restaurants, and packaged-food companies? Do we give consumers a simplified wine offering of, say, six different varietal wines that taste of no more than the grape variety? Or do we opt to present consumers with flavours that are a little more challenging but express the sense of place of the wine? This is undoubtedly a more complicated story, but it is a lot more compelling and culturally and intellectually rich. It sets wine apart from other alcoholic drinks. Isn't it why we love wine? Isn't it what drew us to this wonderful gift of nature in the first place? Why not share it?

In today's wine market, the sweetly fruited, easy-to-drink wines are designed by consumer focus groups. At the other end of the price spectrum (though not necessarily the quality spectrum), monster international fine wines brimming with sweet fruit and oak spice compete for the affection of a single wine "expert" and a score that tells us more about the optical density of the wine than anything worthwhile.

In some ways, we are now spoiled for choice when it comes to interesting, diverse, and authentic wines. The wine world forty years ago was much less diverse, and there were far fewer wines that would fit our definition of authentic. So you could argue that what we have today does not reflect what existed in the past. We would counter by suggesting that the breadth of the wine market as it stands is in part a reflection of strong economies creating a sustained and growing demand for more expensive wine, but also that the basis of the fine wine venture—wines that have a sense of place, grown on sites that are privileged for winegrowing—has been there for many centuries. And in New World wine regions, those who are making the best wines are following in these footsteps of identifying places that suit the production of interesting wines, and are seeking

JAMIE GOODE and SAM HARROP

If employees are happier and safer in their roles and profits are distributed throughout the industry, workers in all sectors of the trade will do a better job growing, making, and selling more authentic wines. In turn, this is likely to result in a more satisfied consumer—the end goal of all serious wine professionals! This will result in a more sustainable model for the trade. Ethical trading should not be a "standard" that organizations sign up to just to sell more wine and at higher prices. It needs to be entrenched in the ethos of individuals and the culture of the organizations working within this industry if it is to be truly sustainable. Many of the most important wine retailers in the UK (at least) have signed up to the ethical trading initiative (ETI), and FairTrade certification has gained a real prominence on the shelves. These are positive signs for the movement but more work needs to be done by all stakeholders in this industry.

Key ethical questions need to be asked of the supply base. It doesn't matter how far away from the winery the buyer is or how minimal his or her perceived influence is. There is an ongoing need for the buyer to demand certain ethics of winegrowing management practices to make real change. Equally, the wineries—with a little help from consumers (of course)—need to ask that retailers and other stakeholders involved in the distribution of wine practice what they preach. It is all very well demanding acceptable ethical standards from your supply base if you are not practicing acceptable ethical standards in your own area of trading. Retailers need to remember that as long as wineries feel aggrieved by the way they are treated by the retailers, they are less likely to listen and act on the demands that are expected of them.

Clem Yates, one of the buying team of the UK supermarket Sainsbury's, has this to say of ethical trading: "Sourcing with integrity is one of Sainsbury's core values and it is something that we take seriously within the wine category. We are founding members of the ETI and expect all our suppliers to follow our Code of Conduct for Socially Responsible Sourcing, which incorporates the base code of the ETI. We are also the world's largest FairTrade retailer and have committed to doubling our FairTrade wine sales in 2011."

to find the appropriate varieties, viticultural regimes, and cellar practices for interpreting these terroirs in a meaningful way.

There is a timelessness about authentic wines. They are neither hidebound by tradition nor overly modernist. Whatever the particular characteristics of the region they come from and the variety or varieties from which they are made, you can taste authenticity in them. But just as authentic wine requires that growers have the honesty to let it express its sense of place in a manner that is true to its site, growers must have the honesty and wisdom to make sure that their vineyards are managed sustainably because sustainability involves such issues as social capital.

We see a bright future for the wine industry, but we want that to be a common future. We believe strongly that authenticity is the way forward for the whole industry. It would be bad news if there were a schism in the industry: at one pole, the niche of authentic wine, hidden away and found only by a few; at the other pole, the wine "industry" of manufactured, commodity wines, stripped of soul and sense of place, made in a fashion that is unsustainable (in environmental impact and social capital), and becoming the only visible face of the wine industry for the vast majority of consumers. Our hope is that this book will, in some small way, make people think a little about which way to turn at this fork in the road for global wine production.

INDEX

Microoxygenation, 124–129, 162–163, 190
Milanowski, Tony, 161
Millennials, 238–239
Millton, James, 77–79
Millton Vineyards, 50, 77–79
Minerality, 26, 27, 31–36, 72, 77, 133, 163, 210
Mitchelton, 226
Mites, 95
Miticides, 74
MLF. *See* Malolactic fermentation
Mondavi, Robert, 93
Monoculture, 58, 68, 76, 85
Mont Tauch, 227
Moreno, Yerko, 93–94
Morey, Pierre, 58, 71, 73–74
Morris, Jasper, 72
Mosel, 32, 35–36, 44, 45
Mount Difficulty, 12
Mount Etna, 163–164
Mulch, 83, 96
Mychorrhizae, 220

Nacional vineyard, 44–46
Napa Valley, 13, 20, 58, 232–233
Natural fermentations. *See* Wild ferments
Naturalness, 2, 6, 17, 141–168, 247–248
Néauport, Jacques, 149
Nematodes, 95, 97
Nerello Mascalese, 164
New Zealand, 3, 12, 22, 27, 45, 77–79, 88–90,
    99–100, 119, 147, 156–159, 173–174, 175
Niepoort, Dirk, 30, 31, 34, 35, 128–129, 211
Nikolaihof, 49
Nitrogen, 54, 160, 171
Nomblot concrete eggs, 128–129, 151
Noval, Quinta do, 44–46
Nutrients, 34, 122, 201
    Vines, of, 64
    Yeast, for, 60, 171

Oak, 13, 26, 33, 59, 124–129, 153, 156, 165–166,
    183, 189–190
    Alternatives to barrels, 124–125
    Brettanomyces risk, 203–204
    Chips, 124
    Lactones, 124
    Staves, 124–125

Offsetting, carbon footprint, 232
Oidium (powdery mildew), 38, 39, 43, 57, 74, 83,
    86, 99
Orange wines, 166–167
Oregon, 5, 45, 53, 59, 69, 79–82, 87, 90–93,
    129, 147
Oregon Certified Sustainable Wine (OCSW),
    91–93
Organics, 6–7, 49–84, 85–87, 89–90, 93, 101,
    105, 142, 145, 160, 163, 195, 220, 248
    Definition, organic wine, 55
Orion, 30
Overripeness, 26
Oxidation, 114–115, 145, 148, 151–153, 158–161, 163,
    168, 211–217, 226
    Premature, of white Burgundy, 159, 213
Oxygen, 124–129, 132–133, 136, 154, 171, 211–217,
    227
    Pickup, 160–161
    Transmission rate through closures/
        packaging, 153, 202, 210, 227

Paardeberg, 25
Pacalet, Philippe, 145, 149
PAN [Europe] (Pesticide Action Network),
    104–109
Parasitoid, 98
Parducci, 231, 241
Paris, France, 141
Parker, Robert M. Jr., 11–14, 81, 135, 238
Partial root drying (PRD), 188
Pasteur, Louis, 169
Pectinases, 134
Penfolds, 118, 120
Pesticides, 6, 102–109
PET (polyethylene teraphthalate), 225–227
pH, 120, 136, 143, 150, 190, 215
Phenolic ripeness (physiological ripeness),
    184–188, 194–195
Phenolics, 151–153, 173, 186, 195, 212
Pheromone traps, 90, 98
Phloem, 42
Phosphoric acid, 120
Photosynthesis, 185, 193, 195
Phylloxera, 37–48, 73, 81, 85, 164
Physiological ripeness. *See* Phenolic ripeness
Phyterra, 179

INTERIOR DESIGN: Barbara Haines
COMPOSITION: Westchester Book Group
TEXT: 9.5/14 Scala
DISPLAY: Scala Sans
PRINTER AND BINDER: Thomson-Shore, Inc.

The Science of Wine
From Vine to Glass
JAMIE GOODE

"Thorough, fascinating, and comprehensive....
A perfect mix of science and humanity, not unlike
wine itself." —*Gastronomica*
Glenfiddich Drink Book of the Year Award 2006
Copublished with Mitchell Beazley
$35.95 cloth   978-0-520-24800-7

Reading between the Wines
TERRY THEISE
With a New Preface

"A consequential book, rich in ideas and powerful in
feeling." —**Eric Asimov, *New York Times***
Finalist, Drinks Literature, Gourmand World Cookbook Awards
Finalist, André Simon Food and Drink Book Awards
$17.95 paper   978-0-520-27149-4

The Way to Make Wine
How to Craft Superb Table Wines at Home
SHERIDAN WARRICK

"Eminently readable.... Highly recommended to anyone eager to discover the thrills and delights of
making wine at home." —*Gastronomica*
$21.95 paper   978-0-520-26614-8

The Taste of Place
A Cultural Journey into Terroir
AMY B. TRUBEK

"A collection of eclectic information that satisfies, at
least temporarily, the most inquisitive and academic
of gourmands." —***The Wine News***
California Studies in Food and Culture
$19.95 paper   978-0-520-26172-3

Great Wine Terroirs
JACQUES FANET

"A most attractively designed book of remarkable
scholarship.... Fanet's wealth of geological knowledge makes a fascinating start on the long journey
towards a rounded understanding of terroir."
—**Andrew Jefford, *The World of Fine Wine***
Copublished with Hachette Livre
$49.95 cloth   978-0-520-23858-9

www.ucpress.edu